SWEDISH SENSATIONSFILMS

BY DANIEL EKEROTH

TRANSLATED BY
MAGNUS HENRIKSSON

SWEDISH SENSATIONSFILMS:
A CLANDESTINE HISTORY OF SEX, THRILLERS, AND KICKER CINEMA

HTTP://WWW.SENSATIONSFILM.COM

Written by Daniel Ekeroth
Translated by Magnus Henriksson
Produced by Ian Christe
Cover artwork by Wes Benscoter

First published in 2011 by
BAZILLION POINTS BOOKS
61 Greenpoint Ave. #504
Brooklyn, NY 11222
United States
www.bazillionpoints.com

ISBN 978-0-9796163-6-5

Printed in Hong Kong

CONTENTS

Photo by Agnes Cavallin

SWEDEN AND ITS *SENSATIONSFILMS*

BY DANIEL EKEROTH

Hello there! I'm Daniel, your basic regular Swedish guy, relaxing comfortably at my summer house in the remote forest west of Stockholm. The weather is sunny today, and the Scandinavian air is fresh. Butterflies are sweeping over my garden, and small colorful birds are singing the tunes of spring's arrival. If I just had some naked girls cavorting on the lawn, the international poster image of my home country would be complete.

Yes, Sweden is envied as one of the nicest and most stable of the world's nations—a peaceful and idyllic oasis in the north, sheltered from turbulence in modern history. We have avoided war for over two hundred years. Sweden is praised for its social and economic equality. The status of women is far better than in most other places, and our immigrant policy is generous and humane. Our social security system puts that of just about any other nation to shame, and our enviable landscapes are open for all people to wander around freely. This place is well-described as a small piece of heaven on earth. But, as we soon shall see, there are rats in this paradise—and from time to time, they make mutiny in heaven.

As this tome of dark recollections will show, the Swedish film industry has specifically been a source of infection. It did not begin that way. As the film medium emerged in the late 1800s, an innocent Sweden was initially frightened by the fast new form of art. The national government panicked, and in 1911 created Statens Biografbyrå—The National Board of Film Classification—the world's first state-sponsored film censor bureau. The urge to remain decent and apply restraint dominated cinematic expression for decades. While the rest of the world was bogged down with World War I and World War II, the Swedish film industry conquered provincial screens with many *pilsnerfilmer* (beer films), jolly comedies in which fat men sang songs about brotherhood and friendship. But as postwar Europe began to construct a saner future, the Swedish government forgot to sweep out its nest. With the 1950s, Sweden's film industry swerved into forbidden areas—creating the singular breed of Swedish cinema I call *sensationsfilms*.

From 1951 to 1993, over 200 films were produced that reveled in themes of sex and violence. Arne Mattsson's film *Hon Dansade en Sommar* started it all in 1951. Though totally mild by today's standards, the exposure of a bare female breast stirred the entire world, firing a warning shot to Hollywood that soon forced the end of Hays Code censorship in America. After Mattsson's original nip-slip, Swedish films quickly earned a reputation for being sexually liberated, an extension of the social upheaval and push for sexual freedom in the country at the time, for women in particular. Facing an ever-flowing stream of films—

including Ingmar Bergman's bare-breasted 1953 entry *Sommaren med Monika*—Swedish censors fought valiantly but ultimately had no choice but to gradually accept the increasing prevalence and intensity of on-screen sexuality. During the 1950s, Swedish boobs probably knocked out more men than world champion boxer Ingmar Johansson's "toonder and lightning" right fist!

As this sexual revolution rolled into the 1960s, the only evident victories won by women were the rights to stroll around topless at the beach and participate in sleazy movies. Soon, Swedish *sensationsfilms* became known internationally as a powerful force of exploitation. Even Ingmar Bergman participated, kicking off the decade with Oscar and Golden Globe prizes for *Jungfrukällan* (1960). Though generally praised as a masterpiece, at its heart the film is clearly a *sensationsfilm* thanks to its rape-revenge plot and first-ever on-screen depiction of vomiting. Following the trail of this giant into the swamp, Swedish directors of talents large and small dug deeper into sexuality. Among countless similar pictures, Vilgot Sjöman's *Jag Är Nyfiken – Gul* (1967) is probably the most famous. Despite its rather serious political content, the film made waves around the world for outspoken sexual content and countless scenes of intercourse between young girl Lena Nyman and mature man Börje Ahlstedt.

Though rather explicit, *Jag Är Nyfiken – Gul* stopped short of depicting real sex scenes. Within months, though, another *sensationsfilm* went there. With *Dom Kallar Oss Mods* (1968), director Stefan Jarl presented gritty social commentary about the marginalization of troubled teenagers, but again the film became notorious for a scene of actual copulation between young hipsters. Trying to preserve their battered dignity, the Board of Film Classification censors immediately banned the movie, but minister of culture Olof Palme intervened and ordered that *Dom Kallar Oss Mods* be released uncut.

With the government on their side, the seedier Swedish filmmakers really got down to business. Also in 1968, Mac Ahlberg delivered the first *sensationsfilm* masterpiece, *Jag – En Kvinna 2. Äktenskapet*, an all-out exploitation follow-up to his more serious *Jag – En Kvinna* (1965). The sequel wallowed in perverted sex, Nazi memorabilia, and psychedelic music, melting all into an unholy pot of sleaze. Then in 1969, the notorious *Kärlekens Språk* was released, basically the first film anywhere to dress up truly graphic scenes of authentic sex for mass consumption—real *sensationsfilm* sleaze disguised as a documentary.

Disguised became the operative word. Aboveground, the 1960s were cool, free, and loving. Beneath the surface, some serious exploitation was starting to occur. Some Italians could smell a rat accurately, and in 1968 director Luigi Scattini helmed the phony documentary *Sweden – Heaven and Hell*, a mondo portrait of Sweden as a place of meaningless sex, alcoholism, and suicide. Though everything about the film was fake, the makers might have been onto something: Their effort spawned a host of fake Swedish knockoffs worldwide. But there was nothing like the real thing! Supervised by the notorious Dr. Håkan Åström, the Swedish government began providing free drugs for users at the end of the 1960s. Of course, this genius plan created a massive increase in drug users and prostitutes (as Stefan Jarl later revealed in his alarming *Ett Anständigt Liv,* 1979).

Into this rising whirlwind of madness, I was born, in 1972. As the '70s came along, all limits were forgotten, and the *sensationsfilm* industry kicked in with a vengeance. A new breed of Swedish starlet was minted, combining purity, youthful enthusiam, lack of inhibition, and—regarding Christina Lindberg and Diana Kjaer, at least—real dedication to acting. Of course, not every leading actor bothered to learn his or her craft. Sweden was flooded with sexually explicit films of every kind, violent gangster movies, and tons of nasty pornography. Women burned their bras in the streets, and everyone's behavior became unzipped in the name of freedom; a freedom that tolerated child pornography, tons of porn theaters in Stockholm, and numerous brothels—which we learned were often visited by politicians. All morals were gone. Film directors such as Bo A. Vibenius and Mac Ahlberg took full advantage of the times with sensational tales such as *Thriller – En Grym Film* (1974) and *Jorden Runt med Fanny Hill* (1975). Vibenius all but vanished after pioneering the insertion of hard-core sex scenes into violent fiction films, and giving Quentin Tarantino the inspiration for his *Kill Bill* saga. Ahlberg actually escaped to the United States and became cinematographer of cult films such as *Re-Animator* (Stuart Gordon, 1985). Even the original *sensationsfilms* director Arne Mattsson sank deeper into the swamp, abandoning his earlier brand of sensual films and mild thrillers. His fantastic *Smutsiga Fingrar* (1973) is probably the most unpleasant Swedish crime thriller of all, reveling in mad scenes of rape, drugs, and senseless violence.

In the wake of the unsuspected crossover success of *Deep Throat* in 1972, two foreign directors took advantage of the prevailing chaotic climate to produce pure pornography in Sweden. The Romanian Andrei Fehrer made a slew of porn flicks starring Swedish blondes, and the American Joseph Sarno created the most notorious Swedish porn film of all: *Fäbodjäntan* (1978). For the next decade, this film was seen by every Swede, young and old. It was the first pornographic film I ever saw, and come to think of it, probably the first one my parents saw as well—which makes me kind of uneasy. Yet the most unsettling and unusual pornographic film ever made came from a Swedish director, the former Ingmar Bergman pupil Bo A. Vibenius. With *Breaking Point* (1975), he crushed all boundaries of comprehension, mixing equal parts perverse sex and psychological torment into something out of this world. The *sensationsfilm* had reached perfection. The censors were evidently completely at a loss; they cut large parts of the film, and still barely left a mark.

As the 1980s arrived, something had to be done about all this craziness, and a perfect scapegoat soon appeared in the form of the videocassette recorder. In December 1980, the TV debate show *Studio-S* tried to settle the question once and for all. An episode titled "Who Needs Video?" offered an outraged mob of conservative politicians, Christian leaders, and angry parents a platform to attack the video business and their dirty films. With *The Texas Chain Saw Massacre* (Tobe Hooper, 1974) as a prime target, the coalition concluded that the VCR itself should be banned from Sweden for the good of all children. What happened next should have been obvious—a surge of shocking publicity caused my entire generation to become obsessed by violent films. We rushed out to rent them all. In my early teens, I consumed everything violent that crossed my path, just like everyone else my age in Sweden. My friends and I became obsessive video film collectors. The climate was great.

Most of the videos we could find were low-budget horror and locally produced sex films. Sleaze flourished wild and free, while the big film companies—with Disney leading the charge—continued to fight a losing battle against the VCR, refusing to license tapes for release in Sweden. Even if we wanted to watch something pleasant, we could not.

As the VCR continued to wear down the bloated and bland mainstream film industry in the 1980s, the world of *sensationsfilms* receded. After the heyday, only true lunatics with ultra-low budgets continued the quest. Mats Helge Olsson's early films *I Död Mans Spår* (1975) and *The Frozen Star* (1977) were scarcely seen, and with good reason. But after making his entrance with Swedish westerns, Mats Helge ventured into the arena of bloody action films. His incredible *The Ninja Mission* (1984) set the new *sensationsfilm* standard with its shoestring budget, countless explosions, roaring bullets, and inept script. For some reason the movie was an international hit, and Mats Helge continued on his violent path. He was only outdone by Björn Carlström and Daniel Hübenbecker, whose *War Dog* (1986) reveled in brutal violence against men, women, and especially children. Meanwhile, the Cold War raged, and our schools preached the horrors of American and Soviet nuclear aggression. Just imagine the proportions of this after a Russian submarine became stranded in Swedish waters during the 1980s. Of course, we watched sick movies and listened to extreme music to drown out all the alarms.

Aside from our homegrown Swedish treats, violence infiltrated mainstream youth culture through films like *Karate Kid* (John G. Avildsen, 1984) and *Rocky IV* (Sylvester Stallone, 1985). Out in the streets, signs of destruction appeared. Phone booths all across Sweden were kicked completely to pieces, and the blame was placed—quite accurately—on unruly kids who had seen too many violent films. Something drastic needed to be done, so the Swedish phone company Televerket devised a perfect plan: To stop the violence, they would to make a film about violence! Without pausing for a moment to think things through, they hired notorious Stockholm youth criminal Paolo Roberto and produced *Stockholmsnatt* (1987). The taxpayer-funded film depicted the daily life of teenagers kicking down people in the streets and having a great time. The next step was to show this "masterpiece" in every school in Sweden to inform the children that violence was wrong. Instead of putting a stop to the vandalism and fighting, the film just made us all incredibly excited to hit the streets for some serious kicking. In blissful ignorance, the government had come full circle, now financing and promoting the exact kind of film they initially created Statens Biografbyrå to censor. In Sweden, irony tastes both salty and sweet.

Soon the Berlin Wall toppled, and the reign of Swedish sleaze collapsed, too. The last film of importance was *Sökarna* (1993), starring Liam Norberg—one of Paolo Roberto's old friends from the kicker days. Basically a darker and sleazier version of *Stockholmsnatt*, the film took on new power when Norberg was convicted of a massive bank robbery shortly after its release. It turned out that the film had actually been produced with stolen money—and a healthy infusion of government funds, naturally. *Stockholmsnatt* kindled my fear of the dark side of Stockholm, and *Sökarna* seared those feelings inside me permanently.

Just as the authorities had accepted that violence and explicit sex could not be stopped, the Internet arrived and got the job done almost immediately. Suddenly, all the dirty little Swedish *sensationsfilms* seemed quaint. In 1996, after eighty-five years of bungled service, Statens Biografbyrå all but gave up. They declared they would no longer cut or ban films, and would only to set recommended age limits for viewers. In the wake of satellite TV and the Internet, there seemed little point to carrying on their crusade. Sadly, the last veterans of Swedish *sensationsfilms* felt the same way. The last emperor, Mats Helge Olsson, fled the country one step ahead of tax collectors, and nobody remained to claim his throne. The original *sensationsfilm* auteur, Arne Mattsson, passed away in 1995 with little notice, his main body of work in danger of being forgotten.

Yet even now, as I look back on decades of depravity, I hear the rustling of an ill wind in my garden. A Swedish sleaze director has recently been caught in an armed confrontation with police. King of kickers Paolo Roberto has again become a TV star, and a new generation of kickers is learning terrifying moves from grainy clips on YouTube. The bank robber turned actor Liam Norberg is making a comeback as a born-again Christian. And the rape-revenge, violent subway attacks, and sinful incest of Stieg Larsson's novels and film adaptations are again reminding the world of Sweden's hidden sensations.

I will just stay here in my little cabin and review the treats and terrors of the golden age of Swedish *sensationsfilms*. It's safer that way—as the long Scandinavian night falls over my garden, the climate suddenly seems cold and dark, and full of predators. The butterflies are all gone, the birds sing no more, and I can hear the crawling of hungry rats from the swamp wandering through the tall grass.

CHRISTINA LINDBERG, EXPOSED
AS TOLD TO RONNY BENGTSSON

G rowing up in Gothenburg, we tended to go down to the beaches a lot, and that's where I was discovered. The city newspapers like *Göteborgs-Posten* and *Hallandsposten* had a beach girl spread in every issue, kind of like the English tabloids have today. I was the beach girl in those papers and a few others. I was in my first photo session at sixteen.

Men's magazines were incredibly popular during the '70s. They could sell around 300,000 copies a week by mixing serious journalism with undressed girls. Most Swedish journalists of importance actually started out in *Fib Aktuellt*. While visiting a rock club, I met celebrity photographer Siwer Ohlsson, who worked for *Fib Aktuellt*. He saw me dancing in the nightclub, and asked if I would participate in a photo shoot featuring a cavalcade of Gothenburg girls—and, in addition, he wanted me to take some undressed pictures.

I was in high school when I did my first centerfold for the men's magazine *Lektyr*. When I came to school after the publication, the whole place was virtually wallpapered with the pictures. I really had to stay mentally strong. I had no social control at all from home—my siblings and I grew up with divorced parents, so I didn't get much guidance from the adult world. I took care of myself and relied on my own decisions most of the time.

With the big circulation of these magazines, fame came kind of naturally. Soon enough, different movie producers started to get in touch with me; one of them represented the American production company behind my first movie, *Maid in Sweden*.

Maid in Sweden was shot in Stockholm. Since I was still in school, I had to play hooky. During the filming I settled in at Grand Hôtel. I felt a whole new world opening up to me, absolutely fantastic. I felt instantly that this was for me. The movie was shot in two weeks in different locations all over Stockholm. Among others, I acted with famed Swedish actor Gösta Ekman's brother Krister Ekman and his wife Monica.

Then *Rötmånad* came along. Two days after graduating high school I moved to Hotel Reisen, my first home in Stockholm. I didn't get the part in *Rötmånad* by applying, the producer, Bengt Forslund, had simply seen my magazine photos. Over four hundred girls had applied for the part, but Bengt called director Jan Halldoff and said that he had found the right girl. "I am the one in charge," Bengt told Halldoff. I guess Bengt thought I had the right attributes for marketing the movie.

A couple of years earlier, Halldoff had made the acclaimed movie *Korridoren*, which was seen as very serious. This led to a very mixed reaction for *Rötmånad*. I guess the reviews were fairly good, but the movie clearly agitated and divided the critics.

Along came *Smoke*, directed by Torbjörn Axelman and starring Lee Hazlewood. The production was pretty small, as Torbjörn's main media was television. *Smoke* was initially meant to be an American feature. I portrayed a girl similar to comic strip character Little Orphan Annie, with short hair. Axelman offered to double my fee—which was low to begin with—if I would cut my long hair, but the limit of my integrity had been reached! We used a wig. Torbjörn has always been pretty odd and peculiar, I think he felt a bit excluded.

Next came *Exponerad*, which costars many of the big Swedish acting names of the time, like Janne "Loffe" Carlsson, Heinz Hopf, Tor Isedal, and Bert-Åke Varg. *Exponerad* become incredibly famous, and was screened at the film festival in Cannes. I guess you could call me the commotion of the year, since they dropped me from a helicopter onto a pier in the middle of the Mediterranean. I remember it being windy like you wouldn't believe. I had custom-made clothes to wear around the festival palace, and a manager who made sure I was constantly in the spotlight. There were tons of photographers everywhere, so the pictures spread throughout the world. Around that time, I recorded a single, produced by old country singer Alf Robertson. I howled and sang to the best of my ability, but there were no efforts made in order to improve my vocals, so it sounded like it sounded.

After that, I was very busy. I participated in two productions by Joe Sarno, *Young Playthings* and *Swedish Wildcats*. He liked going to Stockholm to look for Swedish girls. He was fairly productive and today a lot of people have reassessed his movies. I also made four *Schulmädchen* movies in Germany. The Germans love their uniforms, it's as simple as that. It was disciplinary, up early in the morning and all around very German. I also had a split-second part in *Jorden Runt med Fanny Hill*—if you blink, you'll probably miss me.

Thanks to the heavy publicity from *Exponerad*, I got the opportunity to go to Japan and work for one of the biggest production companies there, Toei, participating in two movies, *Sex & Fury* and *Journey to Japan*. I incidentally bumped into representatives from Toei on an airplane when I was heading to France for a photo shoot.

The Japanese and I really hit it off. I am pretty shy, reserved, and small. They liked that for some reason, and when I acted in movies there, I easily adjusted to their lifestyle. They wanted me to sign a long-term deal, which I probably would have done, but I received a telegram from Sweden asking me to star in *Anita – Ur En Tonårsflickas Dagbok*. I had been in Japan for three months already, and was getting a bit homesick. For them I was probably something out of the ordinary. In many ways, Japan was perfect for me.

My costar in *Anita* was the now world-famous actor Stellan Skarsgård. Strange as it may sound, back in those days I was actually more famous than him. Stellan had a passionate interest in movies, he was virtually a movie freak, but first and foremost he loved the theater. He had been in the *Bombi Bitt* series (sort of the Swedish *Huckleberry Finn*), and to really establish himself in the world of theater he worked as a dresser at the Royal Dramatic Theatre. He never had any formal education in acting. Aside from theater he worked in movies. We did another movie together, *Lätt Byte*, but it was never finished. He was a very soft-spoken and pleasant person, somewhat shy, like I was. Stellan sometimes distances himself from his early career, and I think that's a shame.

For a few years during the 1970s, many established names of the Swedish film business acted in these movies, or worked behind the camera. For example, we used the same technicians as Ingmar Bergman. These were big productions made with the most prominent cinematographers, actors who had worked for the Royal Dramatic Theatre and other established personnel. Things worked this way up until about 1974, when the industry for these movies collapsed and transitioned to pornography—which obviously led to these actors not wanting to participate.

In 1972, I began work on the movie I am best known for, *Thriller – En Grym Film*. It was a pretty cruel production as well. Bo A. Vibenius was an emotionally detached person. I had to take both karate and weapons classes, and I ended up looking like one big bruise. Bo was pretty keen on things looking authentic. Fair enough: I was of the opinion that if I was supposed to be beaten, then beat me, but do it in one take! His rough approach was probably for the best; if you do it like that, you can tell it is for real.

I was excited to be part of *Thriller*. My character, Madeleine, doesn't have many lines, an ingenious decision by Vibenius. Since I wasn't a professionally trained actress, my strength did not lie in expressing myself with my voice. While shooting the movie, I was brought in to see the police as a criminal menace. In one scene, I stop short in my car and throw myself out of it while cradling a gun. Suddenly, I saw people running desperately for their lives. Since we were shooting with cameras low to the ground, they weren't very visible, and apparently people thought everything was for real: A mad girl coming at them with a black coat, an eye patch, and sporting a weapon.

Only Vibenius can verify how the infamous eye-cutting scene was accomplished. I heard he knew a doctor at Karolinska University Hospital, and that they had the body of a girl there who had committed suicide. They supposedly put on some makeup around the eye and poked it with a scalpel. As for the sex scenes, as far as I remember I didn't know of them, but there was a clause in my contract mentioning that there would be inserted scenes. Those scenes were shot separately at an old sex club where they had intercourse onstage.

As far as my costar Heinz Hopf, he was a wonderful person, and I became very close with him. He was intellectual, interesting, and intelligent. Unfortunately, he doubted his calling to act. He did go back to school to become a doctor, but returned to acting when he got a part in the TV series *Varuhuset*. We had already worked together in *Exponerad*, but otherwise there was no comparison between the two movies. The director of *Exponerad*, Gustav Wiklund, was pretty laid back and bohemian, quite a charming man. Vibenius was rough and demanding, so the two Swedish directors had very different personalities.

Thriller fascinated me a lot, and it was enormously criticized when it came out. Personally, in all my naïveté, I was mostly happy about finally getting a challenging part. I think that the movie was somewhat ahead of its time. You can clearly see how later movies, like *Kill Bill*, have used its themes. In a way, *Thriller* lives on, through strong women in subsequent films. I am very flattered, of course. Vibenius planned to make a sequel, but for some reason he never came around. *Thriller 2* would have been pretty cool, wouldn't it?

After *Thriller*, I was supposed to get the lead role in *Natalie*, but I ditched it. Or to be honest, I ran away from the movie shoot. I was there for two weeks, but during a chat with the director, Gerard Damiano, he told me that they were shooting genuine porn scenes in the basement, and that the movie would end up being hard-core pornography. I ran away. He said, "I think you are too serious and talented, you should just get out of this production, as I plan on doing so myself." I brought Marie Ekorre with me. We escaped early one morning and then waited at the airport, shivering, until the first airplane came. The German producer tried to hunt me down for years, threatening to sue.

As promised, Damiano also left, so I don't know who finished directing that film. I remember Damiano was a nice guy. I don't buy all that talk about him forcing Linda Lovelace to do all kinds of things in *Deep Throat*. I simply think she had second thoughts after the reviews came out. Damiano was not the kind of person who would force anyone to do anything.

Other than Heinz Hopf, I didn't have close relationships with many of the actors I starred in films with. Most of them, like Jan-Olof Rydqvist, always portrayed unlikable characters, and you could probably find a lot of themselves in the parts they played. I was so young and most of the others much older than me. There was a fairly wide gap between the generations in those days, so mostly we didn't connect to any wider extent. I liked hanging out with the technicians better, so I became closer with the machinery behind the camera.

I applied to the National Academy of Mime and Acting. I made a few audition cuts, but it somehow grew too big. I got nervous, so it didn't work out. I found a real job instead. I tried out journalism in the mid-1970s. Studying at Poppius School of Journalism in 1975 led to part time work at *Se*, *Fib Aktuellt*, and a few magazines within the Bonnier group. Most notably, I did sauna interviews, where I took famous people with me into a sauna. I also contributed a number of sex columns, but actually got fired from that since they thought I was too much of a prude. There is probably some truth to that—it really wasn't my thing.

In 1977, I had one of those split-second parts portraying a nurse in *91:an och Generalernas Fnatt*. The man I eventually shared my life with, Bo Sehlberg, also participated in that movie. I met him in 1973. But I decided that he damn well needed to see what it meant to make a movie. A film set is not as glamorous or cool as it may seem, but rather an endless wait. A couple of years later, we did a short together, *There Is a Sunrise Every Morning*, a fascinating movie made by a man named Björn Örtenheim. It's so cool. He had full insight into the changing climate: The film was kind of a short version of Al Gore's *An Inconvenient Truth*, but in 1979. It serves as a warning for what all the pollution will lead to. Among other characters, I played a Stone Age woman and a housewife, and the effects of climate change are displayed exactly as they are still discussed today.

Since I have always been passionate about the environment, I brought up that movie a lot while doing publicity for other films. I talked about it when I returned to Japan. When I spoke about what I knew about the mercury disaster in Minamata, I guess the Japanese didn't find me as polite anymore. I really wish that *Sunrise Every Morning* could be made available now. Nowadays, Björn leads a pleasant life in Thailand, and the movie remains in his daughter's basement in Stockholm, so we are working on that. I have to say, I think it's pretty cool that they knew exactly what they were talking about back in the mid-1970s.

During the 1980s, my screen time dropped to a few short moments. I had a small role in *Attentatet*, in the very beginning of the movie. I recall shooting at least parts of it in Mats Helge Olsson's apartment in Lidköping. Around that time, Per Oscarsson's *Sverige åt Svenskarna* came out, and I had another small part. That movie can be described as hysterical. I imagine Mats Helge suffered financially from both of those films.

In the following years, my life became about almost anything but celebrity or cinema. To this day, I am a mushroom fanatic. I spend all year waiting on that first day when it's time to head outside and pick those first little summer chanterelles. It's such an astonishing feeling to pick mushrooms, kind of like hunting but without the blood. In the 1990s, my husband-to-be, Bo Sehlberg, and I produced the short *Christina's Mushroom School*, an introduction to twenty different kinds of edible mushrooms. In my own teaching style, I explain how to break them apart and how to cut them open.

I am passionate about nature, animals, and the environment. I would not have had such a wonderful life without them—they give life purpose. I like animals just as much as people. As of now I live with two Siamese, Merlin and Moritz. Meanwhile, a whole range of wild animals roam freely outside my house. I live in a mansion that I cherish, and I love taking care of it and the surrounding property. The neighbor's horses graze on my land. Biological diversity is an understatement when describing my life. I guess I am a bit of a fanatic.

I haven't abandoned acting entirely. I acted in *Ingen Kom Ner* in 2009, a suggestive horror thriller. Otherwise it is mostly a matter of time. After all, I have a business, a house, and land to look after. I get many suggestions from enthusiasts about participating in movies. In the 1980s, the interest was virtually dead. No one cared about the 1970s any more. Now there is an incredible new interest; I think it's great. As of now, it just keeps growing.

That makes me proud. I really tried to create something good, something beyond the skimpy-clothes deal. Though I don't like watching myself on film, people usually say that I was the only one in my pictures who had enormous ambition. I tried to find a purpose and goal with these films, even if others just thought they were goddamn liquor movies.

Now I look back on my life with a lot of humor—it was fun. It might not sound as cool today, but I was probably one of very few to even travel outside of Sweden in the 1970s. It wasn't very common. I got to act with many of the biggest names in Swedish film, and when I see any of them around town, I still greet them politely. I danced with King Carl Gustaf when he was crown prince. He spent a lot of time at Alexandra's club in Stockholm with his friends. I imagine they must have had a table reserved constantly, and they always invited over hot girls. I got to ride in his sports car, and later danced with him at Princess Christina's party in the castle.

I look back with genuine joy. I am so very happy I could be a part of the '70s; it was so incredibly interesting. I carry it with me; it is a part of me. I would never deny being in *sensationsfilms*. I know that a lot of people do so, but I just had a blast.

Thank you to Rickard Gramfors for invaluable expert assistance.

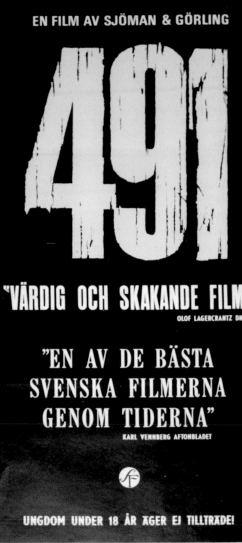

Clockwise from top left: Stylish and sensual poster for 491 masks a bleak, nihilistic movie;

"A dignified and unsettling film"... "One of the best Swedish films in history"..."Youths under 18 not allowed to enter";

Totally spoiler-free Italian poster for Ådalen '31—not a labor riot in sight

491

Six juvenile delinquents are persuaded to take part in a questionable therapeutic experiment—and if they refuse they will be sent to jail. Young, enthusiastic idealist Krister (Lars Lind) will host the reluctant gang while they conduct group therapy by conversation. The purpose of this is not totally clear, and things quickly get out of hand. One of the young men, Nisse (Leif Nymark), gets especially out of line, spending his days harrasing and abusing everyone, stealing things, and pimping a girl from the group. This lout crosses the final line when he steals all the Nietzsche and other important books from the study and trades them for booze. Things turn even sourer when one of the instigators of the experiment abuses Nisse sexually. The project implodes when one of the guinea pigs kills himself, and the whole group ends up being picked up by the police after all.

Based on a controversial book by Lars Görling, *491* is a brutal story about ruthless juvenile delinquents under the control of an equally ruthless sociopolitical institution. Shock waves rocked Sweden when the movie came out. The film was banned altogether in 1963, and only after the minister of education supervised a number of cuts could the film be shown in theaters.

When finally rereleased in full uncut glory in 1975, audiences were confronted by bad language, sex, drinking, physical abuse, and of course the most disreputable scene, involving off-screen nonconsensual sex with a dog. (The sound effects of the groaning dog had been among the first elements to fall under the shears of the king's censor.) Though not as high-impact today, *491* is actually still quite powerful. The movie version, however, is inferior to Görling's totally unrelenting original novel.

Director:
Vilgot Sjöman

Cast:
Lars Lind
Leif Nymark
Stig Törnblom
Lars Hansson
Sven Algotsson
Torleif Cederstrand
Bo Andersson
Lena Nyman
Frank Sundström
Åke Grönberg

(1969) ÅDALEN 31

Director:
Bo Widerberg

Cast:
Peter Schildt
Marie De Geer
Jonas Bergström
Kerstin Tidelius
Roland Hedlund
Stefan Feierbach
Martin Widerberg
Anita Björk
Olof Bergström
Olle Björling

A 1931 labor strike in the region of Ådalen in northern Sweden gets out if hand, escalating into violence as scabs are dragged away from the job and battered by enraged strikers. The police are powerless in the chaos, so the military must mobilize in order to calm the situation. This does little good, though, and the scene intensifies. A fierce clash erupts in the village of Lunde between demonstrators and the military. Circumstances degrade further, and the military loses all control, opening fire and killing five people.

This historical drama depicts the happenings in Ådalen in the early '30s, when the people in power killed a number of demonstrators over a labor dispute. Though the film is actually a serious political drama, there is something undeniably exploitative about making entertainment out of a historic tragedy. Oh, there is also an unpleasant sequence in which a man hypnotizes a girl in order to have her take her clothes off. That's uncalled for—intrusive, considering the nature of the story—and by all means sensational.

Ådalen 31 hit the jackpot at the 1969 Cannes Film Festival, taking home the jury's special prize. Everyone in France was horrified by the shabby appearance of the Swedish filmmakers, who apparently lacked any kind of elegance or proper clothes. The film was also nominated for an Academy Award for Best Foreign Language Film that year.

Director Bo Widerberg often injected unnecessary elements of *sensationsfilm* into his otherwise serious productions. In his final film, *Lust och Fägring Stor* (1995), he finally went over the top and put his own son, Johan, in all the sex scenes. He further amused himself in that same movie by making a twelve-year-old girl strip nude for his hungry camera. And then he died.

Alternative title: *Adalen Riots*

ÄLSKANDE PAR
[Loving Couples]

In 1914, three women come together in a maternity ward to give birth, and by coincidence they must also free themselves from dead children in their pasts. In flashbacks, we get insight into the lives of the women.

Mai Zetterling's feature debut is a powerful version of Agnes von Krusenstjerna's notorious novel *Fröknarna von Pahlen* (The Misses von Pahlen), a source of great controversy in the early 1930s—a kind of *sensationsbook*, if there was such a thing. Scenes from the hospital are totally anxiety-ridden, with an eerie audio backdrop of squeals, echoes, and screams. Several long flashbacks bring to life a wide variety of bizarre motifs such as copulating dogs, veiled homosexuality, bare breasts, a pastry-gobbling pedophile, a hound getting shot to death, and a dead fetus being thrown into a wastebasket—with a few authentic scenes of childbirth thrown in to complete the audacious stream of consciousness. Add a young Heinz Hopf as a sleazy upper-class brat, and *Älskande Par* rates as a minor masterpiece.

(1964)

Director:
Mai Zetterling
Cast:
Harriet Andersson
Gunnel Lindblom
Gio Petré
Anita Björk
Gunnar Björnstrand
Jan Malmsjö
Heinz Hopf
Eva Dahlbeck
Anja Boman
Frank Sundström
Hans Strååt
Inga Landgré
Dan Landgré
Bengt Brunskog
Margit Carlqvist
Toivo Pawlo
Catharina Edfeldt

ÄNGLAR,
FINNS DOM...

REGI: LARS-MAGNUS LINDGREN

JARL KULLE
CHRISTINA
SCHOLLIN
EDVIN
ADOLPHSON
SIGGE
FÜRST
ISA QUENSEL
GUNNAR SJÖBERG

FÄRGFILM
MUSIK:
EVERT TAUBE
TORE
LUN

Sandrews

Christina Schollin and
Jarl Kulle—about as
sensational as Swedish
films got in 1961

ÄLSKANDE PA

en film av Mai Zetterling med Harriet Andersson Gunnel Lindblom Gio Petr
Gunnar Björnstrand Jan Malmsjö Anita Björk Eva Dahlbeck m.fl.   Sandrew

Happy title (Loving Couples),
happy marriage, happy poster—
dark, dark movie

ÄNGLAR, FINNS DOM?
[Angels, Do They Exist?]

(1961)

Here lies a simple love story about a poor boy meeting a rich girl—what possibly could be sensational about that?

Though *Änglar, Finns Dom?* appears sweet and innocent by today's standards, at the time of its premiere the film was seen as very daring. In particular, the theme of a woman recognizing her own sexuality was considered totally improper. I guess the women of 1960 were expected to be home doing the dishes and raising children; forget about how those children were conceived—nobody was supposed to know about that. Fortunately, Swedish directors returned to this theme with great vigor hundreds of times in the following years, and countless subsequent *sensationsfilms* soon cleared up everything anybody could possibly want to know about female sexuality.

Back in 1961, however, *Svenska Dagbladet*'s reviewer was genuinely offended by the intense intimacy: "It is frankly terribly disturbing!" Nonetheless, leading couple Jarl Kulle and Christina Schollin became very popular following the release of this film, and they acted together again in several movies.

Alternative titles: *Do You Believe in Angels?*; *Love Mates*

Director:
Lars-Magnus Lindgren

Cast:
Jarl Kulle
Christina Schollin
Edvin Adolphson
Sigge Fürst
Isa Quensel
Gunnar Sjöberg
George Fant
Margit Carlqvist
Åke Claesson
Elsa Carlsson
Toivo Pawlo

ANIMAL PROTECTOR

Director:
Mats Helge Olsson
Cast:
David Carradine
A. R. Hellquist
Camilla Lundén
Mats Huddén
Timothy Earle
Frederick Offrein
Bo F. Munthe
Bruno Wintzell
Eva Andersson
Lars Lundgren
Eva Ostrom

While safely sequestered on a remote island, away from peering eyes, military scientists perform horrendous experiments on animals in order to produce chemical weapons. The corrupt military management does not hesitate to turn to murder to protect its interests. But when the island is invaded by both the CIA and an all-female animal rights group calling themselves Animal Protectors, a full-scale war erupts.

Mats Helge Olsson's substandard effort sends ripples across the screen with a smattering of Ak 5 Swedish assault rifles, poorly choreographed fights, and broken English. The plot is thin even by Olsson's standards, but the movie makes up for its lack of story with action, as people are shot and burnt to bits on a regular basis. In one especially vile sequence, a boat captain unlucky enough to end up on the island is tied to a chair to be tortured and shot for seemingly no reason. All this wicked violence in combination with the arrival of the foxy '80s-style ladies of the animal rights group makes this film somewhat more enjoyable than the rest of Olsson's productions from the same time period. For anyone in the right mood, this colorful action spectacle is worth a look. I enjoyed it more than *Iron Man* (Jon Favreau, 2008).

ANITA – UR EN TONÅRSFLICKAS DAGBOK
[Anita: From a Teen Girl's Diary]

(1973)

Director:
Torgny Wickman
Cast:
Christina Lindberg
Stellan Skarsgård
Danièle Vlamnick
Michel David
Per Mattsson
Evert Granholm
Arne Ragneborn
Jörgen Barwe
Erika Wickman
Berit Agedal
Thore Segelström
Jan-Olof Rydqvist

Listless teenager Anita (Christina Lindberg) feels rejected at home by her cold parents, and she doesn't fit in with a judgmental society. Her restlessness leads to rebellious nymphomaniac behavior, and the young girl seeks out sex encounters with an assortment of dirty old men, staggering drunks, hallucinating drug addicts, and other questionable individuals. This untamed lifestyle takes her on a journey through the dirtier parts of Stockholm, including junkie central, Plattan square; the lawless central train station; some sex shops; porn clubs; and a dope den on Västmannagatan, a street in the fashionable Old Town of Stockholm.

Young psychology scholar Erik (Stellan Skarsgård) becomes involved in Anita's life, and tries to help her get back on track. His unorthodox solution to her troublesome nymphomania is to push her to reach orgasm, and toward that end he launches a series of "experiments." Erik treats Anita like a rare spider, and he gets very upset with his colleagues when they fail to understand his unorthodox approach to her rare affliction. For some reason, they just think she's a dirty girl. However, various attempts to have sex with a bunch of rough Italian junkies end up with everyone but Anita reaching sexual climax, and another liason with a shy office girl just seems bleak for everyone involved. The solution turns out to be true love—which she finds in the understanding and comforting Erik—and he cooks! All's well that ends well.

This is one of a string of movies based and obsessively focused on the stunningly gorgeous body of Christina Lindberg. There is a great deal of nudity, especially once the protagonist lands a job working at a strip club with several other girls. The dirtiest sequence depicts Anita, still in her pursuit of an orgasm, visiting a dope den overflowing with roughneck Italians ready to vent their sexual frustrations on the little girl. Mercifully, the final seconds of that scene occur off-camera.

Director Torgny Wickman's efforts were heavily criticized after the Swedish premiere. "*Anita – Ur en Tonårsflickas Dagbok* is a wretchedly bad story," wrote Monica Tunbäck-Hanson in *Göteborgs-Posten*. Yet all in all, this is a very good movie, if a little slow at times. Lindberg literally acts the pants off of Skarsgård. All hail Lindberg!

Alternative titles: *Anita*; *Anita: Swedish Nymphet*; *Les Impures*

Christina Lindberg and one of her many dirty old boyfriends (in this case, film director Arne Ragneborn) find a love nest in Anita – Ur en Tonårsflickas Dagbok (Anita: From a Teen Girl's Diary)

Courtesy of Klubb Super 8

Ann och Eve – De Erotiska (Ann and Eve: the Erotic Ones)*'s Gio Petré in firm Italian arms*

ANN OCH EVE – DE EROTISKA
[Ann and Eve: The Erotic Ones]

(1970)

Director:
Arne Mattsson
Cast:
Gio Petré
Marie Liljedahl
Francisco Rabal
Julián Mateos
Olivera Vuco
Heinz Hopf
Bozidarka Frajt
Nevenka Filipovic
Erik Hell
Agneta Prytz

Two Swedish journalists, Ann (Gio Petré) and Eve (Marie Liljedahl), slip away for an Italian vacation just prior to Eve's impending marriage. On arrival, Ann persuades her soon-to-be-wed friend to engage in an Italian love affair, and that act escalates into a number of sexual adventures with men as well as women. Before long, the focus shifts to unsettled matters between Ann and her ex-husband, against whom she plotted and whose death she ultimately caused. At the end, Eve heads back home to get married, and Ann scampers off to a film festival on the arm of an Italian film director.

This odd English-language sex thriller by the prolific auteur Arne Mattsson was obviously made for a foreign market, but it's hard to imagine how it could have been well received abroad. For one thing, the plot is very vague. Like many art-house productions, the movie floats freely, seemingly headed nowhere. Among a multitude of peculiar sequences are three singing performances; these include one in Swedish, and another featuring a midget on piano—the same midget who years later became widely known across Europe for his role in the hit TV show *Fort Boyard*. One of a heap of sex scenes that cannot go unmentioned entails stunning international star Marie Liljedahl, who is used by a band of dirty Italians on a truck bed after they toss her in the betting pot during a game of cards! Also of note is Heinz Hopf as the smarmy skipper who appears at the beginning of the movie.

Not surprisingly, critiques by the contemporary media were ruthless: "Let us all hope that Mattsson can move along and escape the stalemate his bitterness has put him in," wrote Elisabeth Sörensson in *Svenska Dagbladet*. My advice is to ignore the critical voices—and enjoy this classic Swedish sleaze flick to the fullest!

Alternative titles: *Ann and Eve*; *Anybody's*

(1979) ETT ANSTÄNDIGT LIV
[A Decent Life]

Director:
Stefan Jarl

Cast:
Kenneth "Kenta" Gustafsson
Eva Blondin
Patric Gustafsson
Majken Gustafsson
Gustav "Stoffe" Svensson
Lena Löfgren
Jan Löfgren
Sven-Åke "Skåning" Dyhlén
Elisabeth "Bettan" Backe
Jan "Jajje" Klingryd

In this freestanding sequel to quasi-documentary *Dom Kallar Oss Mods* (see page 51), eleven years have passed since we last met the pair Kenta and Stoffe, who have here reunited for the film. Kenta is now an employed family man who seems to get by fairly well. For Stoffe, things have accelerated downward, and he is completely stuck in a rut of drugs and alcohol. Kenta tries to persuade Stoffe to try to break away from his substance abuse, but he fails utterly. Instead, Stoffe dies from an overdose in a dirty toilet early in the movie. Kenta finds himself on his hands and knees, scrubbing up gallons of blood from his mother's apartment floor after she is arrested for stabbing her abusive boyfriend to death. Thus the second chapter of the Mods Trilogy serves up a bitter reflection on the beaten and socially marginalized.

Misery, desperation, and death find their victims in the distressed world of narcotics. The little spark of hope from *Dom Kallar Oss Mods* is totally extinguished and the result is a deeply frightening and dark movie. The refined balance between fact and fiction that Jarl presented in the first movie is totally broken down. All the suffering of the demolished people on the screen resonates in your soul, and you cannot help but wonder where the creators got the energy to just keep on arranging and staging this bitter production. This is a movie where the camera follows its subjects literally to the death.

While running for prime minister, Olof Palme campaigned on themes drawn from *Ett Anständigt Liv*, specifically the drug problem in Stockholm. As cultural minister, he had lifted the ban against the first Mods film in the late 1960s, and he was shocked to see that the protagonists had seemingly aged forty years in less than a decade. A powerful figure in the Swedish film world during the *sensationsfilm* era, to be sure, Palme even appears in *Jag Är Nyfiken – Gul* (see page 104), and his public assassination in 1986 (while leaving a movie theater) coincides with the end of the era.

Alternative title: *A Respectable Life*

ATT ÄLSKA
[To Love]

(1964)

Director:
Jörn Donner
Cast:
Harriet Andersson
Zbigniew Cybulski
Isa Quensel
Thomas Svanfeldt
Jane Friedmann
Jan Erik Lindqvist
Nils Eklund

Recently widowed, Louise (Harriet Andersson) must break out of her boring, petit bourgeois existence in order to become an independent woman. Initially reserved and inhibited, Louise embarks upon a journey that allows her to explore her sensuality, foremost through her encounters with Fredrik (Zbigniew Cybulski). In the end, she learns how to feel free, and looks forward to enjoying her life.

Jörn Donner is a distinguished Swedish-Finnish intellectual who has published more than thirty books. In 1984, he received an Oscar for producing Ingmar Bergman's *Fanny and Alexander*. *Att Älska* is hardly one of his more daring movies, but it still possesses the curious nuances that distinguish his productions. Though the boldest scene is rather tame—Louise dreams about being a stripper—a certain peculiarity pervades the entire movie, and thus the work qualifies as a *sensationsfilm*.

Att Älska was screened at the 1964 Venice Film Festival, but hardly anyone remembers seeing it. As was customary in southern European productions, the film was shot with each actor speaking in his or her native tongue. Afterward, Polish actor Cybulski's voice was overdubbed by well-known Swedish actor Sven-Bertil Taube, son of notorious Swedish folksinger Evert Taube, who wrote many songs of sailing the world in search of women and something to drink.

ATTENTATET
[The Violent Attack]

Director:

Thomas Johansson

Cast:

Willie Andréason
Christina Lindberg
Per Oscarsson
Marina Lindahl
Stig Törnblom
Carl-Erik Proft
Vivian Falk
Dan Lindhe
Thomas Johansson
Roland Johansson

Attentatet travels ten years into the future, all the way to the impossible-to-imagine 1990s, when a fictionalized Sweden has been plagued by civil war for eight years. A professor and a group of women are held hostage by three men in an apartment. After a nerve-racking siege, the standoff ends in a bloody confrontation.

This is indeed a violent depiction of the future, produced by the guru of Swedish trash cinema, Mats Helge Olsson. He cut costs by filming scenes at his apartment in Lidköping. The media completely ignored the film—it was not reviewed anywhere. As far as actors go, we are humbled by Christina Lindberg and Per Oscarsson, the best of two worlds—the most beautiful girl and the craziest *sensationsfilm* star.

During the 1960s, Oscarsson was invited to sing on a popular TV variety show. Instead of a nice song, he unexpectedly delivered a lengthy monologue on the subject of how to speak to children about sex. He stripped to his underwear on prime-time television, then removed them to reveal another pair of underwear. As his lecture progressed, he continued to peel off layer after layer of undergarments, in the process shocking the entire nation of Sweden to its core.

Alternative title: *Outrage*

AWOL – AVHOPPAREN
[AWOL: The Defector]

(1972)

Director:

Herb Freed

Cast:

Russ Thacker

Isabella Kaliff

Glynn Turman

Lenny Baker

Dutch Miller

Stefan Ekman

Heinz Hopf

Fed up with the Vietnam War, an American deserter (Russ Thacker) takes off for Stockholm. After getting fired from his initial job, as a porn actor, he soon lands under the wing of a clan of young left-wing revolutionaries. He takes a liking to Inger (Isabella Kaliff), who regrettably ends up getting shot by the police during a demonstration in the tragic climax of the film.

In 1972, Hollywood remained completely silent on the subject of Vietnam, but, interestingly enough, this Swedish–American co-production was completed successfully—in spite of the total disagreement that existed between the two countries concerning the war. Swedish exploitation king Heinz Hopf is an especially creepy highlight of the film, thrown in for good measure in a minor role as a porn director.

Movie critic Jonas Sima saw right through the topical subject matter and denounced *AWOL* to *Expressen* readers as "a sick, political porn movie." Probably Sima still had his distaste for this film in mind fifteen years later, when he launched an unsuccessful national campaign to ban such films as Peter Jackson's *Dead Alive* (1992).

BÄDDAT FÖR LUSTA
[Bed Made for Lust]

Director:
Rune Ljungberg
Cast:
Lajla Senf
Miss de Lee
Lajla af Stockholm

A virgin named Amy visits a sex counseling agency to gather some information on sinful adulthood. The sex consultant quickly leads Amy into a hidden side room, where a great number of sexual acts take place before her eyes. Before Amy knows it, she finds herself involved in the lustful games with men as well as women.

This listless and amateurish movie is basically a porn film where we see a young girl confronted with all sorts of sexual desires. No offense to the actors, but the most exciting parts of the movie are in fact all the fabulous 1970s paraphernalia, such as the clothes, the furniture, the music, and even the great wallpaper! Wristwatches are never removed when performing sex, a detail that probably says a lot about the commitment of the participants. And yet *Bäddat för Lusta* is the first Swedish porno recorded in 35 mm color. Unfortunately, this breakthrough did not disrupt the amateur-hour flavor. Overall, *Bäddat för Lusta* is a pretty boring affair.

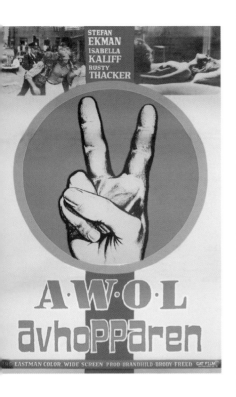

Clockwise from top left:
"Sick, political porn"? AWOL
– Avhopparen (AWOL: The
Defector) *poster;*

*You don't have to understand
Swedish to enjoy the
unforgettable* Baksmälla
(Hangover) *poster, but it helps
("baksmälla" literally
means "ass smack")*
Courtesy of Klubb Super 8;

*Jörn Donner and Diana Kjaer
in* Baksmälla
Courtesy of Klubb Super 8

(1973)

Director:

Jörn Donner

Cast:

Jörn Donner

Christine Hagen

Diana Kjaer

Rolf Bengtsson

Lisbeth Vestergaard

Birgitta Molin

Guy Durante

BAKSMÄLLA
[Hangover]

After an exceptionally booze-fueled party, worn-out car salesman Lasse (Jörn Donner) wakes up with a terrible hangover and a strange woman in his bed. The bad news piles up when an insurance agent passes by to examine Lasse's paperwork. Our protagonist's day seems to reach rock bottom when his wife (Diana Kjaer) asks for a divorce—quite understandable considering the circumstances. Yet by bragging about former sexual escapades, Lasse somehow manages to stabilize the situation and intrigue his wife anew. Afterward, he still has sex with the unknown woman before her boyfriend eventually picks her up. The wife does not let the interloper bother her, though, and the couple reconciles with champagne, food, and sex. Happy endings all around—no matter how unlikely the story sounds!

Baksmälla is a surreal potpourri of erotic flashbacks, severe hangovers, naked women, nice boozing, and cool jazz. The director's choice to cast himself in the role of womanizing protagonist can be seen as nothing less than a gigantic ego trip. Donner's lack of acting ability does not help anything, reducing the movie to an involuntary farce. The best of the erotic flashback sequences involves immorally hot sleaze queen Diana Kjaer as one of the car salesman's conquests. In contrast, the shabbiest moment of the movie occurs when "the woman who spent the night" pets herself vigorously with a telephone receiver. The abundance of nudity and the reasonably erotic atmosphere make for a decent movie. The critics did not agree. "Miserable dialogue by Donner. The photography and editing is severely lacking," chided *Nordvästra Skånes Tidningar*. "Is there anything positive to say about this movie? No." This did nothing to tarnish the Oscar statue sitting on Donner's fireplace for his work on *Fanny and Alexander* (Ingmar Bergman, 1982).

By the way, *bäksmalla*, the Swedish word for "hangover," literally means "ass-smack," which explains this film's seemingly gratuitous but assuredly unforgettable poster artwork.

Alternative titles: *Danish Love*; *Romantic Memoirs*

BARNENS Ö
[Children's Island]

(1980)

Director:
Kay Pollak
Cast:
Tomas Fryk
Anita Ekström
Ingvar Hirdwall
Börje Ahlstedt
Lars-Erik Berenett
Hjördis Petterson
Sif Ruud
Lena Granhagen
Majlis Granlund
Malin Ek

Eleven-year-old Reine Larsson (Tomas Fryk) does not feel like going to summer camp at Children's Island, so instead he decides to spend the summer on his own in Stockholm. After successfully manipulating his neglectful mother, he ventures out into the big, sprawling capital city, ready to spend one last summer on the streets as a child. Scared of growing pubic hair, yet curious as to what adolescence will bring, he encounters a theatrical group, some rowdy hustlers, a gang of juvenile delinquents, and other charmers. Through a string of adventures and discoveries, and with the help of his creepy portable tape recorder, Reine gradually realizes what becoming a man is all about.

This critically acclaimed and successful youth drama is a remarkable reminder that movies don't always turn out to be exactly what they claim. Though *Barnens Ö* has a number of artistic qualities, make no mistake: This is also a genuinely sensationalized movie that wallows in dirty words, drinking, nudity, and other dubious attributes. Quite exceptional is the director's fixation with young Fryk's penis, which is displayed fully erect—sleazy exploitation in its most questionable form! In the same vein, a scene where Börje Ahlstedt has sex with a very young girl in a car can only be described as highly disagreeable. Honorable mention goes to Ingvar Hirdwall, who is immensely unsympathetic in the role of the mother's lover.

Enhanced by the music of Jean-Michel Jarre, *Barnens Ö* is a highly commercial *sensationsfilm* that holds up to repeat viewings. Fourteen years later, director Kay Pollak received an Oscar nomination for his musical drama *Så Som i Himmelen* (US title: *As in Heaven*)—a movie far inferior to *Barnens Ö*. Though *Barnens Ö* won a slew of Swedish awards, the Russians still felt obliged to cut out all the child nudity for their release. Nuclear bombs, Gulags, and non-stop espionage were fine, but even the Soviets couldn't stomach child exploitation at the level we tolerated in Sweden.

Fans of Swedish music should note that if eleven-year-old Reine had gone to summer camp on Children's Island like he was supposed to, he might have met Nicke Andersson, Alex Hellid, and Leif Cuzner, who in fact met there as thirteen-year-olds around that time and formed Nihilist, which later become Entombed, the best-known of all Swedish death metal bands.

(1973)

Editing:
Lasse Lundberg

DET BÄSTA UR KÄRLEKENS SPRÅK-FILMERNA
[The Best of the Language of Love Movies]

This is a sloppily edited compendium of clips from Torgny Wickman's four pseudo-documentaries starring Danish sex geniuses Inge and Sten Hegeler: *Kärlekens Språk* (see page 126), *Mera ur Kärlekens Språk* (see page 166), *Kärlekens XYZ* (see page 127), and *Kär Lek – Så Gör Vi. Brev Till Inge och Sten* (see page 122). Having quickly pointed that out, this is a movie no one needs to see—so let's forget about it immediately.

BEL AMI

Journalist George Duroy (Harry Reems) arrives from periodical *Ny Moral* (ahem, "New Morals") to cover an art exhibition by competing magazine *Playhouse*. His angle is that fine art is rapidly declining into pornography. As you might expect, the innocent Duroy is soon lured into the pleasures of the flesh himself, as every lady of the *Playhouse* staff displays a heated interest in this attractive young man. Only the beautiful girlfriend of his colleague Gordon (Bent Warburg) appear uninterested. However, when George ends up becoming editor in chief of *Playhouse*, the fringe benefits include free access to the desirable Anita (Christa Linder).

This is a typical Mac Ahlberg mix of hard-core pornography and slapstick. The film was a coproduction between Sweden, Finland, France, Holland, and Spain—everybody wanted some! Notable leading man Reems was costar of *Deep Throat*, and thus one of the bigger porn stars of the 1970s. His "grandeur" is evident, as he is the protagonist in every porn sequence of the movie. (He also keeps his wristwatch on in all the scenes—impressive!) Marie Forså is the brightest shining star among his female counterparts, and sex scenes with her are the movie's erotic highlights. As is typical of the genre, the coarse humor often takes the edge off of the erotic atmosphere, rendering scenes humorous rather than arousing. Trivia buffs might like to know that the movie is shot at Ängsholm castle near Stockholm, probably without the owners' knowledge.

Director:
Bert Torn
(Mac Ahlberg)
Cast:
Harry Reems
Christa Linder
Maria Lynn
(Marie Forså)
Bent Warburg
Bie Warburg
Jacqueline Laurent
Lucienne Camille
Preben Mahrt
André Chazel
Pia Rydberg
Lisa Olsson
Evert Granholm
Rune Hallberg
Christina Hellman
Göthe Grefbo
Lars Lennartsson
Charlie Elvegård
Lotte Cardy

(1988)

Director:

Joakim Ersgård

Cast:

Kjell Bergqvist

Lena Endre

Johannes Brost

Joanna Berglund

Patrik Ersgård

Bernt Lundquist

Lena Lindholm

PG Hylén

Mats Lundberg

Leif Grönvall

BESÖKARNA
[The Visitors]

Frank (Kjell Bergqvist) moves to a remote villa with his wife, Sara (Lena Endre), and their two kids. As soon as they are settled, Frank begins having trouble at work, and strange things start to occur at the house. Wallpaper peels off the wall for no apparent reason, eerie sounds echo in the night, and an evil aura emanates from a sealed room in the attic. To sort this mess out, Frank calls an occultist (Johannes Brost) from a tabloid, and the expert immediately recognizes that he must bring out the big guns. Armed with several energy-based gadgets, the team sets out on an exorcism, *Ghostbusters* style. The occultist dies during the procedure, however, and Frank soon lands in the middle of a police investigation. Sara now thinks that her husband is just plain crazy, so instead of assisting him she leaves him there. In the end, the handy Frank gets down to business and solves his ghost problem once and for all.

Dead set on making a horror film in Sweden, brothers Joakim and Patrik Ersgård spent over a year trying to secure funds from the Swedish Film Institute. Eventually, they realized they should do what the producers of the recent Swedish horror film *Scorched Heat* (see page 217) had done, and they launched their own company just to finance this single film. This was very risky business, since their film cost a staggering amount for a Swedish B movie—nearly two million dollars. More than a million people would have to buy tickets to see it for the brothers to break even, something that was just not going to happen in a nation of eight million people. Still, they dubbed all the sound in postproduction so they could sell international versions to make up for some of the losses. Nevertheless, their debt kept the brothers out of the film business for five years.

The film itself is a rather competent horror story about a haunted house, featuring a few explosions and a car chase. It's a shame *Besökarna* doesn't contain more sensations—blood, gore, sex, and nudity would certainly have helped the film break even. Eventually, Joakim Ersgård paid off his debts and came back to the film business, relocating his company to the more suitable environment of Los Angeles (changing his name to Jack Ersgard in the process). After *Rancid* (2004), he seems to have disappeared again, probably working off another financial deficit after that film's commercial failure and plotting his next return.

BLÖDAREN
[The Bleeder]

Director:
Hans G. Hatwig
Cast:
Åke Eriksson
Danne Stråhed
Mia Hansson
Sussi Ax
Agneta Öhlund
Eva Pettersson
Maria Landberg
Tony di Ponziano
Eva Danielsson

While touring northern Sweden, the all-girl hard rock band Rock Cats is stranded in the middle of nowhere due to an engine failure. Perhaps unwisely, they leave their bus to seek aid on foot, and soon they arrive at a mysterious deserted house. When it turns out that the house is inhabited by a deranged killer, the band finds itself in a grim scene of horror where it's hard to know who will survive.

Blödaren is a deplorable Swedish horror movie, shot in 1982 with a trembling video camera. The story is remarkably insufficient, and the acting is catastrophic. Even the thrill scenes are well below par. Despite the title, there is almost no blood to be found, beyond that which pours naturally (by reason of birth defect) from the evil title character's eye sockets. To add insult to injury, one of the main characters is portrayed by Swedish *dansband* singer Danne Stråhed, a complete cornball despite the fact that he was named the most prominent person from the province of Skåne in 1999. The only highlights in this mess are Thord Widlund's soundtrack—an homage to John Carpenter's *Halloween* score—and the truly intimidating portrayal of the mentally disturbed killer by Åke Eriksson, better known as drum virtuoso "Doktor Åke" from Swedish rock bands Wasa Express and Attack.

Before the premiere, Swedes ran amok, inflamed by rumors that Kiss front man Gene Simmons played the main character, which of course was untrue. The origin of the rumor was probably a picture in the Swedish music magazine *Okej!*, in which Simmons appeared holding a VHS copy of *Blödaren* in his mouth. Granted, there are distinct similarities between the totally unappealing Doktor Åke and Simmons, but the source of the rumor was most likely director Hans G. Hartwig, also editor in chief of *Okej!* Even without the demon of Kiss, a group of high school media students could produce a better film than this in a matter of hours.

Blödaren was released on video in Sweden by Mariann, a record label run by the notorious Bert Karlsson that trafficked in immensely succesful Euro-*schlager* artists such as Carola (active in the cult Word of Life) and Herreys (three brothers sworn to the Mormon church—probably the only Mormons in Sweden). Not satisified after selling millions of records appealing to the basest public instincts, Karlsson went into politics in the early '90s with the arrogant Count Ian Wachtmeister. The pair's extremely racist right-wing party, Ny Demokrati (New Democracy), received under 10 percent of the vote in the 1991 election and promptly dissolved.

(1958)

Director:

Robert Brandt

Cast:

Mark Miller
Lars Ekborg
Anita Thallaug
Birgitta Ander
Erik Strandmark
Stig Järrel
Dagny Helander
Norma Sjöholm
Ruth Johansson
Eva Laräng
Anita Edberg
Sangrid Nerf

BLONDIN I FARA
[Blonde in Danger]

After American journalist Larry (Mark Miller) is dispatched to Stockholm to write a series of articles about Swedish morals, he quickly discovers that the entire country is populated with nothing but easy blondes. While enjoying a drive in the countryside, Larry, eagerly keeping his eyes peeled for more girls, gets into an accident and wrecks his car. He hitches a ride with the unpleasant Max (Lars Ekborg), who runs an traveling strip show. Larry soon figures out that Max is dealing drugs, and naturally starts investigating further. When Larry's cover is blown, Max's hoodlums try to eliminate him, but the American sleuth gets off with nothing more than a good scare after a violent chase through the fun house at Gröna Lund, Sweden's oldest amusement park.

The film's international title *Blonde in Bondage* unfortunately gives false hopes, as there is no bondage to be found. We are treated to a strip show—a tease that definitely would have been considered more daring in the '50s than nowadays, as it disappointingly ends with the girl in her giant bra and panties. On the plus side, the movie offers a couple of reasonably intense punch-ups, and some neat sequences set in dirty streets and bars. For the modern audience it all comes across as very innocent. Though it sounds gritty on paper, the story never completely captivates, but all in all, this is still a fairly good movie.

Alternative titles: *Blonde in Bondage*; *Narkotika*; *Nothing but Blondes*

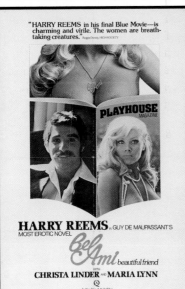

Clockwise from top left: The tense finale of Blondin i Fara
(Blonde in Danger), *as* Dan Ekborg *lies in wait for Mark
Miller during a chase through Gröna Lund fun house*
Courtesy of Klubb Super 8;

As undressed as it gets in Blondin i Fara
Courtesy of Klubb Super 8;

*Frederick Offrein in a gunfight and a naked groupie
avalanche rescue—a sample of the boundless entertaining
sensations in* Blood Tracks;

Harry Reems and Christa Linder grace the cover of
Playhouse *on the* Bel Ami *poster*

(1985) BLOOD TRACKS

Director:
Mike Jackson
(Mats Helge Olsson)

Cast:
Jeff Harding
Naomi Kaneda
Michael Fitzpatrick
Brad Powell
Peter Merrill
Thorsten Wahlund
Zinny Zan
Kee Marcello
Freddie Von Gerber
Alex Tyrone
Chris Lynn
Harriet Robinson
Tina Shaw
Frances Kelly
Karina Lee
Helena Jacks
Mats Helge Olsson
Frederick Offrein

Always up for a wild adventure, the rock group Solid Gold decides to record their new music video in an old abandoned factory up in the mountains. Trapped by an avalanche, they are soon forced to realize that everything is not as it should be. The decrepit facility turns out to be the home of a murderous family, and soon the video production crew starts to disappear.

Blood Tracks is the terminally sensational Mats Helge Olsson's unbelievably inadequate stab at making a 1980s slasher film. He produced a perfect turkey here, jam-packed with the three obligatory B-movie ingredients: breasts, beasts, and blood. The couple of snuggly sex scenes are hilarious, as the non-gender-specific glam rockers and their groupies intermingle in a nude tumble of teased-up hair and studded bracelets. As far as *sensationsfilms* go, this is a great one. Don't miss the scene in which a naked girl is dragged from a snowbound Volvo by an overeager gang of rescuers.

The biggest attraction is surely old trustworthy Swedish rockers Easy Action, here portraying fictional '80s hair farmers Solid Gold. Fact and fiction blur together in an almost uncanny fashion, and the priceless theme music would make Dokken weep! Not content with this career high point, guitarist Kee Marcello of Easy Action soon joined Sweden's titanic hair metal band Europe (of "Final Countdown" fame), while singer Zinny Zan (if that is his real name) moved to America and formed Shotgun Messiah.

Alternative title: *Heavy Metal*

BÖDELN OCH SKÖKAN
[The Executioner and the Harlot]

(1986)

Director:
Hrafn Gunnlaugsson

Cast:
Niklas Ek
Stephanie Sunna Hockett
Kjell Bergqvist
Per Oscarsson
Kjell Tovle
Sune Mangs
Kent Andersson
Lennart Tollén
Kim Anderzon
Britta Forsberg
Moica Ring
Solveig Wikander
Björn Gedda
Tor Isedal
Lasse Petterson
Olof Rhodin
Thorsten Flinck
Staffan Götestam
Emy Storm

In the late seventeenth century, a blacksmith (Niklas Ek) is wrongfully sentenced to death for assisting a band of robbers. Trouble occurs when the executioner (Kent Andersson) rapes a woman the night before the beheading, earning a spot on his own chopping block. To solve this mess, the blacksmith is freed and hired as executioner. After dispatching his first death sentence, the blacksmith realizes his new job is far from glorious. People throw mud at him on the street. Also, while relaxing at the local brothel, only the most overweight prostitute in the house is willing to service him—and only from behind, with no groping. Fortunately, a fresh new prostitute, Ursula (Stephanie Sunna Hockett), arrives at the brothel, oblivious to her customer's shameful occupation. Now the executioner can make love any way he desires. He apparently shows talent, because the couple's relationship goes from strictly business to emotional in a matter of minutes. In the romantic swirl, Ursula becomes pregnant. The blacksmith buys her from the brothel and prepares to marry her honestly. Unfortunately, things sour when Ursula's former master (Kjell Bergqvist) appears on the chopping block. A downward spiral ensues, ending badly for all.

Icelander Hrafn Gunnlaugsson directed this gloomy melodrama between his great Jokull-Western *Korpen Flyger* (see page 134) and his boring *Korpens Skugga* (see page 135). The result falls in the middle—it's great but boring. Though plenty dirty and sensational, the movie first aired on national Swedish television December 29, 1986, effectively ending the Christmas holiday and leaving a sour taste in the champagne glasses before New Year's Eve. Bloody decapitations and dirty brothel action are not family fare for the holidays—not even in Sweden. Everything about the whorehouse is unpleasant. The prostitutes are scuzzy and overweight, the customers all have limp unwashed penises, and everyone inside is drunk and miserable. The pacing is awfully slow, making the mood all the more depressing. But the real drawback is the headsman himself, as actor Niklas Ek mainly walks around looking stupid, apparently unaware that the camera is rolling. He was originally a dancer and probably should have kept hopping around. Sunna Hockett as prostitute Ursula fails to impress, but at least she can blame it on her inexperience—the poor thing was only fifteen years old! Yet she is exposed fully nude, acting in sensual sex scenes with Ek, twenty-seven years her senior and several steps down on any beauty scale. No wonder she never acted again.

(1975) BREAKING POINT

Director:
Ron Silberman Jr.
(Bo A. Vibenius)

Cast:
Anton Rothschild
(Andreas Bellis)
Irena Billing
(Barbro Klingered)
Per-Axel Arosenius
Jane McIntosh
Susanne Audrian
Bertha Klingspor
Liza June
Adolf Deutch
Joachim Bender
Marilyn Inverness

Hats off to the definitive Swedish *sensationsfilm*! A frustrated and solitary middle-aged family man, Billing (Anton Rothschild), suffers during his monotonous days working at an office. He lives in a surreal future, where everyone knows that 89 percent of all women are sluts waiting to be raped, and where a ceaseless war rages in "Africa"—a distant hell that is more or less an Africa of the mind. When our hero's family goes on vacation, his existence turns into a mesh of sex, rape, weapons, and model railroads; the boundaries between feverish fantasy and sordid reality are hardly distinguished. Among several staggering adventures, Billing tricks a female colleague into drinking from a cup of coffee spiced with his semen. In one dream sequence, he amuses himself by shooting a rubber band at his very erect penis. General insanity continues throughout the movie, until the completely unhinged modern man finally picks up his family at Stockholm's Arlanda Airport.

Breaking Point is without a shadow of a doubt one of the oddest and most fascinating Swedish movies ever. Judged by the perverse level of strangeness, no other movie even comes close to Bo A. Vibenius's curious opus. *Breaking Point* lacks action sequences and an understandable plot, but compensates handsomely with an array of unsettling hard-core pornography. The audience the creators of this movie were aiming for is completely impossible to discern, since the monotonous abstract story could hardly have drawn either the porn audience or the trash movie fiends. Among other curiosities, Anton Karas's classic "Harry Lime Theme" from *The Third Man* (Carol Reed, 1949) was stolen for the soundtrack. Not to mention that the movie's creators hide behind pseudonyms such as Adolf Deutsch, Oscar Wilde, and Urban Hitler!

This is unquestionably Swedish *sensationsfilm* at its most erratic and insane, and one of the most bizarre movies ever made anywhere. Today, the bleak office tower where Billing spends his days has become a university specializing in social problems, but the environment remains far too bleak for learning. Vibenius had worked with Bergman, and developed his own reputation with *Thriller – En Grym Film* (see page 258), but he shied away from directing films after this movie. Allegedly, the hard-to-pigeonhole director tried to coproduce some work with artist and filmmaker Carl-Johan de Geer during the 1980s based on the "Bill & Ben" books—a 1960s paperback series depicting the sexy and action-filled cowboy life of the American Wild West.

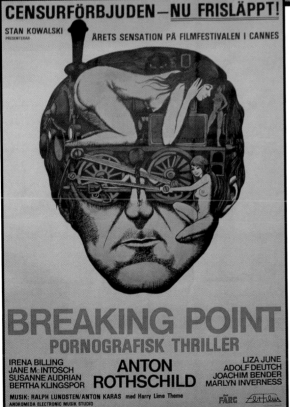

Clockwise from top left:
The controversial Il Capitano*;*

Sensationsfilms *queen Marie Forså's last hurrah,* Chez Nous*;*

Sex and model railroads on the mind on the graphic poster for Bo Arne Vibenius's odd and unforgettable Breaking Point

IL CAPITANO

(1991)

Director:
Jan Troell
Cast:
Maria Heiskanen
Antti Reini
Berto Marklund
Antti Vieriko
Harri Mallenius,
Majrut Dahlström
Eva Stellby
Matti Dahlberg
Christina Frambäck
Ingemar Böcker

Il Capitano is a docudrama based on the horrible Åmsele tragedy, a dark episode in 1988 in which two Finnish youngsters murdered a Swedish family of three. The heavy realism almost makes the film seem like director Jan Troell was present during the violent odyssey. Amateur actors Maria Heiskainen and Antti Reini are completely believable in their roles, and the gloomy, foreboding mood builds an atmosphere of impending doom. Troell comes across as respectful, even as he heavily exploits a real-life tragedy.

Even so, the proximity to the actual events—the film appeared just a few years after the crime—must have been painful for the victims' family. The families tried to stop this film production, cheered on by the moral majority of Sweden, and Troell came close to cancelling the whole project in 1989. Despite the heavy protests, the movie received good reviews at its premiere and won several awards internationally, including the Silver Bear at the Berlin International Film Festival. It's a brutal and ruthless masterpiece.

Alternative title: *Il Capitano: A Swedish Requiem*

CHAMPAGNEGALOPP
[Champagne Gallop]

(1975)

Director:
Vernon P. Becker

Cast:
Ole Søltoft

Egil Holmsen

Barbro Hiort af Ornäs

Sue Longhurst

Tina Möller-Monell

Per-Axel Arosenius

Julie Bernby

Bengt Olsson

Malou Cartwright

Charlie Elvegård

Diana Dors

Martin Ljung

Göthe Grefbo

Lars Lennartsson

Börje Mellvig

Billed as "the first lust story in 3-D," this is the story of young Jack (Ole Søltoft), who is growing up and becoming curious about sex. After being introduced to the mysteries of love at a brothel, Jack seeks out a woman of his own—someone who can be his sex coach, and the object of his heart's desires, too. He takes a liking to upper-class girl Alice (Sue Longhurst), and so kidnaps her, brings her to his home, and locks her up in a room filled with sex toys and—oddly enough—Jack the Ripper hiding in the closet. After Jack (the young boy, not the Ripper) thoroughly forces himself on her, Alice falls in love with him and they are soon married, leaving just one paramount unanswered question among several: Will Jack be able to handle his young wife's now insatiable sex drive?

Since Ole Søltoft was the king of Danish softcore, and Diana Dors had been the queen of British nudie films, their 3-D debut together should have been an event of royal proportions. However, if you think what's written above seems stupid, you are not alone. After the Swedish premiere, *Expressen's* Jonas Sima wrote: "Don't let this lifeless sex film lure you in with its atrocious jokes like a flat tasteless soda. Unfortunately, this is out of sync, out of focus, and out of luck. Granted, you do duck for an intrusive nipple from time to time, and close your eyes in shame over Martin Ljung's pitiful freak role. Nothing is worse than this. Shame on you, Europa-Stockholm Film!" Though the film's 3-D effects are admittedly pretty lousy, it's still more interesting than *Avatar* (James Cameron, 2009).

Alternative titles: *Champagne på Sengekanten*; *The Groove Room*; *A Man with a Maid*; *Musfällan*; *My Favorite Butler*; *Teenage Tickle Girls*; *What the Swedish Butler Saw*

(1962)

Director:

Gunnar Hellström

Cast:

Lillevi Bergman
Gösta Ekman
Bertil Anderberg
Åke Fridell
Eivor Landström
Sture Ericson
Åke Lagergren
Hans Wigren
Torsten Wahlund

CHANS
[Chance]

Raggare girl Mari (Lillevi Bergman) is a wild sixteen-year-old rocker, just released from a year at a juvenile detention outside Stockholm. Her wild ways aren't entirely her fault, as she was seduced by her uncle—an incident that led her into this life of booze, drugs, and crime. Seeking out her old gang, she finds that her ex-boyfriend has replaced her with a new squeeze. Crushed by rejection, Mari finds comfort in homosexual drug addict Natan (Bertil Anderberg), who cares for her without asking for anything in return. When this pillar of stability is arrested for possession, Mari finds a new haven with the sympathetic scholar Stefan (Gösta Ekman). Driven by her aggravating alcoholism, Mari tries to reconcile with her old gang, only to be further rejected and abused. In the bitter end, the messed-up girl is again taken into custody by police and sent back to the detention hall.

Based on Birgitta Stenberg's novel of booze, drugs, and carjacking, Gunnar Hellström's film is the roughest and most uncompromising of all the *raggare* movies—the mini-genre of films concerning a strange Swedish young subculture lost halfway been American cars, '50s rock 'n' roll music, and booze. The pessimistic approach and semidocumentary style of *Chans* paved the way for movies such as *Dom Kallar Oss Mods* (see page 51) and *491* (see page 17). Contemporaries in 1962, however, viewed the picture as iffy and shallow, as critics believed there were already too many exploitation movies about kids running completely wild in the streets of Stockholm. They had no idea how many more were still to come.

Alternative title: *Just Once More*

CHEZ NOUS

(1978)

A young girl named Laijla (Marie Forså) is murdered, and the press has a field day when they learn she worked for porn club Chez Nous. The killer, spurred by the attention, seeks out one of the evening newspapers to clarify certain details. As public interest in the case grows, journalists Maria (Ewa Fröling) and Wirén (Sven Lindberg) are sent to investigate the mystery. They take a dark, dirty journey through the misery and criminality of Stockholm's underworld.

Jan Halldoff's *Chez Nous* is a gritty crime drama with a very impressive cast. The incomparable list of actors includes names like Ernst-Hugo Järegård (as a wonderfully sleazy nightclub manager), Örjan Ramberg, and Kjell Bergqvist—all great guys. Exploitation enthusiasts will be pleased to find sleaze queen Forså's name on the list, as she makes one of her final appearances. Despite negligible screen time, she makes a lasting impression by swimming naked in an aquarium and pleasuring herself with an eel—even before the opening credits! The rest of the movie struggles to reach the quality of the great intro, and is too wordy to fully find traction. The actors end up standing in the way of the sensations. Nevertheless, *Chez Nous* is still well worth a look. Screenwriters Anders Ehnmark and Per Olov Enquist insisted the movie was better than their original play.

Director:
Jan Halldoff
Cast:
Ewa Fröling
Ernst Günther
Sven Lindberg
Ingvar Kjellson
Ernst-Hugo Järegård
Lis Nilheim
Kerstin Bagge
Kjell Bergqvist
Olof Buckard
Per Ragnar
Marie Forså
Per Oscarsson
Örjan Ramberg

(1971) DAGMARS HETA TROSOR
[Dagmar's Hot Panties]

Director:
Vernon P. Becker

Cast:
Diana Kjaer
Robert Strauss
Tommy Blom
Ole Søltoft
Anne Grete
Anne-Lise Alexandersson
Tor Isedal
Inger Sundh
Karl Erik Flens
Lars Söderström
Åke Fridell
Cecil Cheng
Bobby Kwan

Swedish lass Dagmar Andersson (Diana Kjaer) works as a prostitute in Copenhagen, but she is on the verge of quitting the business and returning to Sweden to get married. During her last day on the job, Dagmar encounters unfortunate complications, thanks to her difficult brother and some demanding customers. She eventually manages to flee, and locates a brighter future in Stockholm.

Largely uninteresting, this is a poor and dull sex comedy. Thankfully, Kjaer is her usual sinful self as the leading lady, but her presence just isn't enough. The movie is forcefully restrained by annoying slapstick gags accompanied by cheerful music—and altogether too many "tripping and falling on your backside" sequences. Things pick up when Tor Isedal arrives on the scene as a rough and brusque abuser of women, but even that threatening vibe dissolves immediately with a "humorous" scene of Isedal running about without clothes in a stairwell. *Dagmars Heta Trosor* is only recommended to the most devoted admirers of Swedish sleaze.

Alternative titles: *Dagmar & Co.*; *Dagmar's Hot Pants*; *Dagmar's Hot Pants, Inc.*

DAMEN I SVART
[The Lady in Black]

(1958)

Director:

Arne Mattsson

Cast:

Anita Björk

Sven Lindberg

Karl-Arne Holmsten

Annalisa Ericson

Isa Quensel

Nils Hallberg

Lena Granhagen

Lennart Lindberg

A young lady mysteriously disappears one night from the small village of Holmfors, somewhere in the middle of Sweden. The local police seem incapable of solving the crime, but by lucky coincidence ace private investigators John Hillman (Karl-Arne Holmsten) and his wife, Kajsa (Annalisa Ericson), happen to be vacationing in a small cabin nearby. After talking to some locals, the couple hears tales of the old village ghost, "The Black Lady," roaming the streets. Everyone acts suspiciously—not just the rough workers but also an arrogant artist and some neurotic aristocrats. The plot thickens when some other deaths occur, and the once idyllic village is plunged into terror, mystery, and violence. Since none of the locals seems able to function on a sane level, it's up to the Hillmans to crack the case.

This is the earliest of Arne Mattsson's five thrillers based on the Hillman couple, and this Swedish noir series went down extremely well, both with critics and audiences. This first installment flirts openly with horror clichés such as mysterious staring eyes, howling dogs, a tense violin score, and scenes draped in fog and long shadows. Not very sensational, the film is a mild mixture of suspense and humor (mainly courtesy of the Hillmans' goofy assistant, Freddy [Nils Hallberg]), except for a purely unnecessary and grim beheading of a chicken, captured in close-up.

The film's best sequence is set within a large, dark house. When the lights go out, the characters are chilled as they realize that someone with a lit cigarette has entered the room. In moments like this, the black-and-white cinematography of Ingmar Bergman favorite Sven Nykvist really shines. Apart from that, on-screen strangulation and a scene with a floating corpse might have been strong stuff in the '50s, but they wouldn't frighten a fly today.

Next in the series was the superior *Mannekäng i Rött* (see page 159), a film that earned Arne Mattsson a strong critical reputation, which he enjoyed for a few years.

Talk, talk, talk: A poster that fits Dagmars Heta Trosor (Dagmar's Hot Panties) *perfectly*

Young and carefree—Kenta and Stoffe on the poster for Stefan Jarl's masterful Dom Kallar Oss Mods (They Call Us Misfits)

Arne Mattsson's very early sensationsfilm, *the dark* Damen i Svart (The Lady in Black)

DOM KALLAR OSS MODS
[They Call Us Mods]

(1968)

Directors:

Stefan Jarl

Jan Lindqvist

Cast:

Kenneth "Kenta" Gustafsson

Gustav "Stoffe" Svensson

Jan "Jajje" Klingryd

The first film of the Mods Trilogy, this is a quasi-documentary depicting the closely intertwined lives of two struggling young men, Stoffe and Kenta. Through interviews, reenacted natural scenes, and verité observations, we get to know a lot about their upbringing and their seemingly carefree everyday life. The audience follows their journeys filled with beer bottles, hash pipes, arrests, and, eventually, disillusion. The depiction of these fiddling grasshoppers is honest and warm, yet ultimately turns brutal and frightening.

Stefan Jarl's classic portrayal of youngsters on the outskirts of society is overwhelming and touching. The film's open depiction of drugs and liquor must have been shocking at the time, and the portrait remains powerful to this day. The movie also contains what is often credited as the first genuine sexual intercourse in a feature film. Though really quite innocent and sweet, the scene became the source of huge controversy in Sweden, and was initially banned. After an extensive battle with the censors, the film ended up on the desk of Minister of Culture Olof Palme, who demanded that the movie be released with no cuts. Even so, no distributor in Sweden dared touch this volatile work, so it fell into the hands of pornmongers Pallas Film. This led to some confusion as old men in trench coats entered the theater expecting the usual trash and were met with sensitive social realism.

People of supposedly high morals heavily opposed the movie, but serious critics saluted this portrait of youth and its indescretions. Eventually, audiences found the film, and it became one of Sweden's proudest contributions to cinema. *Dom Kallar Oss Mods* remains a classic to be seen over and over again. Sadly, the protagonists never saw the film, as they were both arrested at the Stockholm premiere.

Alternative title: *They Call Us Misfits*

(1985)

DREAMS OF LOVE

Director:
*Andrew Whyte
(Andrei Feher)*

Cast:
*Gabriel Rivera
Marilyn Lamour
Gabriel Pontello
Marie Bergman
Bebi Bess
Ingrid Lindgren
Denise Martin
Ronald Engström
Ingvar Lund
Jeanne Zola*

An aging Casanova looks back on his life while writing his memoirs. As we follow his memories in flashbacks, we witness a whole string of erotic adventures and exploits—the old buzzard had time for a lot of hanky-panky over the years.

Andrei Feher's final film is a dull affair, presenting one mindless sex scene after another. Basically, the entire premise is just an excuse for the director to cobble together some "greatest hits" and commemorate his own life's work. Considering how much of the material is nicked from his own earlier productions, you realize just how watered down *Dreams of Love* really is. To put the most positive spin on things possible: Maybe this could be seen as a last breath of Swedish sex cinema before the makers had to surrender their cameras and make way for poor, homemade video productions.

Alternative title: *Kärleksdrömmar*

EAGLE ISLAND

(1986)

This movie begins badly for Eddie (Tom O'Rourke), a ranking military officer who gets fired from his job on the heavily guarded Eagle Island. His post is taken by a no-good infiltrator who paves the way for Soviet commandos to storm the island. Blissfully unaware, Eddie has a lame new job escorting an unwelcome female birdwatcher back to the mainland. When the birdwatcher finally stops ogling Eddie long enough to mention that her West German colleague remains stranded on Eagle Island, our hero turns the boat around and heads back to the rescue. Unfortunately, the Russians have already arrived and killed the remaining birdwatcher. Eddie takes matters into his own hands, and after a very, very long battle the Russians are defeated and the spy exposed.

Eagle Island was mostly shot at Mölle in the Swedish province of Skåne under the working title *The Ninja Mission 2*. The title is not altogether misleading; the Soviet soldiers at least resemble ninjas in their black costumes and hoods. Director Olsson and writer Madeleine Bruzélius had worked together already on *The Ninja Mission* (see page 182), but at that point the latter was only responsible for costuming. *Eagle Island* marks her debut as a scriptwriter, and it is very obvious she had no prior experience in that field. The plot is lacking, the direction poor, and the pathetic dialogue falls terribly flat. Even the fight scenes are weak and almost unbearably long. A talented director could have saved the Bruzélius script, and with Olsson in charge the film is obviously a lost cause. The results are so astonishingly insufficient that they even stain the already mocked life's work of Mats Helge Olsson (see *Animal Protector,* page 22; *Fatal Secret,* page 64; and too many others to list).

Alternative title: *The Ninja Mission 2*

Director:
Mats Helge Olsson
Cast:
Tom O'Rourke
Willy Boholm
Terry D. Seago
Timothy Earle
Mats Huddén
Lisa Robinson

(1969)

EVA – DEN UTSTÖTTA
[Eva: The Outcast]

Director:

Torgny Wickman

Cast:

Solveig Andersson
Hans Wahlgren
Siw Mattson
Inger Sundh
Göthe Grefbo
Barbro Hiort af
Ornäs
Jan Erik Lindqvist
Arne Ragneborn
Börje Nyberg
Caroline Christensen
Conny Ling
Jan-Olaf Rydqvist
Marie Liljedahl

Eva (Solveig Andersson) is a sad and lonely teen living in a small Swedish town. Since moving to the sticks from Stockholm, she has been treated like an outcast and looked down upon by the locals. In a desperate bid to somehow get even, she commits to a life of free sexuality to shock those around her. When the police start unraveling a prostitution racket, they discover that Eva has sold her body to a whole string of more or less respectable men in the city. When the entire ring is put on trial, at first it seems the men will walk away scot-free, until a young man who has always looked up to Eva speaks out bravely in her support. The perpetrators are convicted, and Eva finally receives the sympathies of all her fellow citizens and neighbors.

This speculative melodrama deals with the hypocrisy and double standards of a small community. There is a great deal of nudity, but the proceedings never become too seedy. Two shabby scenes stick out: one where Eva suddenly exposes her breasts to a police officer during questioning, and another where Eva flashes back on a fairly innocent lesbian adventure. A couple of somewhat daring sex scenes with sucking on nipples also occur. It's pretty vivid for a film from the '60s; more importantly, the movie is one of Torgny Wickman's best. Reportedly, a nudity-free version of the film was released in Catholic countries—too bad for the sleaze enthusiasts in the Vatican.

Alternative titles: *Eva*; *Eva... Was Everything but Legal*; *Diary of a Half Virgin*; *Swedish and Under Age*

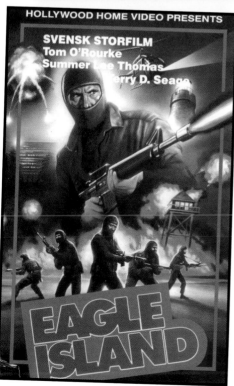

HOLLYWOOD HOME VIDEO PRESENTS

SVENSK STORFILM
Tom O'Rourke
Summer Lee Thomas
Terry D. Seage

EAGLE ISLAND

Clockwise from top left: Solveig Andersson cops a feel in Eva – Den Utstötta (Eva: The Outcast)
Courtesy of Klubb Super 8;

Eva – Den Utstötta's *Solveig Andersson*
Courtesy of Klubb Super 8;

Far away from Hollywood, Mats Helge Olsson's action-packed Eagle Island

Heinz Hopf beats up Tor Isedal as Christina Lindberg watches—the unholy trinity of sensationsfilms *superstars mixes it up in* Exponerad (Exposed)

Courtesy of Klubb Super 8

Janne Carlsson and Christina Lindberg embrace in Exponerad

Courtesy of Klubb Super 8

EXPONERAD
[Exposed]

(1971)

Director:
Gustav Wiklund

Cast:
Christina Lindberg
Heinz Hopf
Tor Isedal
Siv Ericks
Janne Carlsson
Björn Adelly
Birgitta Molin
Håkan Westergren
Margit Carlqvist
Bert-Åke Varg

Lena (Christina Lindberg) is a troubled seventeen-year-old whose life we follow during a few wild summer weeks. With her parents out of town, Lena sets out for adventure, but finds trouble in the form of sleazy and violent scoundrel Helge (Heinz Hopf), who blackmails her into performing any kind of degrading sexual act he wants on the strength of some slutty nude photos he has taken of the experimenting young girl. Tired of being sexually abused in her own home, Lena finally has enough, and she stabs Helge to death. When the unsuspecting parents come home, everything is peaceful once again.

Exponerad is a powerful exploitation film uniting Hopf and Lindberg, the king and queen of Swedish sleaze. Tons of nudity and several daring sex scenes are spiced up by a few dirty flashbacks and fantasy sequences, and a wild soundtrack that makes this an exquisite experience. The scene where Hopf ties down and takes advantage of Lindberg—only to be stabbed to death—is nothing less than fantastic. The foundation of the movie is Lindberg's beauty, and the excitement rises whenever her impeccable body is put on display. Lindberg's fantastic charisma deserves credit—she practically sparkles!

Blind to Lindberg's charms and everything else, the critics disapproved. "Crap equals *Exponerad*," as *Norra Skåne* put it. Nevertheless, ardent exploitation cinema fans will cherish Gustav Wiklund's directorial debut. According to rumor, this classic was banned in twenty-seven countries, stirring controversy nicely as a precursor to the even more destructive relationship Lindberg and Hopf soon brought to life in Bo A. Vibenius's infamous *Thriller – En Grym Film* (see page 258).

Alternative title: *The Depraved*

FÄBODJÄNTAN
[The Farmhouse Girl]

(1978)

Director:

*Lawrence Henning
(Joseph W. Sarno)*

Cast:

*Leena Hiltunen
Anita Berglund
Marie Bergman
Knud Jörgensen
Anne
Tomas*

Little farmgirl Monika (Leena Hiltunen) upsets those around her with her free-spirited sexuality. She discovers that when she blows an ancient wooden horn, all females for miles around will become violently aroused—and I mean violently. Like any normal person, Monika abuses this power to the fullest. She takes maximum advantage of this source of entertainment until every single female in the district, from curious farmgirls to chaste missionary wives, becomes wholeheartedly lost in excessive sexual escapades.

Probably the most notorious film in this book within the confines of Sweden, this movie has been seen by everyone and their parents, and probably their grandparents, too. Most Swedes learned about sex from this movie. Directed by productive American Joe Sarno, this legendary Swedish porn was filmed on location in the beautiful traditional region of Dalarna. The authentic milieu is emphasized by shots of grazing sheep, green meadows, and a soundtrack built around very hearty accordions. There are some flaws in the dialect department, as the supple country Dalarna girls all speak with thick city-slicker Stockholm accents. Also flawed is the acting, utterly horrendous in an indescribable way. There is a total lack of feeling in the delivery of the lines, and sometimes actors stumble, or even simply just restart, saying the sentence over again with little improvement. Very comical! Not a scrap of film was left on the cutting-room floor. Less exciting is the intercourse, as unattractive and hairy actors carry out uninspired lovemaking. We are subjected to a scene including fistfucking, though, which must have been very shocking in the '70s. And of course the infamous scene where a woman gets down with a *falukorv*—a very thick kind of Swedish sausage which only contains around 17 percent meat. Anyone with the slightest interest in Swedish sex films must see *Fäbodjäntan*—if indeed there is anyone left who has not seen it!

Alternative title: *Come Blow the Horn!*

FAIRE L'AMOUR

(1971)

In this international collaboration between French, German, Japanese, and Swedish film companies, the life situations of women in different countries are portrayed. The movie is divided into four parts, and most of the women get educations, families, and other useful things. The Swedish segment, directed by Gunnar Höglund, is about Ingrid (Annabella Munter), who is inspired by the ever-stronger atmosphere of sexual freedom she feels growing around her. After the meltdown of a spontaneous love affair, she comforts herself with several different men. And that's the life situation of a woman in Sweden—at least as far as a *sensationsfilm* is concerned.

After this film, Sweden was never, ever allowed to take part in such an international project again.

Directors:

Jean-Gabriel Albicocco [France]

Thomas Fantl [Germany]

Sachiko Hidari [Japan]

Gunnar Höglund [Sweden]

Cast:

Jean-Claude Bouillon

Nicole Garcia

Raoul Saint-Yves

Colette Régis

Jo Charrier

Jean-Henri Chambois

Annabella Munter

Krister Ekman

Inge Marschall

Michael Kramer

Yukiko Takabayashi

Mikio Saito

(1976)

Director:

Jonas Åberg

Cast:

Anders Lindquist
Agneta Dahlqvist
Inga Kjellgren
Lars-Erik Johansson
Ingemar Sjödin
Torgny Stigbrand
Odd Lindell
Hans Häggmark
Maria Brännström
Jonas Åberg

FALLET CASH
[The Cash Case]

English agent James Cash (Anders Lindquist) arrives in Sweden planning to steal some important data. He is heavily opposed by a notorious pro–Viet Cong liberation group, but they are unable to expose him.

This is a rarely seen and very obscure amateur movie shot on Super 8 by a group of youngsters in Umeå between 1972 and 1976. Still, these mavericks managed to secure at least one theatrical screening of their sole print of the film.

FANNY HILL

(1968)

Fanny (Diana Kjaer) travels to Stockholm from the countryside in order to find a job. Unsuccessful in her search, the young woman is forced to seek employment at a whorehouse. When she meets young Roger (Hans Ernback), he falls in love with her and saves her from the brothel. Roger's father, displeased with his son's new girlfriend, sends him off for a long trip, and lets Fanny know that Roger has left her. Overwhelmed by sadness, Fanny falls into a life of alcohol and nightclubs, which leads to a couple of relationships with older men. When one of them dies, Fanny suddenly finds herself financially independent, as the old man decided she should inherit all his fortune. Eventually Fanny reunites with Roger, and life is all of a sudden nothing but happiness.

A far cry from John Cleland's banned erotic novel, *Fanny Hill* is entertaining but trivial lightweight smut delivered by the productive Mac Ahlberg. The big attraction is leading lady Diana Kjaer, who is supposed to portray an innocent, unkissed farmer's girl but obviously looks unbelievably sinful with those yearning eyes. Despite a couple of dirty sex scenes and drunken nightclub visits on the plus side, overall there is too much drivel and not enough nudity for this to be complete thumbs up. No complaints aesthetically, though—the movie capture the spirit of the '60s perfectly with sharp colors, beautiful clothes, and snappy organ music by Georg Riedel. A short sequence in Venice livens things up, though it serves very little purpose and was probably just added so the film crew could get a nice vacation. Simply put, this is a decent movie that needs a little more indecency.

The smut level was absolutely perfect for the more prim and proper American market, however, and the film's "thick-lipped" blonde bombshells were praised highly. Germany was not so easily conquered—critics there referred derisively to male star Oscar Ljung as "Oscar Ljunk."

Alternative title: *The Swedish Fanny Hill*

Director:
Mac Ahlberg
Cast:
Diana Kjaer
Hans Ernback
Keve Hjelm
Oscar Ljung
Tina Hedström
Gio Petré
Mona Seilitz
Astrid Bye
Bo Lööf
Gösta Prüzelius
Jarl Borssén

*Convincingly neurotic, Arne Ragneborn
in* Farlig Frihet (Dangerous Freedom)
Courtesy of Klubb Super 8

*Director/star Arne Ragneborn takes a
thrashing in* Farlig Frihet
Courtesy of Klubb Super 8

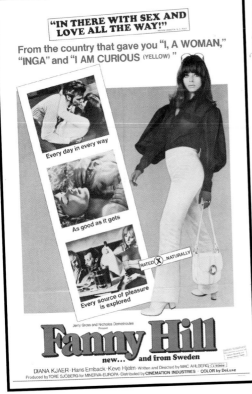

*"New... and from Sweden"—Diana Kjaer
on the US poster for* Fanny Hill

FARLIG FRIHET
[Dangerous Freedom]

(1954)

Director:
Arne Ragneborn

Cast:
Arne Ragneborn
Maj-Britt Lindholm
Carl-Olof Alm
Fritiof Billquist
Sif Ruud
Jan-Olof Rydqvist
Inga Gill
Lars Ekborg
Peter Lindgren
Lars Burman
Åke Grönberg
Bengt Martin
George Skarstedt
Catrin Westerlund
Sven-Axel "Akke" Carlsson

Small-time crook Kristian "Myggan" Strömholm, portrayed by director Arne Ragneborn himself, escapes from jail in order to meet up with his girlfriend, Laila (Maj-Britt Lindholm). Armed with a stolen gun, the two go on a crime spree, breaking into summer cottages and stealing a car. After heading for Stockholm, Kristian joins a gang and start planning a bank robbery. In the end, reality catches up with him; he has a breakdown and is caught by the police after a wild chase through the city.

This is a rather weak early attempt to make some kind of Swedish film noir. Apart from Ragneborn, who is pretty convincing in the role of the neurotic protagonist, there is not much to get excited about. As far as exploitation goes, there are a couple of shots fired, moderate drinking, and some slaps to innocent faces, but it all feels fairly dated and campy. The sexual content is restricted to a simple squeeze of a breast—through a jumper, at that! *Arbetaren*'s reporter Hanserik Hjertén was nonetheless shaken by the immorality of it all, warning: "*Dangerous Freedom* is a dangerous film."

Alternative title: *The Vicious Breed*

FATAL SECRET

(1988)

Directors:

Mats Helge Olsson

*Andrew Nelson
(Anders Nilsson)*

Cast:

David Carradine

Camilla Lundén

A. R. Hellquist

Jonas Karlzén

Eva Andersson

Eva Ostrom

Tina Ljung

Frederick Offrein

Lars Lundgren

Timothy Earle

Mats Huddén

Tina Anger

After an important disc filled with national intelligence secrets is stolen by a narcotics syndicate, the CIA dispatches the hot agent Kim Brown (Camilla Lundén) to retrieve it. Kim swindles her employer, though, and takes off with a big sum of money. Now chased by both the CIA and the hoodlums, Brown experiences a bad turn when her two female colleagues are caught, and the money and the disc go missing. Kim seeks out her old buddy John Mitchell (A. R. Hellquist), and together they pull out all the stops to get the money back, leading to an inferno of gun battles and death.

The summary makes this sound like an interesting movie, but it is not. Terrible music, wretched acting, nonexistent direction, laughable dialogue—basically everything is pitiful here. The film is inadequate even for Mats Helge Olsson, but it features at least a few acceptable sequences. In one, an emotionally unstable villain tries to drag information out of a taped-up woman, and in another, sleazier one, Camilla Lundén exposes herself in sexy underwear. We also get a couple of decently choreographed fights and some really bloody shootings. Otherwise, the most entertaining aspect is the way that the Swedish actors deliver their lines with almost militant apathy. *Fatal Secret* is an unbelievable turkey, and definitely a laugh fest!

FIRMAFESTEN
[The Office Party]

This film begins as a quiet reflection of the goings-on when employees at an advertising agency throw an office party. Things obviously escalate into drunkenness, followed by gossip and adultery. For thrill seekers the most interesting sequence shows two gentlemen wandering into a porn club in the Old City in Stockholm, where they are treated to a live show. The scene where the unimaginably sinful Diana Kjaer tries to have sex with an impotent Bert-Åke Varg in an empty office is wonderfully sleazy as well. Notice a young Stellan Skarsgård as an unbearable poet, and Lars "Lasse" Berghagen as an equally unbearable troubadour and womanizer. Classic!

(1972)

Director:
Jan Halldoff
Cast:
Lauritz Falk
Bert-Åke Varg
Lars Amble
Göthe Grefbo
Siv Andersson
Nils Hallberg
Rolf Bengtsson
Beatrice Järås
Lasse Berghagen
Stellan Skarsgård
Christina Carlwind
Reimers Ekberg
Diana Kjaer

Clockwise from top left: "Is this really what happens?" Firmafesten (The Office Party) *artwork;*

American poster for Flossie*;*

Flossie *climax, billed as "one of the most well made and most wonderful love scenes ever to be put on film"*

Courtesy of Klubb Super 8

FLOSSIE

(1974)

Jack Archer (Jack Frank) is a young man who has recently moved to Stockholm to work for an embassy. He falls in love with the beautiful city and its beautiful ladies. When he meets Flossie (Marie Forså) and Eva (Anita Andersson), they surprisingly ask him to join them at their place. Jack is quickly taken with Flossie, but Eva makes him promise to stay away from the very young orphaned girl. Jack agrees, and good-naturedly makes love to Eva instead. During the act, she lets drop that Flossie has only had lesbian sexual experiences. Eva is suddenly struck with the clever idea that Jack should become her friend's first man! Before long she reverses her ban on sex with Flossie, and the embassy worker and the semi-lesbian orphan are soon embraced in hot lovemaking.

With *Flossie* Mac Ahlberg obviously tried to make a sensual and erotic film, but, unsurprisingly, everything still descends into the usual monotonous sex movie. Jack's inner monologue, in which he apathetically describes his ecstatic emotions, is especially formulaic and laughable. *Flossie* still features an abundance of hot sex and, unlike in other Ahlberg productions, those scenes are long and detailed. The movie wallows in intercourse, group-sex lesbian games between schoolgirls, and so on. The high point must be an early blow job scene that becomes almost surreal with the use of psychedelic music and extreme close-ups! Marie Forså does not disappoint as the title character—she comes across as innocently sinful as only she can be.

According to some informative text on the back of the Midnight Video VHS issue, the climactic sex scene between Jack and Flossie is "one of the most well-made and most wonderful love scenes ever to be put on tape." That's just too funny not to mention.

Alternative title: *Swedish Sex Kitten*

Director:
Bert Torn
(Mac Ahlberg)
Cast:
Maria Lynn
(Marie Forså)
Jack Frank
Anita Andersson
Kim Frank
Gunilla Göransson
Lars Dahlgård
Marianne Larsson
Karl Göransson
Gösta Bergkvist
Tomas Svensson

(1980)

Director:

Torbjörn Axelman

Cast:

Thomas Hellberg
Ann Zacharias
Ernst-Hugo Järegård
Håkan Serner
Agneta Eckemyr
Walter Gotell
Lars Amble
Willie Andréason
Lillebil Ankarcrona
Bob Asklöf

FLYGNIVÅ 450
[Flight Level 450]

Five years into the future—in 1985, that is—the entire Western world is facing a severe shortage of fuel. The Swedish social democrat government wants to solve this by nationalizing all natural resources and joining OPEC. But this plan is only a cover-up for a nefarious scheme to seize control of American oil company IORF. Soon a mysterious accident strikes IORF, and their oil rigs sink and their workers become ill and die of unknown diseases. Even the surrounding flora and fauna start going through unexplainable changes. A notorious terror organization is blamed. But when pilot Göran (Thomas Hellberg) by chance gets on the trail of one of the suggested terrorists, he and journalist Lisa (Ann Zacharias) slowly realize they are dealing with something greater than they expected. Göran suddenly disappears, and Lisa decides to do the same thing. The prime minister is forced to resign after a number of irregularities, and the military seizes power. Don't worry, none of this actually happened in 1985.

This ambitious project is unfortunately a failed attempt to create a Swedish action drama. The producers were initially promised lots of help from the Swedish Army, which has all kinds of unused weapons, soldiers, and cool vehicles just sitting around. When the Minister of Defense realized what was going on, he became outraged and sternly put a stop to the arrangement, calling the idea absurd. He was right. The sole highlight is the wonderful Ann Zacharias in the female lead. Other than her the film offers nothing of interest—no nudity, no violence worth mentioning, nothing. The long list of prominent actors, including Ernst-Hugo Järegård and Thomas Hellberg, does not help matters. See Torbjörn Axelman's superior movies *Het Snö* (see page 88) and *Kameleonterna* (see page 120) instead of this snooze fest.

DE FÖRSVUNNA
[The Missing]

Director:

Sergio Castilla

Cast:

Nelson Villagra

Leonardo Perucci

Elizabeth "Ely" Menz

Hugo Medina

Adelaida Arías

Juan Seoane

Jaime Hernández

Ana L. Renteri

Max Ropert

Tomás López

Welcome to Chile, where what once was a pleasant middle-class suburban home in Santiago is now transformed into an examination prison by the dictator Pinochet's police. *De Försvunna* follows a group from the resistance as they meet their torturers and executioners. Their agonies and terror persist until death, and no light is ever spotted at the edge of the darkness.

In this Swedish-Cuban coproduction, Chilean expatriate Sergio Castilla explores the darker conditions of his motherland with brutal intensity. *De Försvunna* may not be considered an exploitation movie per se, but it includes a number of overwhelming sequences of abuse, forcing viewers to witness a string of cruelties, including torture with electricity, simulated executions, and degrading rapes. It's intimidating, painful, and grim.

Alternative title: *Prisioneros Desaparecidos*

(1976) FÖRVANDLINGEN
[The Transformation]

Director:
Ivo Dvorák

Cast:
Peter Schildt
Ernst Günther
Gunn Wållgren
Inga-Lill Carlsson
Per Oscarsson
Jan Blomberg
Augustin Benka
Per-Arne Ehlin
Claire Wickholm
Chris Wahlström
Sture Ericson
Grynet Molvig

Around the turn of the century, a young man wakes up to realize he has been transformed into a bug. Anxiety strikes: How will he be able to support his family? His friends and family observe the transformation in horror and initially try to help him, but as they grow more disgusted by him, they start hating him, and even long for his death. Unable to do the killing themselves, they find it best to simply persecute and loathe him. When he finally dies, everyone is happy.

This is a very odd film directed by Czech refugee Ivo Dvorák, based on Franz Kafka's story "The Metamorphosis." In a curious case of fact emulating fiction, after the release of this film the director—like his protagonist—was totally neglected and ignored by audiences, critics, and the Swedish Film Institute forever.

Alternative title: *Metamorphosis*

FRÄNDER
[Kinfolk]

(1985)

Director:
Peter Borg
Cast:
Peter Borg and friends

Director Peter Borg is a real go-getter in the Swedish film industry. In 1985 he made this obscurity using an 8 mm camera and some friends, and, according to the director himself, this was the first Swedish splatter movie. Today the film is seemingly impossible to track down, and apparently never got any kind of distribution when it came out. Since I don't know anyone who has actually seen this lost film, I can't even confirm its existence. Anyway, Borg claims that everything was set up for a massive American launch of the movie, but that things fell apart when the financiers decided to put their money into *The Evil Dead* (Sam Raimi, 1981) instead—which is curious, considering that Sam Raimi's classic movie came out four years before *Fränder*. Peter Borg hasn't forgiven Raimi since, and reportedly the pompous American director won't even return Borg's phone calls anymore. If you look at Peter Borg's later horror films *Scorched Heat* (see page 217) and *Sounds of Silence* (see page 241), you will probably realize that this cannot have been a film with enough production value for a wider release, but it might still be interesting. But, as with Mats Helge Olsson's *Silent Chase* (see page 218), the film has yet to be tracked down for a proper review.

Alternative title: *Next of Kin*

THE FROZEN STAR

(1977)

Director:
Mats Helge Olsson
Cast:
Isabella Kaliff
Willy Carlsson
Roland von Rainals
Lennart Eriksson
Paul Eriksen
Hans-Gunnar
Erlandsson
Gert Nilsson
Karl-Axel Dahlgren
Gustav Hallin
Bengt Erlandsson

A young stranger named Willy arrives in a remote region that is controlled by gunslinger Bart. When Willy falls in love with the prostitute Rose, Bart gets furious and chases him off. The courageous young man soon returns, though, this time with a posse, to get even with Bart and his band. The final gunfight at the saloon sees Bart meet his fate.

Mats Helge Olsson haunts us with his second movie, and just as with his debut, *I Död Mans Spår* (see page 95), he delivers a red-hot Swedish western. This movie was actually produced in 1974, even though it premiered in 1977, so it should be seen as his maiden voyage. Unfortunately, it is close to impossible to track down today; there was never a video or DVD release. The original print was only screened once for about ten people at the Metropol theater in little Värnamo, and even that was probably only to fulfill the government funding requirement by the Swedish Film Institute. Legend says the only existing copy was burned to a crisp in a car accident, probably during production of a later Mats Helge Olsson action movie.

As *Aftonbladet* proclaimed, probably correctly: "The worst movie in the world just premiered—it will never be screened outside of the province of Småland." So far, it never has been.

G

(1983)

Director:
Staffan Hildebrand

Cast:
Sebastian Håkansson
Joakim Schröder
Niclas Wahlgren
Ulrika Örn
Ulf Brunnberg
Ewa Fröling
Lasse Strömstedt
Magnus Uggla
Dominik Henzel
Niels Jensen
Rebecca Pawlo
Jerry Williams
Olle Ljungström

Robban (Joakim Schröder), Alexander (Sebastian Håkansson), and Kim (Niclas Wahlgren) are three sixteen-year-old guys set free from high school, exploring their first summer as semi-adults. Things in the wild city of Stockholm are not easy, though, and they all struggle with its many delights.

Robban explores the magic of hashish, which makes him a target for police and criminals alike. Even worse, he wears shoulder-length hair, which enrages every adult he encounters. Alexander, on the other hand, gets an offer to join a big rock band, which makes all of his teenage friends angry as hell—somehow he has let them down. Things are toughest for Kim, who struggles with his sexual identity and is torn between feelings for his girlfriend and a cool male DJ. In the disapproving way of all adults in the world of *G*, his mother tells him he is not normal. After a few days of crazy adventures, everything turns out well, and the boys' problems evaporate when they get haircuts, find jobs, abandon their rock dreams, and fuck girls instead of boys. The end.

Stockholmsnatt director Staffan Hildebrand somehow secured a big budget for this film, and he marshaled those resources to deliver one of the most overblown and insane moralizing cinema sermons ever. The message of *G* is simple: Stay away from homo-sexuality, drugs, and rock 'n' roll, and your life will turn out fine. Nevertheless, in depicting these things that kids are deeply curious about, he touched the hearts of all Swedish teenagers and had a gigantic hit. You can't really overestimate this film's importance for the 1980s generation. We all learned about sex, drugs, and rock 'n' roll from this film, and immediately dedicated ourselves to getting our hands on some sex, dope, and rock 'n' roll as soon as possible. It all just looked so good!

The sleaziest moment of the film is a backstage sequence in which a nude girl is whipped and made to lick the boots of a stern Olle Ljungström, still a real-life pop star in Sweden. *Sensationfilm* veteran Ulf Brunnberg is also great as a slippery manager. *G* is by far Hildebrand's most professional and successful film, but as sensations go he really hit the jackpot with *Stockholmsnatt* (see page 246) a few years later. By then he was barely even pretending that he believed in the very, very old morals of *G* anymore.

Alternative title: *G – Som i Gemenskap*

Androgyny, drugs, and new wave on the home video box for Staffan Hildebrand's G

Old-wave criminal Clu Gulager, fresh off the train, ready to wreak havoc in idyllic rural Sweden in Gangsterfilmen (Gangster Movie)

GANGSTERFILMEN
[Gangster Movie]

(1974)

Director:

Lars G. Thelestam

Cast:

Clu Gulager

Ernst Günther

Per Oscarsson

Gunnar Olsson

Ulla Sjöblom

Peter Lindgren

Carl-Axel Heiknert

Gudrun Brost

Tor-Ivan Odulf

Gunnar Ossiander

Lou Castel

Accompanied by a gang of companions, American gangster Glenn Mortenson (Clu Gulager) settles down in a small, picturesque Swedish town. Officially, he is there in order to learn about Swedish democracy, but in reality his agenda is more tightly directed toward ruthless killing and rape. Finally, a few locals muster the courage to face down this beastly gangster.

This debut from director Lars G. Thelestam delivers an action-packed and dark reflection on how easily evil can dominate the little people. Gulager's portrayal of the cold rapist is truly chilling, and a sense of doom lingers throughout the whole production. Fans of European exploitation cinema will welcome the sight of Swedish actor Lou Castel, veteran of various Visconti, Fassbinder, Wim Winders, and Damiani Damiani productions.

Critic, director, and member of Sweden's film funding board Jörn Donner went on the record with an official assessment of the profitability potential of the original novel, written by children's book author Max Lundgren. The system saw piles of Swedish kronor in this dark tale. "A movie [based on the book] would have the potential to be just raw enough, just vulgar enough, and just commercial enough," Donner said. Raw and vulgar, yes, but on the commercial question they totally failed.

Alternative title: *A Stranger Came by Train*

(1979)

GANGSTERS

Director:
Mac Ahlberg

Cast:
Nai Bonet
Tony Page
Michael V. Gazzo
Peter Iacangelo
Dino Laudicina
Vicki Sue Robinson
Raymond Serra

George (Tony Page) is a merciless gangster who runs his night-club with no compromises. His real business, an illegal casino, is located in the basement. Rich clients are lured there to gamble by beautiful female nightclub singers. George also dabbles in dia-mond smuggling, a sideline carefully hidden away from his boss, the Godfather (Michael V. Gazzo). When George's favorite girl, Loretta (Nai Bonet), tries to break away from the decadence and violence to start a new life with a man she has met, George grows furious and has her lover killed. The situation spins out of control, until George is forced to meet Loretta and the Godfather face-to-face in a bloody confrontation.

This Italian-produced crime flick ended up being Mac Ahlberg's last movie in Europe before he headed to Hollywood for a suc-cessful career as cinematographer. He directed some great movies, such as *Jag – En Kvinna 2. Äktenskapet* (see page 108), but seems sick of all the hard work at this point, as this is a very tired and uninspired affair. Things liven up a bit with a couple of assaults and a tiny bit of nudity in the sweaty dressing room of the club. Otherwise, it feels like the movie is heading somewhere but never reaches its target. A number of lousy song performances, mostly by Nai Bonet, who also wrote and produced this dreck, don't help at all. Let us forget about this nonsense and remember Mac Ahlberg for his groundbreaking Swedish *sensationsfilms*, including mile-stones such as *Jorden Runt med Fanny Hill* (see page 114) and *Jag – En Kvinna 2. Äktenskapet*.

Alternative title: *Hoodlums*

GRÄSÄNKLINGAR
[Grass Widowers]

(1982)

Director:

Hans Iveberg

Cast:

Gösta Ekman

Janne "Loffe" Karlsson

Börje Nyberg

Sten Johan Hedman

Peter Harryson

Lennart R. Svensson

Lena Olin

Mona Seilitz

Marika Lindström

Lena Nyman

Joel Fänge

Ulrika Jansson

Lina Lundblad

Cecilia Tryselius

Svante Grundberg

Christina Lindberg

This film is worth mentioning only as Christina Lindberg's final film appearance during her classic period. Her involvement is just a few seconds long. She stands wearing sinful black underwear in the background during a magic show. If you blink or don't know what to look for, it's easy to miss her entirely. Too bad that Lindberg is wasted as a simple extra in a throwaway scene in this uninvolving and dull comedy. Bigger parts went to three other Swedish sex symbols: the good Lena Olin, the bad Lena Nyman, and the ugly Mona Seilitz. If Lindberg had replaced any of them, the film would have been twice as good.

And so Christina Lindberg made her unworthy exit at the end of a magnificent career in Swedish *sensationsfilms*. As she is still worshipped like a goddess around the world to this day, there can never be any other end for director Hans Iveberg but tar and feathers.

Alternative title: *One-Week Bachelors*

(1980)

GRÄSÄNKOR PÅ SKANDALSEMESTER
[Grass Widows on Scandalous Vacation]

Director:
Andrew Whyte
(Andrei Feher)

Cast:
Barbi Andersson
Marie Bergman
Gabriel Poutello
Daniel Trabet
Allen Plumer
Guy Royer
Ingrid Josephson
Jack Gatteau
Birgitta Svensson
Patty Ekman

Housewives Barbro (Barbi Andersson) and Ulla (Marie Bergman) spend their days having an enormous amount of sex with their husbands. When the two girlfriends head for Paris, they unsurprisingly end up in bed with a couple of Frenchmen. These turn out to be professional con men, however, and they spike the girls' drinks in order of rob them of all they have. Barbro and Ulla quickly adapt to the situation—they turn out to be pretty good con artists themselves, and one sexual adventure soon follows another. Men and women come and go in their beds, and if no one else is around they play with each other. In the end they return home to their husbands and everything goes back to normal.

"Stockholm at 8 PM. The streets are empty, but the seductive Swedish ladies are not being idle..." This commentary (over a collage of beautiful Stockholm views) sets off this energetic mix of graphic sex and slapstick by the uncompromising director Andrei Feher. As usual when it comes to Feher (and other Swedish porn from the late '70s), the high point of the movie is the unreasonably indolent dubbing. According to the Swedish video release on Videodepoten, the movie contains "French massage, oral erotica, virgin sex, rump fumblers, and Negroes set on fucking"—quite a mixed bag of selling points! The director's son Thomas Whyte worked as production manager here, before straightening up and launching a more sensible career as a dentist.

Alternative titles: *Crazy Swedish Holidays in Paris*; *Deux Suédoises à Paris*; *Blue Erotik Movie*

Don't be fooled by the interesting-looking poster for Gangsters

"An indecently funny porn flick"

A quiet bus ride becomes exciting. From Arne Mattsson's final Hillman film, Den Gula Bilen (The Yellow Car)

"The whole movie has charm, humor and e-x-c-i-t-e-m-e-n-t"— Den Gula Bilen *poster*

(1980)

GROSSISTEN
[The Wholesaler]

Director:
Torbjörn Lindqvist
Cast:
Alexander Bengtsson
Catarina Genberg
Marianne Hafström
Åke Persson
Benny Rask

John works in wholesale, but he spends most of his time in shady bars and bouncing around between prostitutes. He finances his decadent lifestyle by dealing heroin smuggled in from Amsterdam. Two of his friends soon sense something is wrong, and they start prying into his life. Despite their well-meaning meddling, John carries on full-speed ahead, until in desperation he kills a prostitute who threatens to reveal his wicked ways. Once the police are on his tracks, the situation quickly spins out of hand. The end comes on a beach, as John is shot to death by his drug companions before the police get a chance to arrest him.

This witless attempt at a crime movie never managed a real theatrical release—probably hampered by its nonexistent budget, lousy acting, and deplorable dialogue. The story itself is mindless and about as believable as the front page of *Expressen*, the Swedish equivalent of tbe *New York Post*. For example, the viewer is left wondering why John, if he indeed makes that much money on his heroin deals, wears the same stupid clothes every day and returns to the same musty bar night after night. He never washes his hair, and he restricts himself to only the cheapest hookers. The suspense builds when the drug king invites John over for an after-party, but even that all ends up with the two outlaws just having a quiet cup of coffee together. The movie does benefit from the dystopian portrayal of otherwise fun town Malmö, and also from a totally unjustified sequence of a teen girl exposing her breasts. But otherwise this is just bad.

Alternative title: *Djävulens Vita Guld*

GROTTMORDEN
[The Cave Murders]

(1990)

Director:

Mats Helge Olsson

Cast:

Taggen Axelsson

Magnus Cederblad

A. R. Hellquist

Gareth Hunt

Camilla Lundén

Frederick Offrein

A highly dangerous mental patient is mysteriously freed from his institution, leaving behind a string of corpses. At the same time, daring reporter Peter Savage (A. R. Hellquist) is researching an old legend about a boy who disappeared in a nearby cave twenty years earlier. Peter heads for the caves, bringing along a production team to make some kind of documentary about the case. The escaped lunatic naturally ends up in the same cave, and a lethal game of hide-and-seek commences. It is soon exposed that the madman's cold and calculating businessman brother, Mr. Tanner (Taggen Axelsson), is ruthlessly using the maniac as a weapon. Also, the little boy was heir to a large fortune, and Tanner has reasons to keep the ghosts of past remaining silent. His men are now out to get rid of the TV team and control the fortune of the cave once and for all.

Grottmorden is an unstoppable low-budget action movie so unbelievably bad that you gasp for breath just trying to wrap your head around how poor it is. When measuring the quality of this movie, don't overlook the scene where Hellquist gets out of a bath wearing totally dry shorts. As in most of Mats Helge Olsson's movies, the script is in English, but in this case the horrendous forced dialogue sounds more like the Swedish chef from *The Muppet Show* than an actual language. There is no nudity to speak of, apart from the male actors' peculiar habit of ripping off their shirts as soon as a fight is about to happen. If you are out for breasts, make a beeline for Mats Helge Olsson's *Blood Tracks* (see page 40) instead. There are not even that many murders in this film—it's safe and calm, like New York these days!—and the ones we get are listless and lousy. The creepiest part of the movie is probably A. R. Hellquist's eerie haircut, lush, like that of George Michaels in his prime, which brings forth sinister memories of bygone times. Another Mats Helge Olsson movie that is just indescribably bad.

Alternative title: *The Forgotten Wells*

(1963)

Director:

Arne Mattsson

Cast:

Karl-Arne Holmsten

Nils Hallberg

Ulla Strömstedt

Barbro Kollberg

Semmy Friedman

Toivo Pawlo

Kotti Chave

Carl-Olof Alm

Tor Borong

Gunnar Skoglund

Laila Westerlund

Roland Söderberg

DEN GULA BILEN
[The Yellow Car]

While on vacation, Dr. Kerstin Björk (Ulla Strömstedt) happens to film a terrorist attack against President Hurkas (Roland Söderberg), leader of some unidentified country in southern Europe. Hurkas is hidden by the police, but the inspector who stands in for him on the bus ride home is shot while enjoying some jolly singing with other travelers. Always up for a challenge, private investigator John Hillman—who luckily happened to also be on the bus—makes it his duty to solve the case. His only clue is a suspicious yellow car spotted by the fellow traveler Kerstin, but the good doctor is unfortunately soon kidnapped, drugged, and locked up in a mental hospital. Hillman sets out on an adventurous rescue mission that takes him on an action-packed ride through the underbelly of organized crime and international politics.

Though the story is definitely his wildest, this is the last and least effective installment in Arne Mattsson's quintet of Hillman films that began in 1958 with *Damen i Svart* (see page 49). The problem here is probably that the focus has shifted to action away from horror. This is the only crime film of the series, and it seems barren compared to the others, which were all atmosphere-laden thrillers. Putting aside the confusing, nonsensical plot and lack of suspense, at least Mattsson has finally cut down the "comic" sequences starring the hopeless actor Nils Hallberg. (Whoever came up with the character of Freddy should be tortured and shot!) Notably, the violent "film within the film" at the heart of the action comes across as sinister and authentic. The final sequence features a car that will explode if it slows down, curiously anticipating *Speed* (Jan de Bont, 1994) by three decades.

All in all, *Den Gula Bilen* makes a suitable warm-up for the sick crime thrillers Arne Mattsson directed in the 1970s, hinting at the twisted motifs to come. After this film, the critics started to abandon Mattsson, and during the rest of the '60s he went from respected to accepted. In the early '70s he went from tolerated to hated, after which he fled to Yugoslavia to direct films nobody cared about. He ended his career on a sad note in the late '80s, as an assistant director to the talentless Mats Helge Olsson.

HALLO BABY

(1976)

This autobiographical film tells the colorful story of Marie-Louise De Geer Bergenstråhle's childhood and transformation into a grown woman. After an early adolescence portrayed as very difficult, with a dominant and perverted father, in her teens she arrives in the vibrant late 1960s art scene of Stockholm. There she matures into a grown woman, and finally gives birth to a little baby girl.

Hallo Baby is more of a live art exhibition by scene decorator Carl Johan De Geer than a fictional film; its tone is quite similar to the movies of Chilean filmmaker Alejandro Jodorowsky. Marie-Louise wrote the script and plays the lead role. She also hired her then-husband as director and ex-husband as scene decorator. The inimitable De Geer Bergenstråhle is no stranger to provocation in the name of art—she is most infamous for covering herself in human excrement and standing in front of Stockholms Enskilda Bank (a big corporate bank in Sweden), and shouting at pedestrians and bypassers that the stench came from the bank itself.

In *Hallo Baby* she eagerly displays her nude body. Several men and women come and go through her bedroom more or less dressed, but it's just nonsense. We also get to witness male and female masturbation, some limp penises, and a needlessly violent scene, thrown in for good measure. The highlight of the film is when Marie-Louise, disguised as a black woman, visits her mother at the hospital. "Do you have to look like that when you visit me?" her mother asks, not the least impressed or grateful. The film premiered in January 1976, and was seen by 135.000 people in the cinemas around Sweden according to the official records—despite heaps of bad reviews.

Director:
Johan Bergenstråhle
Cast:
Marie-Louise De Geer Bergenstråhle
Toivo Pawlo
Siv Ericks
Håkan Serner
Keve Hjelm
Anders Ek
Malin Gjörup
Manne Grünberger

EN HANDFULL KÄRLEK
[A Handful of Love]

Director:
Vilgot Sjöman

Cast:
Anita Ekström
Gösta Bredefeldt
Ingrid Thulin
Ernst-Hugo Järegård
Sif Ruud
Per Myrberg
Evabritt Strandberg
Frej Lindqvist
Anders Oscarsson
Gunnar Ossiander
Chris Wahlström
Bibi Skoglund
Claire Wikholm
Ernst Günther
Marie Ekorre

This movie follows the life of working-class woman Hjördis (Anita Ekström) during 1909, the year of the big national labor strikes. She lives with her socialist boyfriend Daniel (Gösta Bredefeldt), and works for the well-to-do Crona family as a chambermaid. When her sleazy master (Ernst-Hugo Järegård) impregnates Hjördis, Daniel decides to leave her. The servant then musters the courage to break away from the predatory Crona family, hiding herself and her child among the poorest souls of Swedish society.

This criminally long and boring historical drama is directed by Vilgot Sjöman. As always, Sjöman seems borderline obsessed with showing off his male actors fully nude, giving the movie a sensational streak. When it comes to acting, Ernst-Hugo Järegård is unbeatable and wonderfully slippery.

This movie was praised by the cinematic establishment—among other honors it received a *Guldbagge* award, a Swedish Oscar—yet it was heavily criticized by the press. "Vilgot Sjöman has made a properly bad film," ran the report in *Arbetaren*. "Proper and bad." No argument here. Despite Järegård's best efforts, this was probably Sjöman's biggest commercial flop.

HÄR KOMMER BÄRSÄRKARNA
[Here Come the Berserkers]

(1965)

Director:
Arne Mattsson

Cast:
*Carl-Gustaf
Lindstedt*

Dirch Passer

Åke Söderblom

Elisabeth Odén

Karl-Arne Holmsten

Walter Chiari

Nils Hallberg

Loredana Nusciak

Carl-Axel Elfving

Valeria Fabrizi

Curt Ericson

Olof Huddén

Daniela Igliozzi

Viking chieftain Hjovard the Greedy (Åke Söderblom) is an old widower whose economic assets and sexual conquests grow fewer and fewer with each passing season. When his sons Glum the Flylover (Carl-Gustaf Lindstedt) and Garm the Stupid (Dirch Passer) return empty-handed from raids against the Christians down south in the weaker parts of Europe, the old man is beyond disappointed. Things worsen when he finds out that what little booty they did hoist has already been stolen by rival chieftain Olav the Cranky (Karl-Arne Holmsten), to settle some stupid debt Hjovard owes. In an act of desperation, Hjovard sells his sons to an envoy from Constantinople, where the two berserkers will be forced to work in the dangerous arena as vicious gladiators.

The combination of barren Viking surroundings and Mediterranean Roman decadence sounds like a great breeding ground for a movie overflowing with sex and violence. Unfortunately, all that over-flows from *Här Kommer Bärsärkarna* is poor slapstick. The only details worth noting are a couple of grand brawls, and an excess of skimpily dressed Viking wenches and Roman maidens in tunics. In the end, this is another one of Arne Mattsson's weakest moments. Stay away when these Viking ships appear.

Alternative titles: *Bärsärkarna*; *Vi Vilde Vikinger*

Clockwise from top left: Barren Viking
atmosphere and Roman decadence
combine via Carl-Gustaf Lindstedt and
a suspciously Swedish-looking Roman
handmaiden in Här Kommer Bärsärkarna
(Here Come the Berserkers)
Courtesy of Klubb Super 8;

Dirch Passer and Carl-Gustaf Lindstedt
loaded with props and ready to raid
Courtesy of Klubb Super 8;

"The <u>NEW</u> Swedish porn sensation," reads
the misleading poster for the not-so-new,
not-so-sensational Hemmafruarnas
Hemliga Sexliv (The Secret Sex Lives of
Housewives)

HEMMAFRUARNAS HEMLIGA SEXLIV
[The Secret Sex Lives of Housewives]

(1981)

Director:

Heinz Arland

Cast:

Titti Wallin

Bertil Svensson

Lydia Caroli

Harry Andersson

Kim Jarén

Bo Landros

Shabby pornography all the way through, this is a very small movie about a pornmonger who uses his own wife as a model. Apart from being behind the camera, he is no stranger to throwing himself into the action to join his wife and the other models in erotic festivities. There is not much left to say about this very unprofessional and amateurish movie—even to call it a proper movie is to stretch the bounds of reality. The poster itself made excuses for the film's poor audio quality, chiding viewers who expected high-fidelity sound from a sex film. Nonetheless, no fewer than six 35mm prints of the movie were circulated in theaters, extravagantly replicating a rather meager display of talent and resources. Possibly you might appreciate the almost documentary look that the poor production values create. But overall, this is as tranquilizing as NyQuil.

(1968)

Director:
Torbjörn Axelman

Cast:
Ernst-Hugo Järegård
Sven-Bertil Taube
Grynet Molvig
Ulf Brunnberg
Margareta Sjödin
Håkan Serner
Ingvar Kjellson
Ulf Johansson
Joakim Bonnier

HET SNÖ
[Hot Snow]

While young journalist Michelle (Grynet Molvig) is on assignment in Paris, she witnesses drugs being secretly planted inside a race car. The car belongs to young, handsome race driver Bobby Flyckt (Sven-Bertil Taube), who is unaware that he is being used for narcotics smuggling. In order to investigate the situation further, Michelle befriends Bobby and hitches a ride with him back to Sweden. After their arrival, the two attend a party hosted by Bobby's sponsor, Lennart Stenhäll (acclaimed Swedish actor Ernst-Hugo Järegård, star of Lars von Trier's *The Kingdom*), and they soon agree that something suspicious is in the works. Michelle's sleuthing leads her to believe that Stenhäll is involved in wholesale narcotics dealing, and suddenly someone tries to murder her. After being saved by Bobby, Michelle finally spills the beans about the drugs in his car, and he furiously decides to confront Stenhäll. The gangster syndicate is hot on their trail by now, and Michelle is soon gorily killed with a knife. Bobby is struck unconscious. Stenhäll gets his just desserts in the end, as he is confronted and killed by a girl whom he drove into drug addiction.

Axelman's rough thriller is often cited as the first modern Swedish crime movie, painting a gloomy picture of Stockholm's underworld, ruled by drugs and degradation. The violence is pretty explicit for its date of production; the scene where the young journalist's throat is slit must have seemed especially intense. The cast (Järegård, Taube, Ulf Brunnberg) is indeed impressive, but none of the actors really stand out. The most screen time unfortunately goes to the irritating semi-attractive Norwegian actress Grynet Molvig, who restrains the dirty atmosphere with her chipper presence. Just imagine the awe-inspiring Gio Petré (*Jag – En Kvinna 2. Äktenskapet,* see page 108) or Christina Lindberg in the lead instead! Still, this is definitely worth tracking down, and please note the cameo by pro race car driver Joakim Bonnier during a scene at the track. Also of note, famed Swedish cornball director and Disney collector Lasse Åberg worked as set designer here.

Peek-a-boo! Grynet Molvig hams it up in Torbjörn Axelman's fine effort Het Snö (Hot Snow)

"Hetaste Liggen (The Hottest Shags) is the most notorious porno feature on the continent right now, with Marilyn Lamour—a complete copy of the original Marilyn Monroe in the leading role"

(1983)

Director:

*Andrew Whyte
(Andrei Feher)*

Cast:

*Marilyn Lamour
(Olinka Hardiman)*

Gabriel Pontello

Solveig Viberg

Richard Hemming

Ingrid Lindgren

Marcel Barbey

Ronald Engström

Ingvar Lund

Britt Backlund

Pierre Dumas

Guy Troyer

Carl Thum

Karin Englund

Ulla Wilmertz

G. Scott

A. Hansson

Elly Beck

Loulou Hult

Christian Mazagran

Marianne Aubert

Dominique St. Clair

Cathy Ménard

Moanie

Dominique Aveline

Alban Ceray

Piotr

HETASTE LIGGEN
[The Hottest Shags]

Set in the grimy underworld milieu of the pimps of Paris, this seedy porno flick is as sleazy as it gets. The plot is secondary, but in short the story involves a stunning new prostitute who causes a rumble among rival businessmen. Of far greater importance than the story are the indecencies we are treated to: Buzzing dildos, bearded rapists, rough whips, forced oral sex, upper-class orgies, masked kidnappers, and the businesslike auction of a "certified" virgin are all included. The hard-core rape scenes are notable, and get way out of line as the victims start enjoying the treatment after a while. The disorder of time and space and all the monotonous sex create an almost surreal but mostly sleep-inducing atmosphere. Lead actress Olinka Hardiman was some kind of international pornographic star in those days, basically due to her resemblance to Marilyn Monroe. She's also the most competent person involved in this whole production.

Alternative titles: *Hate and Love*; *International Gigolo*

THE HIRED GUN

(1989)

This film opens with a quiet view of the ocean at sunset. While the opening credits roll, mercenaries Mike (Frederick Offrein) and Tom (Sam Cook) are shown fighting together in Africa. They survive a hail of explosions and become friends for life. Whew! Five years later, some neo-Nazis in Germany are searching for a metal box full of secret World War II documents. For some reason, the box is located in an old cave bunker in Denmark, where some archaeologists are studying it closely. Bad news for the neo-Nazis—the bunker happens to be located under a US Army base. The army doesn't care at all about the old Nazi secrets, but they don't want anyone messing around on their grounds. So the neo-Nazis hire soldier of fortune Mike to retrieve the box. He calls up Tom, and the two of them get down to business, running all around the base and the cave system (a bunch of drab office building hallways). After some ridiculous twists, everything ends with a shoot-out, explosions, and a high five between the main actors.

Right after *The Mad Bunch* (see page 152), Mats Helge Olsson directed this ultra-turkey with basically the same terrible cast, awful score, and nonexistent script. As with the previous film, he tried linking Arne Mattsson to the damn thing by claiming the poor old man codirected it. No doubt this was a 100 percent Mats Helge production, filled with all the characteristics of his lousy career. Mattsson's only effort might have been to finally put a decent actor in a Mats Helge film, as Heinz Hopf shows up as a sleazy doctor. The rest of the movie is basically standard fighting, armed combat, and explosion sequences, loosely linked together by a wafer-thin plot that makes no sense. I bet half the budget was spent on explosions for the opening credits, which has nothing at all to do with the rest of the movie. Lead actor Offrein looks more stupid than ever in his lousy haircut and silly beard, and his constant drinking in this film must have been for real considering his awful performance. The script doesn't help. One line from Offrein basically shows that even the fictional characters are confused: "I know it's ridiculous, but we have to do it."

Everything sucks incredibly in this film, yet it mysteriously manages to entertain on some very low level. It's a shame that Arne Mattsson would stain his name with two awful Mats Helge Olsson productions at the very end of his otherwise great career. Luckily for Mattsson, this film got no distribution at all, and the only existing release is an obscure Greek videotape.

Directors:
Mats Helge Olsson
Arne Mattsson
Cast:
Frederick Offrein
Sam Cook
Heinz Hopf
Lars Gunnar Andersson
Helena Michelsen
Timothy Earle
Paul Smith
Harley Melin
Olof Huddén
Mats Huddén
Lars Lundgren

(1951)

Director:

Arne Mattsson

Cast:

Ulla Jacobsson
Folke Sundquist
Edvin Adolphson
John Elfström
Erik Hell
Irma Christenson
Sten Lindgren
Nils Hallberg
Sten Mattsson
Gunvor Pontén
Gösta Gustafson
Berta Hall
Erich Conrad
Margaretha Löwler
Arne Källerud
Axel Högel

HON DANSADE EN SOMMAR
[She Danced One Summer]

New university graduate Göran (Folke Sundquist) heads for the country in order to spend the summer doing some good honest manual labor. On arrival he falls in love with beautiful young Kerstin (Ulla Jacobsson), and she falls for him likewise. Yet the conditions for their love are bleak, because Kerstin, the daughter of a priest, is kept on a very short leash by her father at home at the vicarage. The tension soon escalates into a downward spiral, and before long there is a tragic death in the family.

Director Arne Mattsson's adaption of Per Olof Ekström's novel *Sommardansen* is fairly innocent in its overall reflection of Swedish barn dances, summer love, and midsummer holiday celebration, but this is arguably the first Swedish *sensationsfilm*. The most legendary and startling sequence that shocked the world, especially America, was a skinny-dipping episode rounded off by Ulla Jacobsson's young breasts being exposed. The movie became a huge international success, praised by critics and adored by the general public. As Mattsson's movies became rougher during the '60s, all interest in his work diminished. His sleazy productions during the 1970s (such as *Smutsiga Fingrar,* see page 229) were flat-out mocked by the critics.

Alternative title: *One Summer of Happiness*

Clockwise from top left: Poster from Bo A. Vibenius's debut as a film director;

One of many, many shoot-outs in Mats Helge Olsson's unbelievably hurting The Hired Gun

An innocent hand-holding start to it all: Ulla Jacobsson and Folke Sundquist in Arne Mattsson's landmark sensationsfilm, Hon Dansade en Sommar *(She Danced One Summer)*

Courtesy of Klubb Super 8

(1969)

Director:
Bo A. Vibenius

Cast:
Fredrick Becklén
Madeleine Onne
Sune Mangs
Birgitta Andersson
Anita Lindman
Rolf Bengtsson
Astrid Fröberg
Gösta Roos
Jan Tillborg

HUR MARIE TRÄFFADE FREDRIK, ÅSNAN REBUS, KÄNGURUN PLOJ OCH...
[How Marie Met Fredrik, Rebus the Donkey, Ploj the Kangaroo, and...]

This is a children's movie concerning two kids who meet a kangaroo and a donkey, and drive a lot of go-carts. It contains nothing at all shocking or sensational in any way, but there is a very good reason to include it in this book. *Hur Marie Träffade Fredrik...* was the first of only three films ever directed by Bo A. Vibenius, the other two being the ultra-sleazy *Thriller – En Grym Film* (see page 258) and the mind-bending *Breaking Point* (see page 42).

Though obviously lacking grim and vengeful sex scenes, this film has a surrealist atmosphere similar to that of *Breaking Point*, though that can be explained by the lack of a script for reference during production. Another thing worth pointing out about this atrociously titled film is that it is super-heavy on product placement. Vibenius obviously couldn't raise the funds for the project, so he incorporated many scenes in which the children promote certain brands of bread and other products in long, long talky sequences.

A final thought: Can you imagine what terror went through the minds of the parents of the child actors in this film just a few years later, when Vibenius's subsequent productions arrived in their unflinching *sensationsfilm* glory? Oh, the horror, the horror...

I DÖD MANS SPÅR
[On Dead Man's Trail]

(1975)

Director:
Mats Helge Olsson
Cast:
Carl-Gustaf Lindstedt
Tor Isedal
Sune Mangs
Sten Ardenstam
Carl-Axel Elfving
Isabella Kaliff
Solveig Andersson
Urban Sahlin
Ramon Sylwan
Lars Lundgren

Old gold prospector Tom (Tor Isedal) is forced to flee from Dick Logan (Urban Sahlin) and his band of brutes, who are after an old treasure map Tom possesses. Before the villainous Logan reaches him, Tom gives the map to his daughter Isabella (Isabella Kaliff). And then he dies. Isabella tracks down her father's old friend Ben Walker (Carl-Gustaf Lindstedt) and persuades him to help her find the gold. Together with Walker's old gang, they embark on a lethal journey, all the while with Logan's band hot on their trail. Unsurprisingly, the chase ends with a duel that sees Walker gunning down the wicked Dick Logan.

Arriving well after *Wild West Story* (see page 280), this movie still helped coin a new term by launching the ultra-tiny "lingonberry western" film genre. Lindstedt plays a gunslinger and Sune Mangs is a bartender in this unbelievable western with dialogue strictly in Swedish. As is probably obvious already, there is no stopping the campiness of this movie. Words can't describe how stupid it looks to see Lindstedt riding around on horseback in the southern Sweden birch forests. As the icing on the cake, this movie also suffers for constant slapstick distractions, coupled with by unstoppable overacting. Some scenes work surprisingly well, especially a couple of macho bar fights and some raging gun battles. In addition, a number of unjustified scenes reveal Kaliff in all her naked glory—impressive, considering how few western films internationally thought it was necessary to include any nudity at all.

This is mythical director Mats Helge Olsson's first release, and he really deserves a lot of credit for courageously setting out to make a Swedish western. *I Död Mans Spår* was largely shot at Småland amusement park High Chaparral, and was coproduced by the park's notorious manager and dignitary Big Bengt Erlandsson, which probably contributed to the festive atmosphere. In fact, the park was only permitted by the Swedish government under the pretext that the buildings would be used as movie sets, even though this is the only known film to be made there. The amusement park is still going strong, decades later. Erlandsson is famed in Sweden for attempting to build a giant statue of himself outside the cowboy park, but he ran out of money after only finishing the pedestal. Even that is one of the largest structures in all of Sweden. As you can see, the revolutionary Swedish cowboy genre is steeped in madness and surrounded by controversy.

Clockwise from top left: American poster for a film seen by almost every typical Swedish family on some awkward Friday night—I Lust och Nöd (For Better and for Worse);

Director Mats Helge Olsson sure knows his camera angles. Carl-Gustaf Lindstedt shoots to kill in I Död Mans Spår (On Dead Man's Trail);

Pioneering lingonberry Western video box cover

I LUST OCH NÖD
[For Better and for Worse]

(1976)

Director:
*Paul D. Gerber
(Gerhard Poulsen)*

Cast:
Elona Glenn

Ulf Brunnberg

Per-Axel Arosenius

Marie Ekorre

Caroline Christensen

Åke Brodin

Jim Steffe

Ted Cegerblad

*Jane Sannemode
Lopez*

Göran Söderberg

Dennis Andersson

Katarina Lindström

Frederic Pavese

Free-spirited Elisabeth (Elona Glenn) is torn between her fiancé Dennis (Ulf Brunnberg) and her insatiable appetite for other men and sexual adventure. Her strong sex drive takes her on many erotic exploits, driving Dennis mad with jealousy. However, as the wedding day grows near, Elisabeth tones down her overly sexual side for a while out of respect for common decency. But rest assured, she is soon back again at the mercy of her raging libido, and as her desires escalate she slides effortlessly into lesbianism and group sex. In the midst of this tangle of eroticism and sex adventure, the movie abruptly ends.

Not a porno film, but on the verge, this is pleasant and well-acted sleaze. Gerhard Poulsen directed many daring and enjoyable scenes, including one in a dark movie theater where the protagonist is fingered by a strange man. Of course the juicy orgies toward the end are unique. The poor broken English of many of the actors fortifies the already dreamlike atmosphere throughout the movie.

Keep in mind that in the early 1980s these sleazy movies were often rented by many families, because the only offerings available to rent in video stores were sexy Swedish *sensationsfilms* and violent Italian slashers like Lucio Fulci's *New York Ripper* (1982). Sex and violence were the only options, because all the big film companies from Disney on down were too busy trying to ban the VCR out of fear that it would kill the movie business. Well, they had it all wrong.

Jonas Sima of *Expressen* was, as always, unimpressed: "I haven't seen anything as stupid, uneventful, and dull as this, even in the old innocent boulevard cinema. We have hit rock bottom."

Alternative titles: *Ceremony*; *Liz*; *Private Pleasures*

(1988)

Director:
Staffan Hildebrand

Cast:
Izabella Scorupco
Håkan Lindberg
Anki Lidén
Stig Engström
Kim Anderzon
Marcus Trapp
Mårten Thomasson
Dominik Henzel
Ulf Granqvist
Patrik Ehrman
Andrej Anderzon-Möller
Paolo Roberto

INGEN KAN ÄLSKA SOM VI
[No One Can Love Like Us]

As sixteen-year-old Annelie (Izabella Scorupco) grows tired of the disco-party lifestyle in Stockholm, she decides to go find her estranged father in the remote northern region of Norrland. There she falls in love with another teenager, and finally she meets her father. The fucking end.

Sweet Lord, this is a slow-moving film! Staffan Hildebrand obviously didn't have a clue what he was doing here, as simply nothing happens at all. This is just a seventy-five-minute buildup to a love scene between the young couple, which seems exactly like something shot for a porn film, except there is no sex or nudity. Finally, Scorupco reveals her tits for a few seconds, probably the whole selling point and idea for this atrocity. She would later go on to have a short career in Hollywood, starting off by playing the Bond girl in *GoldenEye* (Martin Campbell, 1995).

Riding high on his recent *Stockholmsnatt* (see page 246) fame, Paolo Roberto lends a cameo, and Joakim Schröder, who played Robban in Hildebrand's *G* (see page 73), gets writing credit.

After this abomination, Hildebrand made just made a few TV documentaries, with Roberto now reduced to a truly supporting role as his personal driver. Instead of exiting from the Swedish film industry forever, in a last bid for glory he teamed up with *Sökarna* (see page 232) director Daniel Fridell. The pair traveled to Brazil, South Africa, Egypt, Germany, and Thailand to make something called *Juvenis: The Global Generation* (1995). Though I haven't seen it, I'm a bit concerned about everything connected with the idea and the production itself. Well, my mother worked as an assistant on a Hildebrand TV shoot, and she survived. I should just relax.

Clockwise from top left: A young Stellan Skarsgård contemplates his sensationsfilm career in Inkräktarna (The Intruders) **Courtesy of Klubb Super 8**;

A movie best forgotten—Staffan Hildebrandt's Ingen Kan Älska Som Vi (No One Can Love Like Us);

Just a typical Nobel Prize ceremony afterparty? The awesomely sleazy Inkräktarna **Courtesy of Klubb Super 8**

(1974)

INKRÄKTARNA
[The Intruders]

Director:
Torgny Wickman

Cast:
Börje Nyberg
Jacqueline Laurent
Stellan Skarsgård
Gilda Aranico
Chris Chittell
Jim Steffe
Evelyne Deher
Anita Ericsson
Bert Bellman

Paula (Gilda Aranico) and Richard (Chris Chittell) are two hippies on motorbikes who coincidentally end up in an old mansion in the countryside. The master of the mansion (Börje Nyberg) turns out to be a Nobel Prize winner in chemistry living with his wife (Jacqueline Laurent), his son Peter (Stellan Skarsgård), and a couple of chambermaids. We soon witness a perverted sexual carousel, in which everyone has sex with everyone else under loving, degrading, and even hateful circumstances. Paula manages to fall in love with Peter, while Richard is smitten with Lisa (Evelyne Deher), the secretary. Unfortunately, Richard becomes obsessed with the idea of stealing a new invention from the Nobel Prize winner, and he starts acting more and more unpredictable and mean. In the end, Peter proposes to Paula, and she agrees to marry him. Less fortunate Richard and Lisa die in a motorcycle accident as they try to take off with the priceless invention.

In this country manor, juicy sex and nudity abound, complete with skinny-dipping and very steamy saunas. Stellan Skarsgård's presence in such a sleazy movie is odd but entertaining when compared to his later roles in movies such as *Breaking the Waves* (Lars von Trier, 1996), *Good Will Hunting* (Gus Van Sant, 1997), and *Angels and Demons* (Ron Howard, 2009). The absolute high point of this movie is Chris Chittell as Richard. What a jerk. His antics include blackmailing the Nobel winner's wife to have sex with him, forcing her to crawl around on all fours and beg while he verbally abuses her without mercy. When not blackmailing or abusing others, Richard drinks and insults people in a way unprecedented in Swedish cinema. This is high-quality Swedish sleaze, without a shadow of a doubt one of Torgny Wickman's best movies—and possibly one of Skarsgård's best, too.

Alternative titles: *Fait Acompli*; *Let Us Play Sex*; *Swedish Sex Games*

JACK

(1977)

Twentysomething wannabe-author Jack (Göran Stangertz) is up to no good. He wastes his days drinking loads of booze and slacking around the streets of Stockholm with his lowlife friends. In their wild search for kicks, the guys catch a boat to the island of Gotland, where they bicycle around, drinking and smoking loads of pot stolen from a botanical garden. After returning to Stockholm, Jack reconsiders his lifestyle and ultimately turns over a new leaf when he decides to write a book about his wild life.

The 1976 novel *Jack* by superstar Swedish author and singer-songwriter Ulf Lundell is hands down the best-selling Swedish book of all time. A blatant rip-off of Jack Kerouac's *On the Road*, this touchstone novel has urged at least two generations of Swedes to shirk all their obligations in order to just drink and raise hell. Once director Jan Halldoff—known from *Rötmånad* (see page 208) and *Stenansiktet* (see page 243)—got his hands on the book, he quickly secured the film rights and released this big-screen version the same year.

Though drinking and stealing things might seem like excellent inspiration for hard sensations, the film is restrained and down-tuned. A couple of nude scenes, many drinking sessions, and a totally discouraging pot-smoking episode are all the audience can expect. Well, there is a genuinely dirty episode about a heroin addict, but that almost seems beside the point. On the whole, the film is extremely slow-moving. You get the idea that two misty-eyed middle-aged men (Lundell and Halldoff) just wanted to relive their youth via the on-screen adventures of the wooden Stangertz. At the time of this film, however, Lundell was only twenty-eight and Halldoff was thirty-seven—they were way too young to be so over the hill.

Director:
Jan Halldoff
Cast:
Göran Stangertz
Kjell Bergqvist
Örjan Ramberg
Gunnel Fred
Tove Linde
Bibbi Unge
Åke Lindström
Nils Eklund
Kerstin Bagge
Gunilla Nyroos
Ola Sandborgh
Christer Skeppstedt
Stig Törnblom

(1968)

Director:

Vilgot Sjöman

Cast:

Lena Nyman
Börje Ahlstedt
Sonja Lindgren
Hans Hellberg
Bim Warne
Hanne Sandemose
Gunnel Broström
Vilgot Sjöman
Bertil Wikström

JAG ÄR NYFIKEN – BLÅ
[I Am Curious (Blue)]

This movie, a parallel of sorts to the infamous *Jag Är Nyfiken – Gul* (see page 104), offers almost exactly the same kind of content as its precursor but did not receive even close to the same amount of attention or success. The shock value of the first movie had diminished, and the sexual revolution was no longer as sensational as it had been six months earlier. The political aspect seemed tame at that point, and all the attention director Vilgot Sjöman probably hoped to receive was instead channeled toward a considerably more powerful movie that premiered at the same time: Stefan Jarl's *Dom Kallar Oss Mods* (see page 51).

Alternative title: *Jag är Nyfiken – En Film i Blått*

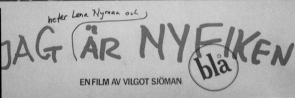

Clockwise from top left: "Angry, shameless and smart"... "It claws, burns and irritates"... "Talked about and discussed!";

The unreserved Lena Nyman hurls herself full force into the depths of sexual freedom;

The face of Swedish sexuality on the American poster for Jag Är Nyfiken – Gul *(I Am Curious [Yellow])*

JAG ÄR NYFIKEN – GUL
[I Am Curious (Yellow)]

(1967)

Director:

Vilgot Sjöman

Cast:

Lena Nyman

Börje Ahlstedt

Peter Lindgren

Magnus Nilsson

Chris Wahlström

Marie Göranzon

Ulla Lyttkens

Anders Ek

Martin Luther King

Jevgenij Jevtusenko

This landmark movie within a movie trails the sexual and political awakening of Lena (Lena Nyman), a young woman living in an apartment with her father during the tumultuous late 1960s. Her life is made exciting by deep political discussions, aimless sex with her director, and dazed sexual escapades. Her freedom and newfound beliefs are challenged when she attempts to start a relationship with the traditional Börje (Börje Ahlstedt). Her fictional story is broken up by strictly authentic segments and interviews.

Vilgot Sjöman's *Nyfiken* movies can be considered the very first serious cinematic attempt to truly portray sex and nudity in a straightforward manner. There are no efforts made to romanticize sexual curiosity, and no cheesy insinuations. People are exposed just the way they actually behave. With every detail and every defect, the blunt sex scenes almost seem authentic. The explicit nature of the movie shocked audiences around the world, and *Jag Är Nyfiken – Gul* was heavily censored almost everywhere. (The only countries to show the totally unedited version at the time of the film's release were apparently Sweden, Denmark, and the Netherlands). In the United States, the film was nearly banned altogether but slipped past the censors, and to this day remains the most successful Swedish movie ever released in the American market. In conclusion, it is rather incredible that the whole world decided to disregard the movie's dense political message and instead wallow in its sexual aspects!

Alternative title: *Jag Är Nyfiken – En Film i Gult*

JAG – EN ÄLSKARE
[I, a Lover]

Beatrice (Jessie Flaws) is trapped in a stagnating marriage, and things do not pick up when her husband, Peter (Jørgen Ryg), develops an erection problem. After taking off for Paris, Beatrice swiftly finds a lover, while her impotent husband stays behind in Sweden, pondering his problems while watching porn. Fortunately, he soon meets a woman who is madly attracted to his manhood complications, and after a couple of hot encounters between them Peter's impotence is history. Once Peter's world has changed, he runs into nothing but hot, willing girls, and when Beatrice returns to Sweden a bright and lustful future appears on the horizon.

One among many Swedish-Danish coproductions that followed the success of Mac Ahlberg's *Jag – En Kvinna* (see page 106), the movie *Jag – En Älskare* is based loosely on a novel of the same name—and probably should have stayed just a novel. The eroticism drowns in poor attempts at humor, and things never really take off. There is some nudity, but nothing more than brief flashes of breasts. For lovers of bearded, carefree Danes nonchalantly dangling cigarettes in the corners of their mouths as they flash creepy smiles at young girls, this movie is a must. The rest of us might as well skip it.

(1966)

Director:
Börje Nyberg
Cast:
Jørgen Ryg
Axel Strøbye
Jessie Flaws
Ebbe Langberg
Paul Hagen
Dirch Passer
Kerstin Wartel
Marie Nylander

JAG – EN KVINNA
[I, a Woman]

(1965)

Director:

Mac Ahlberg

Cast:

Essy Persson

Tove Maës

Erik Hell

Preben Kørning

Preben Mahrt

Bengt Brunskog

Jørgen Reenberg

Frankie Steel

Ebba With

Siv (Essy Persson) is a young nurse on the brink of discovering her sexuality. Starting innocently with Siv exploring and caressing her body, the film gets spicier when she starts seeing an older married patient. When Siv's fiancé finds out about this affair, he is outraged. His girlfriend's carefree attitude toward sex disgusts him. She ignores the cuckolded fuddy-duddy, though, and continues her sexual journey, steadily increasing her range of exciting locations and partners. Eventually, all her lovers are scared away by Siv's excessive lust—the mere thought of her sexual freedom leaves them all feeling insecure and powerless.

This Danish-Swedish coproduction marks legendary Swedish auteur Mac Ahlberg's directorial debut. The explicit nudity caused much controversy at the time, but actress Essy Persson sprang into fame as something of a sex symbol. The commotion the movie caused at its premiere seems a bit foreign today; the film has lost much of its controversial edge, and comes across as harmless and innocent—more about feminist liberation than sleazy sex. A few scenes hold up to this day, including one at a busy strip club and another where Siv is spanked good by her one of her lovers. This was a mere warm-up for Ahlberg, though, and he provided an astonishing lineup of erotic movies during the following decade.

From Sweden...A totally new concept in artistic motion pictures for adults!

RADLEY H. METZGER
presents

"I, a woman"

wiTH **ESSY PERSSON**

BASED ON THE NOVEL BY SIV HOLM A co-production of Nordisk Film, Copenhagen and AB Europa Film, Stockholm
Directed by Mac Ahlberg–Distributed by *Audubon Films*

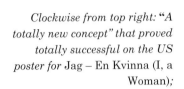
Recommended for THE MATURE ADULT!

Clockwise from top right: "A totally new concept" that proved totally successful on the US poster for Jag – En Kvinna (I, a Woman)*;*

Essy Persson and lover in Jag – En Kvinna
Courtesy of Klubb Super 8 *;*

Essy Persson and a different lover in Jag – En Kvinna
Courtesy of Klubb Super 8

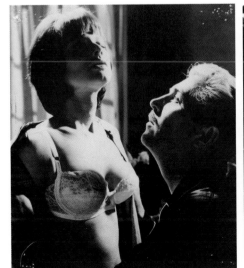

JAG – EN KVINNA 2. ÄKTENSKAPET
[I, a Woman 2: The Marriage]

(1968)

Director:
Mac Ahlberg

Cast:
Gio Petré
Lars Lunøe
Hjördis Petterson
Bertel Laurig
Klaus Pagh
Kate Mundt
Karl Stegger
Carl Ottosen
*Bjørn Pugaard-
Müller*
*Sigrid Horne-
Rasmussen*

The once super-liberated Siv (Gio Petré) is now stuck in a stagnating marriage with her cynical husband, Hans-Henrik (Lars Lunøe), who focuses more on his collection of antiques than on his wife. Unfortunately, his love for old things has placed the couple in debt, and Siv is forced to put out to an old antiques dealer in order to pay down the account. The degrading treatment spawns hatred for her husband, so Siv returns to her job as a nurse—and also to the relationship she had with one of the doctors. At the hospital, she also meets Hans-Henrik's ex-wife, who tried to kill herself after being forced into prostitution by him. The hatred only grows stronger in Siv. When she realizes her husband has a history as a Nazi, she leaves him. Unable to handle the rejection, Hans-Henrik ends up being comforted by his old mother, while he lies pathetically on the wood floor of his apartment.

Mac Ahlberg unleashed this incredibly questionable sequel to his hugely successful *Jag – En Kvinna* (see page 106), this time in color and with Gio Petré taking over the role of the main character. While the first movie was pretty sensible—almost serious filmmaking, this is wall-to-wall sensation. The greedy camera explores Petré's body even during the opening credits, and the lewdness never slows down. The perverted plot includes a large quantity of degrading and exploitative sequences, reaching an almost psychotic pitch in tandem with the wild soundtrack. Almost every sex scene is somehow perverted, like the one in which Siv is forced to have sex with one of her husband's dirty colleagues while Hans-Henrik watches, cynically smirking. No matter how gritty this gets, nothing beats the final sequence, in which Siv marches around in full Nazi uniform in a room filled with swastikas and portraits of prominent Nazis. With this supreme sleaze, Mac Ahlberg really found his calling—it's way better than *Ghoulies* (Luca Bercovici, 1985) or *The Wonder Years* (TV series, 1988), for which he much later served as cinematographer!

The criticism was, of course, ruthless: "It is more a matter of linguistics than of taste whether you decide to call this movie blockheaded, absurd, foolish, or simply idiotic," slagged Jürgen Schildt in *Aftonbladet*.

"JAG" – EN KVINNAS DOTTER
["I," a Woman's Daughter]

Director:

Mac Ahlberg

Cast:

*Gun Falck
(Gunbritt Öhrström)*

Inger Sundh

Klaus Pagh

Tom Scott

Ellen Faison

Søren Strømberg

Helli Louise

Susanne Jagd

Tove Bang

Tove Maës

Bent Warburg

When young virgin Birthe (Inger Sundh) returns home after a long stay at boarding school, she accidentally catches her mother (Gun Falck) in bed with a lover. Upset and confused by the unpleasant sight, she starts pondering her own sexuality, and decides to head out into the wild club scene to try her luck. Birthe soon finds herself experiencing all kinds of sex with both men and women, and she experiments with drugs. In the midst of all this confusion, she meets a black man, Steffen (Tom Scott), whom she ends up falling in love with and marrying.

This is a semi-sleazy Danish production directed by the always reliable Swedish *sensationsfilm* auteur Mac Ahlberg. The spicy atmosphere is established instantly, as the opening credits roll over a backdrop of Inger Sundh floating around touching herself. There are a few peculiar moments, like when Birthe kisses a snake, but the main focus of the movie is just plain old sex, of which the lesbian encounters are highlights. The cake is iced by a few tripped-out drug scenes and a poorly choreographed fight started by a biker gang in a hippie club. All in all, it's a pretty decent movie, though not Ahlberg's best.

Alternative titles: *The Daughter*; *I, a Woman 3*

Setting things up for some "fun sex-sadism" in Jag en Markis – Med Uppdrag att Älska (I, a Marquis: With a Mission in Love

Courtesy of Klubb Super 8

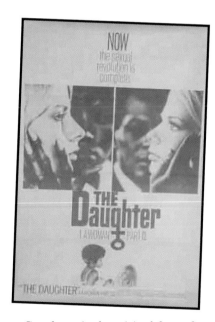

Caught up in the spirit of the age? Mac Ahlberg takes a stand for interracial relationships in "Jag" – En Kvinnas Dotter

When Sweden and Denmark come together... "Jag" – En Kvinnas Dotter ("I," a Woman's Daughter)

Courtesy of Klubb Super 8

JAG EN MARKIS – MED UPPDRAG ATT ÄLSKA
[I, a Marquis: With a Mission in Love]

(1967)

Directors:
Mac Ahlberg
Peer Guldbrandsen
Cast:
Gabriel Axel
Elsa Prawitz
Karl Stegger
Buster Larsen
Ove Sprogøe
Johan Price
Preben Kaas
Poul Bundgaard
Paul Hagen
Lotte Tarp
Jeanne Darville
Lisbeth Lindeborg
Preben Nicolaisen
Carl Ottosen

Reportedly, this Swedish-Danish coproduction is based on a true story—which should hardly come as a surprise to anyone who has ever visited Denmark. Simply by changing his name to "Marquis de Sade," office worker Rasmusen (Gabriel Axel) improves his life situation, which had previously suffered in both the economic and erotic departments. Since everyone assumes Marquis is a descendent of the famous author, they instantly treat him with respect and admiration. Men let him borrow money, and women long to experience sexual adventures with him. After leading a life more and more resembling one eternal orgy, Rasmusen is finally revealed to be a fraud and thrown into jail, while his collection of sex toys is auctioned off to pleasure-seeking women.

We know what to expect from a movie with the tagline "An erotic comedy with fun sex-sadism." The natural high point is the last third, when our office clerk's escalating sexcapades reach a truly Hugh Hefner–like fever pitch. Especially memorable is a masquerade ball that derails and nearly becomes an orgy, with ladies' bottoms getting whipped and their breasts being exposed. De Sade also installs a torture chamber in his basement, but unfortunately that is not used enough in this all-too-lame movie.

Alternative titles: *Greve Porrno och Hans Kvinnor (Count Porrno and His Women); I, a Nobleman; The Reluctant Sadist*

(1968)

Director:

Joseph W. Sarno

Cast:

Marie Liljedahl

Monica Strömmerstedt

Thomas Ungewitter

Casten Lassen

Else-Marie Brandt

Sissi Kaiser

Anne-Lise Myhrvold

Curt Ericson

Lennart Norbäck

JAG, EN OSKULD
[I, a Virgin]

Inga (Marie Liljedahl) has been under the custody of her aunt Greta (Monica Strömmerstedt) ever since she lost her mother in a car crash. Aunt Greta tries to pair young Inga with middle-aged ladies' man Einar (Thomas Ungewitter) in order to be rid of him and halt his advances toward herself. The selfish plans come to nothing, though, as the twenty-one-year-old boy that Aunt Greta fancies falls in love with the stunning Inga and the two youngsters run away together.

"I have no alternative but to warn you against this movie, unless for some reason you are out to bore yourself to death for seventy-five minutes," Lennart Nilsson wrote in *Dagens Nyheter*. For once, the critic's quote is not totally off-target: *Jag, En Oskuld* really is a very dull movie! However, Nilsson is missing a very crucial point: the exploitation value of a very young and incredibly beautiful Marie Liljedahl. As the mere sight of her, the audience is fully protected from the risk of being bored to death. In addition, there are a few slightly sleazy sequences, foremost the one where Inga masturbates accompanied by a wild fuzz guitar— as we all do from time to time. In the end, this is mostly a movie for Liljedahl fanatics.

Alternative titles: *Inga*; *Inga: I Have Lust*; *Inga: I, a Virgin*

The stunning Marie Liljedahl in
Jag, en Oskuld (I, a Virgin)

FILMEN SOM VÅLLAT
CENSURSVÅRIGHETER
FÖR SINA STARKA
EROTISKA SCENER!

JAG EN
OSKULD

*"The movie that has stirred up
censorship problems for its strong
erotic scenes"*

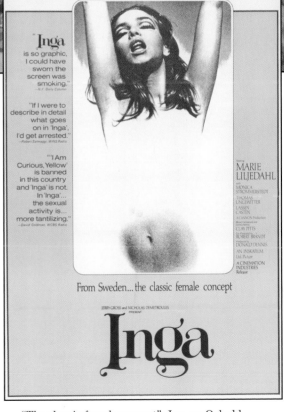

"Inga is so graphic,
I could have
sworn the
screen was
smoking."
—N.Y. Daily Criticism

"If I were to
describe in detail
what goes
on in 'Inga',
I'd get arrested."
—Robert Salmaggi, WINS Radio

"'I Am
Curious, Yellow'
is banned
in this country
and 'Inga' is not.
In 'Inga'...
the sexual
activity is...
more tantilizing."
—David Goldman, WCBS Radio

MARIE
LILJEDAHL

From Sweden... the classic female concept

JERRY GROSS and NICHOLAS DEMETROULES PRESENT

Inga

"The classic female concept": Jag, en Oskuld
airbrushed and renamed for US consumption

(1975)

Director:

Mac Ahlberg

Cast:

Shirley Corrigan
Gaby Fuchs
Peter Bonke
Bo Brundin
Peter Kupier
Marie Ekorre
Gösta Prüzelius
Christina Hellman
Christina Lindberg
Darja Olsson

JORDEN RUNT MED FANNY HILL
[Around the World with Fanny Hill]

Young Fanny Hill (Shirley Corrigan) is unhappy in her awkward marriage to Roger (Peter Bonke), and so manipulates him into divorcing her. Once rid of her husband, Fanny leaves for Los Angeles and soon finds herself lured into the erotic movie industry. As her fame grows, the tabloids pick up her story, and Roger figures out what she is up to. The movie productions take Fanny all around the world, with her jealous ex following her trail. After a number of adventures and mishaps, the two are finally reunited.

Full of confidence following the success of *Fanny Hill*, Mac Ahlberg swiftly arranged this erratic sequel. The fact that the original cast was not available was seemingly of no concern, and new names were randomly cast in the primary roles. For whatever reason, this movie is far more daring than its precursor and includes tons of nudity and explicit sex scenes, even some hard-core sequences. Many of these sex scenes are impressively psychedelic, with tinted colors, kaleidoscopic filters, and slow-motion effects. The constant traveling to new exotic environments provides a fresh and action-packed feeling. Unfortunately, the director could not resist adding a few farcical scenes, but this movie overall remains much more alive and vibrant than *Fanny Hill*. Do not miss Marie Ekorre in an early role, and note that sleaze queen Christina Lindberg appears as a sinful photo model. This alone makes *Jorden Runt med Fanny Hill* worth seeing—it's sleazy, cool, and awesome.

Oddly enough, this film premiered in prudelike Norway, and when it finally turned up in Sweden nobody cared. Only the tabloid *Expressen* bothered to print a review, and they hated the picture: "An unusually uninteresting film with a pompous, boring ending." They were so wrong.

*Clockwise from top:
Christina Lindberg
leaves Sweden, still
manages to find
meatballs in* Jorden
Runt med Fanny Hill
(Around the World with
Fanny Hill)
Courtesy of Klubb Super 8*;*

Swedish Jungfrukällan
(The Virgin Spring)
poster;

French Jungfrukällan
*poster, several degrees
more intimidating*

(1960)

Director:

Ingmar Bergman

Cast:

Max von Sydow
Birgitta Valberg
Birgitta Pettersson
Gunnel Lindblom
Axel Düberg
Tor Isedal
Allan Edvall
Ove Porath
Axel Slangus
Gudrun Brost
Oscar Ljung

JUNGFRUKÄLLAN
[The Virgin Spring]

Sometime in the Dark Ages, a young woman passing through the forest is suddenly raped and murdered by a band of bandits. Later that night, the brutes seek lodging at the house of the girl's unsuspecting parents, who are upset, wondering where their daughter is. When the truth is revealed, the desperate parents get their bloodstained revenge; no mercy is shown, and everybody ends up losing.

Ingmar Bergman's violent medieval saga arguably serves as an important measuring stick for the forthcoming Swedish *sensationsfilm* genre. Never before had acts such as rape and murder been depicted with such intensity. The merciless story is based on medieval folk ballad "Töres Dotter i Wänge" (Töre's Daughter in Wänge). Internationally, *Jungfrukällan* became a success, arguably initiating the whole "rape-revenge" genre, extending to Sam Peckinpah's *Straw Dogs* (1971) and especially Wes Craven's *Last House on the Left* (1972), which is basically a remake of *Jungfrukällan*. John Waters claims Bergman as somewhat of a role model, and cites this as the first movie to portray on-screen vomiting! *The Virgin Spring* is definitely one of Bergman's greatest moments, though he frequently badmouthed the film and surely hated all the trashy low-budget productions it inspired. Regardless, this won awards at Cannes and the Golden Globes, and remains the only Bergman film to win an Oscar for Best Foreign Language Film.

JUSTINE OCH JULIETTE
[Justine and Juliette]

(1975)

Director:
Bert Torn
(Mac Ahlberg)
Cast:
Maria Lynn
(Marie Forså)
Bie Warburg
Kate Mundt
Harry Reems
Felix Franchy
Poul Bundgaard
Bent Warburg
William Kisum
Bert Bellman
Otto Brandenburg
Jim Steffe

Young siblings Justine (Marie Forså) and Juliette (Bie Warburg) are forced to seek their fortune in Stockholm after the death of their parents. The indecent Juliette immediately decides to try prostitution. Virgin Justine wants to lead a more respectable life, but ends up in a destructive relationship. Juliette's immediate popularity as a sex sensation enables her to save Justine, but Justine is not grateful enough to start working at the brothel. She just hangs out there, waiting for something better to happen. When filthy-rich American Don Miller (Harry Reems) visits the brothel, he instantly falls for Justine, and after some wooing he ends up in bed with her. Don dies during lovemaking—but this unbelievable tragedy brings unexpected happiness. It turns out that the rich American with a weak heart had already decided to leave his massive fortune to whatever random person he last had sex with—so almost-virginal Justine in whose arms he died wins a kind of sex lottery. What a stroke of luck!

Mac Ahlberg is in his most hysterical mood here, mixing up soft-core and hard-core sex left and right. The hard-core scenes are notably placed where they could be easily edited out to create a tamer version of the film. Among the notable actors are a very young Marie Forså and of course international superstar Harry Reems, who makes this movie worthwhile with his sprightly ways. Reems's lines were dubbed into Swedish by usually more-respected actor Börje Ahlstedt, who really went gung ho and over the top during sex scenes, screaming in Swedish, "I want to fuck!" at the top of his lungs. The atmosphere gets schizophrenic when all the nasty sleaze is mixed with corny slapstick comedy.

The national press took note of this romp, as it did of many other *sensationsfilms,* if only to annihilate it critically. The review in *Svenska Dagbladet* read: "Even among tough competition, *Justine och Juliette* is a top candidate for stupidest movie of the year. As pornography, it is about as exciting as the children's movie *Barnen från Frostmofjället.*"

Alternative title: *Swedish Minx*

DEN K... FAMILJEN
[The H... Family]

(1976)

Director:

Heinz Arland

Cast:

Anita Westberg
Lasse Berg
Greta Lindner
Monika Viklund
Stig Dahl
Yngve Ericsson
Harriet Sjöberg
Ove Wallin

Here's a standard Swedish sex movie about Anette (Anita Westberg). She recalls her past summer and the sexual escapades she enjoyed—her unforgettable night with Börje (Lasse Berg), how he cheated on her with her mother, how Anette stole her mother's lover, and so on. The most entertaining aspect is the neatly over-dubbed voice-over by Swedish sleaze queen Marie Forså, who delivers an abundance of comical lines with a tone of total indifference. Apart from this mirth, there is nothing much enjoyable to be found here.

Clockwise from top left:
Jarl Kulle and Christina Schollin
make the most out of the short
Swedish summer in Käre John
(Dear John);

Marie Forså and Harry Reems
celebrating in Justine och Juliette
(Justine and Juliette), unaware of
the cruel but comic fate that lies
ahead for one of them
Courtesy of Klubb Super 8;

Torbjörn Axelman's masterful
Kameleonterna (The
Chameleons)

(1969) KAMELEONTERNA
[The Chameleons]

Director:

Torbjörn Axelman

Cast:

Tor Isedal

Mona Malm

Håkan Serner

Monica Stenbeck

Pär Ericson

Monica Nielsen

Ulf Brunnberg

Åke Fridell

Yvonne Lombard

Elisabet Gustavsson

Claude Kazi-Tani

Sten Ardenstam

Eivind (Håkan Serner) is a filmmaker headed for success. For his latest film, he hires chameleon expert Lisa (Monica Stenbeck) as an advisor and quickly falls in love with her. The financier of this project is questionable businessman Dick (Tor Isedal), a cynical crook simmering in a bad marriage. Before long, the movie production turns sour. A couple of mysterious deaths create a bad atmosphere on the set. Then Dick rapes a defenseless Lisa while she is passed out drunk, and things really become awkward. When Eivind's movie, *The Chameleons*, finally premieres, it totally bombs at the box office and everyone abandons him.

This satire of the Swedish cultural establishment and the way films are produced in Sweden takes the form of a psychedelic thriller. Isedal is wonderfully dirty as the rich asshole, and Åke Fridell is good and sleazy as the murderer. Completing a trinity of unholy performances, Ulf Brunnberg overacts incredibly as a movie director—the scene where he loses it during a shoot is priceless. Among a slew of hard-boiled scenes, Dick's rape of the strung-out Lisa as his unhappy wife listens sticks out. Other bizarre sequences portray a hand being devoured by ants, and shots from inside the freezer of a slaughterhouse, with dead animals hanging everywhere. Counteracting the violence and tension and providing a nice equilibrium, there are sequences shot in some kind of kaleidoscope fashion, accompanied by sitar, which will surely put even the most hardened modern audience into a hippielike dream state. The mix of mayhem and flower power overshadows the substandard production and directing.

As expected, the snobby contemporary media came down hard on this movie. "Axelman's new movie is a catastrophe," warned Lasse Bergström in *Expressen*.

KANINMANNEN
[The Rabbit Man]

(1990)

Director:
Stig Larsson
Cast:
Börje Ahlstedt
Leif Andrée
Stina Ekblad
Björn Gedda
Eva Engström
Dominika Posserén
Erika Ullenius
Krister Henriksson
Tomas Pontén
Sven Holm

After a long career as a crime reporter, Bengt Nääs (Börje Ahlstedt) takes a new job as an editor for the cynical TV channel TV9, whose ratings are built on nothing but the most juicy and exploitative content. (The station is a blatant spoof of then newly launched TV3, Sweden's first adventure in tabloid television.) What could be better for ratings than a series of reports about sexual abuse of underage girls during the same time that a real serial rapist is on the loose in Stockholm? Bengt soon suspects that his own son (Leif Andrée) might be the perpetrator, and the movie hurtles into a downward psychological spiral.

Stig Larsson (the sleazebag director, not the author) struggled for over a decade looking for backers willing to finance this risky movie, deemed a blatant speculation in pornography and violence. The subject matter is controversial to say the least, yet the film avoids the temptation to surrender to visual shock effects. Without sensational imagery to match the story, the movie becomes more of a melodrama than a proper exploitation film. Despite this, *Kaninmannen* is dark and unpleasant throughout. Ahlstedt is brilliant as the leading man—he won the Guldbagge movie prize that year. The movie reaches an extra dimension of unpleasant-ness when one consider Larsson's often publicly stated real-life preference for young girls. Even the nerve of calling a serial rapist "the rabbit man" is unsettling. All in all, *Kaninmannen* remains a good specimen from the end of the *sensationsfilm* era.

KÄR LEK – SÅ GÖR VI. BREV TILL INGE OCH STEN [Love Play – That's How We Do It. Letters to Inge and Sten]

(1972)

Director:
Torgny Wickman

Cast:
Inge Hegeler
Sten Hegeler

In the fourth and last installment of the sex-education movie series directed by Torgny Wickman, the two relationship experts Inge and Sten Hegeler again guide the trip. This time around, the sex life of the family is the focal point, illustrated by the actual Hegeler clan as they hang out in a summer cottage in Småland and discuss some of the letters they have received over the years. In addition, they go skinny-dipping and take saunas with some visiting students from Copenhagen. After a while, we inevitably get to see filmed adaptations of the situations described in the letters. The scenarios include several sexually "defiant" games, including erotic role-playing with raincoats in the shower, massage oil and finger-painting experiments, and a sequence where a husband pretends to be his wife's gynecologist.

The format that Wickman and the Hegelers employed with the relatively dry educational film *Kärlekens Språk* (see page 126) has by now totally degenerated into unstoppable sensationalism. The sex scenes are long and detailed, and the whole movie comes across as thinly disguised porn hiding behind a novelty store professor's beard. Yet the sexuality is distorted by the dry, droning voice-over, to the point that the absurd sex situations become hysterical comedy. This movie is totally wild, and a must-see for all enthusiasts of Swedish *sensationfilms*.

Oh, and what about the press? Yes, they panned it. "I insist: reactionary nonsense in pornographic wrapping," Mario Grut snorted in *Aftonbladet*.

Alternative titles: *Love 4, Love-Play: That's How We Do It...*

KÄRE JOHN
[Dear John]

(1964)

The hardened skipper Johan (Jarl Kulle) falls in love with young waitress Anita (Christina Schollin), and they tumble forward, expecting an intoxicating summer of love. After a few misunderstandings and mishaps, there is indeed a happy ending.

Lars-Magnus Lindgren's second movie with Schollin and Kulle in the lead roles turned out to be an immense international success, and Schollin became a virtual global symbol for Swedish sin. Nominated for an Oscar for Best Foreign Language Film, the movie stirred up an enormous scandal in the US, and was labeled completely immoral by the forces of decency. Today, it is impossible to understand what was considered so shocking, since the story really is quite clean and decent—unlike Olle Länsberg's more explicit original novel. Then again, someday our grandchildren will probably wonder what we found so offensive about vile filth like *Kärleksön* (see page 129).

Director:
Lars-Magnus Lindgren

Cast:
Jarl Kulle
Christina Schollin
Helena Nilsson
Morgan Andersson
Erik Hell
Emy Storm
Synnöve Liljebäck
Håkan Serner
Hans Wigren

(1967)

Director:

Lennart Olsson

Cast:

Helena Reuterblad
Per-Olof Eriksson
Niels Dybeck
Åke Jörnfalk
Åke Lindström
Halvar Björk
Inger Liljefors

KÄRLEK 1-1000
[Love 1-1000]

Four peculiar young guys live together. The smartest of them (and that's not saying much) is sent out shopping with the last of their money, and in the process is picked up by a mysterious woman in an elegant car. She brings him home and forces him to wear roller skates, as she begins stripping in front of the confused youngster. At the same time, a group of older men are peeping on them from the next room. The remainder of the day is filled with weird experiences for the young man, climaxing in an orgasmic party where everyone fornicates with everyone.

Kärlek 1-1000 is a one-of-a-kind, surreal movie that has to be seen to be believed. The striptease mentioned above is truly out of this world, followed by an abundance of scenes with more or less naked ladies. I guess the director set out to make some kind of clever art movie, but it comes across as watered-down exploitation in a flimsy disguise. This very odd movie is hard to wrap your head around, and the stressed-out jazz soundtrack that constantly rages in the background does not help calm things down.

The previews hinted that this would be the first Swedish hardcore porn movie, but even the critics were bummed by the harmless result. "If by porn you mean a couple of naked breasts and breathless forced make-out sessions, the movie may be labeled porn—otherwise it does not deserve any other label than bawdy slapstick," wrote Göran Sellgren in *Svenska Dagbladet*. In the US, the reaction was even worse, as the distribution print of the film was initially confiscated due to its depraved morality.

Clockwise from top left: Kärlek 1-1000 (Love 1-1000) *lobby card*

Courtesy of Klubb Super 8;

Swedish Kärlek 1-1000 *poster: "The intrigue is funny and the girls are hot. Hats off for this pornographic farce!"…"The bedroom sequence alone is worth half the ticket price"*

Courtesy of Klubb Super 8;

"Intolerance for the partner"—the cinematic veneer of sex education and couples therapy that masks the sleazy heart of Kärlekens Språk (Language of Love)

Courtesy of Klubb Super 8

(1969)

Director:
Torgny Wickman

Cast:
Inge Hegeler
Sten Hegeler
Maj-Brith Bergström-Walan
Sture Cullhed

KÄRLEKENS SPRÅK
[Language of Love]

Notably, *Kärlekens Språk* was the first film including depictions of authentic sexual intercourse ever approved by the Swedish board of censors—and that was only after twenty-two other countries had already exhibited the film. The US and the UK were not among those trailblazers of the sexual revolution, however. This film was confiscated at the American border, and became the center of a court case lasting almost two years. Incredibly, in 1971 an estimated 30,000 Brits, including pop singer Cliff Richard, gathered in London's Trafalgar Square to protest this film's appearance at a nearby movie theater.

All the hubbub was over a classic sex-education setup directed by Torgny Wickman, starring the Danish psychologists Inge and Sten Hegeler as themselves. The theories of these Danes and Swedish sex advisor Maj-Brith Bergström-Walan form the basis of an array of dramatized episodes and authentic sex scenes. The tone is strictly scientific. Wickman calls upon such techniques as screen splitting and animation to shed light on the subject. There was a name for this kind of thing—*upplysningsfilm* (information film), and the makers of this movie abused that premise to the fullest.

Needless to say, as with all the other *sensationsfilms*, neither the language of love nor the language of education is spoken here—only the language of sensation. It all comes across as rather corny today, but at the time of its premiere the movie was very successful, spawning a number of sequels, such as *Mera ur Kärlekens Språk* (see page 166), *Kärlekens XYZ* (see page 127), and *Kär Lek – Så Gör Vi. Brev till Inge och Sten* (see page 122). The film was also widely talked about internationally, confirming Sweden's emerging hot-to-trot reputation. An American knock-off, *Sexual Practices in Sweden* (1970), purported to be produced under the auspices of the "Svenska Institute of Sexual Response."

Martin Scorsese must have been impressed on some level—*Kärlekens Språk* is the highly inappropriate film Travis Bickle takes Betsy to see on their date in *Taxi Driver* (1976).

KÄRLEKENS XYZ
[The XYZ of Love]

(1971)

Director:
Torgny Wickman

Cast:
Maj-Brith Bergström-Walan

Leif Silbersky

Inge Hegeler

Sten Hegeler

Joachim Israel

Ola Ullsten

Birgitta Linnér

Rune Pär Olofsson

Lars Engström

Sweden's first certified sex advisor, psychologist Maj-Brith Bergström-Walan, tries to be a serious, scientific force in this third installment of Torgny Wickman's sex-education movies—but in vain. As usual, we are guided through the world of carnal knowledge by Danish sex oracles Inge and Sten Hegeler. In this installment, they discuss a bewildering array of sensational topics, including:

- Whether certain case studies are rape or not;
- Various cures for impotence and frigidity through sex;
- The plusses and minuses of the abortion issue;
- Sweden's secret brothels;
- The legal ins and outs of adultery;
- Pimping;
- The communal sex lives of big hippie families; and
- Group sex.

Plainly, this is nothing but sensationalism in an ill-fitting scientific disguise. Even more so than in the two earlier movies, *Kärlekens Språk* (see page 126) and *Mera ur Kärlekens Språk* (see page 166), Wickman totally fails to keep any scientific distance from the subject, and everything explodes in total titillation. Note celebrity lawyer Leif Silbersky and former leader of the Swedish liberal party Folkpartiet Ola Ullsten in the cast.

"Inge Ivarsson's latest notorious sexual education attempt is a monument to cynical speculation, and totally lacks any pedagogic intelligence," wrote Jan Aghed in *Sydsvenska Dagbladet Snällposten*. He was right. On the plus side, Bergström-Walan is still going strong today at age eighty-six, and probably more curious about sex than ever.

Alternative title: *Love 3*

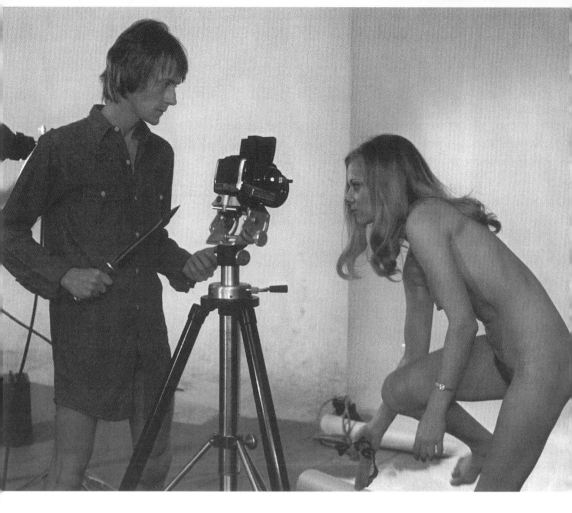

Clockwise from top: Big shirt, big knife, and hard lessons in the phony documentary Kärlekens XYZ (The XYZ of Love)
Courtesy of Klubb Super 8;

"I want to Sleep with Your Lover...," alternative Swedish title for Kärleksvirveln (The Love Swirl);

Joseph W. Sarno's obscene pornographic tragedy, Kärleksön (The Love Island)

KÄRLEKSÖN
[The Love Island]

(1977)

Director:

*Hammond Thomas
(Joseph W. Sarno)*

Cast:

Leena

Sonja

Liza

Thomas

Göte

and their friends

Katrin is a sex-obsessed teen who lives on an island in the Stockholm archipelago. When some summer guests arrive, the feral girl spies on them with great fascination. Soon, she arranges a number of sex dates with the vacationers, luring them into situations where she can sow her wild oats with great enthusiasm.

This 1970s porn by the beloved Joseph W. Sarno sees literally everyone having sex with everyone. Notably, the movie flirts incessantly with incest, escalating in the end into plenty of dirty family sex. Other obscene sequences include Katrin peeing in front of the camera, and masturbating with a hairbrush. A weird, unpleasant mood haunts the movie, so it all comes across as deeply tragic rather than erotic or sensual. Please note the jailbird tattoos on one of the male "actors."

Alternative title: *Love's Island*

(1977)

KÄRLEKSVIRVELN
[The Love Swirl]

Director:

*Andrew Whyte
(Andrei Feher)*

Cast:

*Barbara Scott

Jack Frank

Anne von Lindberger

Jan-Olof Rydqvist

Sonja Rivera

Jan Klevbrand

Ewert Granholm

Arne Sjöholm

Eva Strand

Robert Eriksson

Johan Tall

Thore Karlsson

Lena Blom*

Mr. X (Jan-Olof Rydqvist) is a gangster specializing in art theft, backed up by a gang that includes playboy Romeo (Jack Frank). Problems occur when Gladys (Barbara Scott)—whose husband owns one of the paintings the criminals want to steal—falls in love with Romeo. Complicating this scenario, Gladys's fifteen-year-old daughter Doris (Anne von Lindberger) also falls for the handsome heartbreaker. Ultimately, Gladys shoots Romeo and her daughter, and the resulting rush of angst and dread forces her to take her own life.

At its halfway point, this furious soft-core porn changes course and turns into pure hard-core. Seldom has anyone enjoyed portraying genuine sex on film the way young von Lindberger does, as she huffs and puffs as if possessed while rolling around frantically in bed. Considerably more toned down is Jan-Olof Rydqvist in the role of Mr. X. As usual, he stutters his lines in a fashion completely devoid of feeling, giving one the uncanny sense that he is simply portraying himself. Unfortunately, Rydqvist died some months before the film's premiere, after eating and drinking far too much at his own 47th birthday party. R.I.P.

This very dirty, poorly produced movie deserves a quick look. This was Andrei Feher's first movie in Sweden, and quite possibly his sickest. In my opinion, this is the best Swedish porn movie ever made, but make sure to get the longest cut, as the film exists in many different heavily edited versions—some of them with a stupid happy ending.

Alternative titles: *Swedish Confessions*; *Swedish Love Story; Jag till Ligga med din Älskare, Mamma...*

KATTORNA
[The Cats]

Sixteen women work at a cleaning facility and spend their days chitchatting about love, childbirth, and intercourse. A popular subject of speculation is whether or not supervisor Marta (Eva Dahlbeck) is a lesbian. After Marta is accused of sexually abusing a young girl, animosity grows, and the women hurl terrible accusations around. In the end, everything turns out to be a misunderstanding, and life returns to normal.

This slightly sleazy portrayal of a group of women was directed by Denmark's Henning Carlsen, with cinematography by Sweden's Mac Ahlberg—one of his earliest efforts in the film industry. Ahlberg later had a successful career as a director, with a number of *sensationsfilms* under his belt, before moving on to Hollywood. Veteran Swedish actress Eva Dahlbeck received a Guldbagge Prize for her work here.

Kattorna is an okay movie, but it was dismissed outright by critics: "The director—whose job should be binding things together, toning them down, balancing things out—has instead just thrown out different threads which stick to nothing," wrote Torsten Mann in 1965. "Both he and the photographer stand outside of the intimate world of women, whose inhabitants are grotesquely magnified á la *Gulliver's Travels*, portrayed without any compassion, insight, or tenderness. Needless to say, all the added intercourse is pure sensationalism." And what's wrong with that?

(1965)

Director:
Henning Carlsen
Cast:
Eva Dahlbeck
Gio Petré
Monica Nielsen
Per Myrberg
Lena Granhagen
Hjördis Petterson
Isa Quensel
Ruth Kasdan
Inga Gill
Lena Hansson
Irma Erixson
Gudrun Östbyte
Monica Lindberg
Karin Miller
Celeste Alm
Annika Renström
Margit Nyström

Clockwise from top left: Lesbian misunderstanding? Monica Nielsen and Lena Granhagen in Kattorna (The Cats)

Courtesy of Klubb Super 8

Sex, depression and animal cruelty are the sensations of Komedi i Hägerskog (Comedy in Hägerskog);

Kattorna poster

Courtesy of Klubb Super 8

KOMEDI I HÄGERSKOG
[Comedy in Hägerskog]

(1968)

Director:
Torgny Anderberg
Cast:
Anita Björk
Monica Nordquist
Ulf Brunnberg
Tor Isedal
Bente Dessau
Kerstin Larsson
Åke Fridell
Erik Hell
John Elfström
Lissi Alandh

Dag (Ulf Brunnberg) is a handsome young man, just wasting his life in the one-stoplight town of Hägerskog. He spends his days trying to pick up every beautiful girl within reach, frequently using his elegant sports car to lure his conquests. When the all-important car is hit with a minor malfunction, he suckers a rich elderly lady into simply buying him a new one. This event opens his eyes and makes him question his life's choices. Parallel with Dag's story, we also glimpse into some other people's lives—all of them ruled by impotence, anxiety, moments of passion, loneliness, and death. After these gray scenes, everything ends in melancholy. Nobody's happy.

Despite the gleeful title, *Komedi i Hägerskog* is a very dark movie, distinguished by the presence of energetic Ulf Brunnberg. He moves quickly from one girl to the next, expressing himself with a bag of trademark sleazy mannerisms. In one multifaceted scene, observant viewers can catch a glimmer of his genitalia as he licks a girl's breasts. The most remarkable scene, however, is the one that opens the film, in which a snake is unjustifiably beaten to death for the camera. This gory sequence would probably have stirred up a lot of controversy today, but back then people didn't care as much about animals in Sweden. The exploitative images are brutal and unnecessary—just needlessly sensational, of course. Note that at the tender age of sixteen, schoolgirl-turned-actor Kerstin Larsson was already an emerging nude starlet in the tabloids and dirtier mags.

(1984) KORPEN FLYGER
[The Raven Flies]

Director:
Hrafn Gunnlaugsson

Cast:
Jakob Þór Einarsson
Edda Björgvinsdóttir
Helgi Skúlason
Egill Ólafsson
Flosi Ólafsson
Gotti Sigurðarson
Sveinn M. Eiðsson
Abba M. Jóhannsdóttir
Anna Karlsdóttir
Anna Reynisdóttir
Arnaldur Friðgeirsson
Ármann Ingason

Marauding Vikings raid Ireland, slaughtering the parents of a young boy (Jakob Þór Einarsson) and abducting his sister (Edda Björgvinsdóttir). Sworn to revenge and pledged to reunite with his sister, the boy tracks his enemies for twenty years, at last finding them in the remote wastelands of Iceland. Now only known as "Gest" (Guest), he slowly starts to butcher his enemies and turn them against one another. After loads of bloodshed and confusion, the knife-tossing Gest finds his sister living with his nemesis Thor (Helgi Skúlason) and their young son. Torn between sympathies for her long-lost brother and her son, the sister betrays Gest. Soon the wanderer is trapped and tortured by the ferocious Vikings. Nothing can stop his revenge, though, and eventually he confronts his parents' killer man to man. Gest wins his justice, but in a grim twist his nephew swears revenge on his father's killer. The wheels of retribution start spinning again.

Since we Swedes weren't able to produce a single decent Viking film—as mercilessly demonstrated by *Här Kommer Bärsärkarna* (see page 85)—we had to pay the Icelanders to do it for us. Hrafn Gunnlaugsson did a very fine job with this violent Viking take on the western genre. Everything from the western is here, from the nameless stranger who rides into town to the climactic duel at the end. The film is also violent as hell, with loads of slit throats and bloody stabbings. There's even some nudity, when the Vikings hassle some female slaves in an especially nasty sequence.

The film was a major success with audiences and critics, playing to full houses for a year and winning the Guldbagge (the most prestigious Swedish film award) for best Swedish film in 1984. Unfortunately, it also spawned a lot of Viking worship among rednecks and fed the Scandinavian nationalism trend of the mid-1980s. For a while, the throwing knives used by Gest in this film replaced the stiletto as the weapon of choice among juvenile delinquents. But they were quickly forgotten when Staffan Hildebrand released *Stockholmsnatt* (see page 246), and kicking became the new trend. Though critics tried to coin the term *Jokull-western* (glacier western) to encourage a new genre of Scandinavian action film, nothing came of it except director Gunnlaugsson's own flawed attempt in 1988 to repeat this success with *Korpens Skugga* (see page 135).

Alternative Title: *Hrafninn Flýgurr*

KORPENS SKUGGA
[The Shadow of the Raven]

(1988)

Director:
Hrafn Gunnlaugsson

Cast:
Reine Brynolfsson
Tinna Gunnlaugsdóttir
Egill Ólafsson
Sune Mangs
Kjeld Kristbjörg
Klara Íris Vigfúsdóttir
Helgi Skúlason
Johann Neumann
Helga Backmann
Sigurður Sigurjónsson
Sveinn M. Eiðsson
Flosi Ólafsson
Guðmunda Elíasdóttir

In 1077, northern Europe is in the age of the Vikings. Trausti (Reine Brynolfsson) stumbles into the heartland of his native Iceland after following a raven, and suddenly he finds himself in the middle of a family blood feud over a beached whale. His mother is mortally wounded during an attack, and in a counter-strike his family kills Eirik (Flosi Ólafsson), the leader of the other clan. In the middle of this endless mayhem, Trausti and Eirik's daughter Isold (Tinna Gunnlaugsdóttir) mysteriously finds time to fall madly in love. As is the custom in traditional dramas, death and destruction follow. No one is happy. The end.

This is an obvious attempt to cash in on the unexpected success of Gunnlaugsson's previous Viking film, *Korpen Flyger* (see page 134). Unfortunately, the Swedish financiers apparently wanted a bigger slice of the cake this time, which might explain the appearance of misplaced Swedish actors Reine Brynolfsson and Sune Mangs in leading parts. As a result, this film has nowhere near the impact of the previous one, which was better in every aspect. Instead of presenting a tense atmosphere, this film focuses much more on picturesque landscapes and compositions—a huge mistake. An even bigger mistake is that the director didn't continue the involving storyline of the first film, which had been left open-ended and begging for a sequel. That would have been far more interesting than this religious family drama. Instead of a Jokull-western, this is a ham-handed variation of *Tristan and Isolde*, a fact laid bare by the main characters' awful names. The film delivers a fair share of violence, including a decapitation, but on the whole, the massive 14 million kronor budget was spent carelessly. Notably, *The Girl With the Dragon Tattoo* (Niels Arden Oplev, 2009) star Noomi Rapace made her film debut here as a small child running around in rags. Talk about typecasting.

After this film, Sweden only paid Gunnlaugsson one more time to create a *sensationsfilm*, when in the name of cultural advancement the government coughed up the dough for *Pojkdrömmar* (see page 195) in 1993. In that film there are no Vikings to be seen, though, because Gunnlaugsson blew the entire budget showing off the body of beautiful young Alda Sigurðardóttir. Though gazing at her is a way better pastime than watching the corpulent Pippi Longstocking veteran Sune Mangs, that film's total lack of energy clearly indicated that 1993 was already too late to try to muster a *sensationsfilm*.

KRONVITTNET
[The Crown Witness]

(1989)

Director:

Jon Lindström

Cast:

Per Mattsson
Marika Lagercrantz
Gösta Ekman
Emma Norbeck
Patrik Ersgård
Jessica Zandén
Stefan Sauk
Janne Carlsson
Mimi Pollak
Allan Svensson
Percy Brandt
Sissi Kaiser
Valentin Sköld
Lennart Norbäck
Ylva Swedenborg
János Herskó
Lotta Krook

Thomas (Per Mattsson), a scientist of pharmacology and a sleaze-bag extraordinaire, hooks up with nineteen-year-old Jenny (Emma Norbeck) in a library. They go on a romantic date to Thomas's creepy laboratory, filled with monkeys trapped in tiny little cages and questionable experiments involving cannibalism among rats. The unsavory trysting is only possible because Thomas's wife, Leonie (Marika Lagercrantz), is off at a fertility clinic in Copenhagen. The couple has been unable to have children for ten years, resulting in heartbreak and impotence. Thomas's version of a fertility clinic is the young girl now in his clutches. He takes Jenny on a second date to a restaurant, but this time their heavy drinking ends in a fight, after which Thomas is left on the sidewalk. The next day Jenny is reported missing. A police investigation is launched with inspector Rolf Lambert (Gösta Ekman) at the helm. With a little effort he discovers that Jenny was suicidal, her history filled with abortions and romantic disasters. Considering this evidence carefully, Lambert veers toward the wild conclusion that Thomas has killed Jenny and fed her to his starving rats.

Kronvittnet sounds like an exciting sexual thriller, but the film falls short. The casting isn't the main problem, but with such poor direction the movie did need better actors. Per Mattsson is boring as hell, and Emma Norbeck's phone must have stopped ringing after her unseductive performance. An even bigger problem is Ekman as the libidinous police inspector. What woman would fall for that old bag of bones? Janne Carlsson has a minor role as a lab assistant but doesn't reach the same heights as when he owned the screen in *Exponerad* (see page 57). Throwing him a bone, the director puts Carlsson, one of Sweden's most celebrated drummers, behind a drum kit in a throwaway scene. At least Stefan Sauk is okay as a sleazy lawyer with a ponytail. The lab full of animals and creepy experiments sounds cool, but the director is so dull he must have been soaking his own head in formaldehyde.

One sequence certifies this film as *sensationsfilm* without a doubt; when supreme sex symbol Marika Lagercrantz briefly makes out with a topless Jessica Zandén. Great stuff! The ridiculous plot twist shall remain secret, but keep this in mind: When the truth about the death is revealed, the inspector scoffs at the perpetrators and calls them "amateurs"; yet they have gotten away with everything and are nowhere near being caught. Considering that the director is a Finnish immigrant who used to work as a cabbie, his logic isn't much worse than that of some Swedish directors who were born into privilege and still couldn't figure anything out.

The film that bravely deals with cannibalism among rats, and other pressing issues—erotic thriller Kronvittnet (The Crown Witness)

Tasteful poster for the just as tasteful sensationsfilm Kvinnolek (Woman's Play): "Ingrid said yes. Lisa said yes, and Nils didn't say no!"

KVINNOLEK
[Woman's Play]

(1968)

Director:
Joseph W. Sarno

Cast:
Gun Falck
(Gun-Britt Öhrstrom)
Gunilla Iwanson
Heinz Hopf
Lars Lind
Mimi Nelson
Sten Ardenstam
Ulf Brunnberg
Pierre Lindstedt

Lisa (Gun Falck) is a successful but unhappy fashion designer, seeking comfort in the bottle to relieve her anxiety. The root of her misery is suppression of her sexual desires toward other women, and having to put up with a wimpy husband (portrayed by Heinz Hopf, who seems plagued by sexual problems of his own here). As Lisa flees to the countryside one summer, she meets seventeen-year-old bombshell Ingrid (Gunilla Iwanson), who longs for a glamorous life in the big city. The mere sight of this wonderful girl makes Lisa feel alive again, and she brings her new discovery to Stockholm to see if the girl can cut it as a model. The stunning blonde is instantly accosted by a myriad of men, which leads to several erotic encounters, all ending in tragic humiliation. To heal her spiritual wounds, Ingrid finally seeks sexual comfort with Lisa, and they share one great moment of ecstasy.

This early Swedish production was directed by American Joe Sarno, who made a huge impact in the 1970s with hard-core movies such as *Fäbodjäntan* (see page 58). In the '60s, however, the eroticism was still a tad more sensual. *Kvinnolek* is by no means a pansy film, but a wonderfully pleasant high-quality soft-core movie. Among the the most exciting events, Lisa takes the young and inexperienced Ingrid to a strip club. The diligent exposure of the young heroine's body during the final lesbian encounter is remarkably explicit, especially for the '60s. Commendable acting lifts the movie to a higher level; the male trio of Hopf, Ulf Brunnberg, and Lars Lind delivers more than expected.

Apart from the sex and sleaze, *Kvinnolek* actually has artistic aspirations, with stylized black-and-white photography. A number of sequences from groovy '60s parties have great psychedelic music, and parallel French and Italian productions of the time. Note that the movie was retitled *Kom i Min Säng* (Come Into My Bed) after the original premiere, the idea being that the word *bed* would increase public interest.

Though the film is well made and recommended, contemporary critics were ruthless. "Mr. Sarno will surely find himself in Stockholm again soon, ready for new efforts. How about a deportation?" chided Lasse Bergström in *Expressen*.

Alternative titles: *To Ingrid, My Love, Lisa*; *Yes!*; *Yes! (Count the Possibilities)*

KYRKOHERDEN
[The Vicar]

(1970)

Director:
Torgny Wickman
Cast:
Jarl Borssén
Margit Carlqvist
Magali Noël
Diana Kjaer
Solveig Andersson
John Elfström
Dirch Passer
Håkan Westergren
Åke Fridell
Cornelis Vreeswijk

The new vicar (Jarl Borssén) in the parish of Fors is cursed by a witch, and thereby forced to live with an eternal erection. The passionate women of the village generously try to help him out by having lots of sex with him. Though he bones every one of the village's females, the erection refuses to go away until the woman who originally cursed him finally reverses the spell.

The only casting criteria for the female actors in this mundane soft-core sex film seems to have been a willingness to expose their breasts. The requirements for the men are less clear, but in the peculiar final scene the vicar has apparantly grown two penises, since two girls ride him at the same time. Now a famous actor, Borssén is probably very embarrassed today over this career move. Cornelis Vreeswijk makes a great cameo as a shabby troubadour in this otherwise pointless production.

Critics uniformly hated this movie. "In all respects—script, direction, photo, acting, everything—*Kyrkoherden* is so immeasurably substandard and simpleminded that without a shadow of a doubt it falls way behind any other rubbish that has premiered in Malmö during the last couple of years. Above all, it is abnormally boring," complained Jan Aghed in *Sydsvenska Dagbladet Snällposten*.

Alternative title: *The Lustful Vicar*

(1980)

Director:

Jan Halldoff

Cast:

Lena Löfström

Anki Lidén

Pelle Lindbergh

Gunvor Pontén

Niels Dybeck

Carl-Axel Heiknert

Nikola Janic

Bo Halldoff

Dennis Agerskog

Tove Frisch

LÄMNA MEJ INTE ENSAM
[Don't Leave Me Alone]

Fifteen-year-old Sofi (Lena Löfström) is headed for trouble. Her relationship with her parents is bad, and her boyfriend Magnus (Pelle Lindbergh) seems more interested in his motorcycle and hanging out with his chums at the local boxing club. So Sofi haphazardly ends up at Malmskillnadsgatan, a famous prostitution spot in Stockholm, and befriends hooker Pia (Anki Lidén). Before she knows it, Sofi is also employed in the sex trade, and her everyday routine veers unhappily into violence and degradation. Magnus figures out what has happened to his girlfriend, but unfortunately he breaks up with her and goes out of his way to tell her parents what has been going on in their daughter's life. All the while, Sofi gets beaten up by her lousy pimp.

The precursor to this film, *Chez Nous* (see page 47), was a relatively mild depiction of Stockholm's underworld, but this time Jan Halldoff really digs deeply into the dirt to deliver a movie full of prostitution, violence, and misery. The dystopian atmosphere is not diminished when one learns that the director claims the movie is based on events from his own life. Painting Stockholm even more disagreeably, one of many porn shop showcase windows seen in the background openly displays—without any concern—a *smörgåsbord* of child pornography!

Wallowing in grit, this is one of Halldoff's dirtiest and best movies; a relic from the most insane period in Swedish history—when child pornography and prostitution were legal, yet horror movies were uniformly banned by censors, and homosexuality was by law considered a mental illness. It's a miracle any kid survived those years—and I should know!

Immediately after this film's release, star Lindbergh left *sensationsfilms* behind for a far more successful career as goalie for the Philadelphia Flyers hockey team. He made repeat All-Star appearances and won the prestigious Vezina Trophy for best NHL goaltender, and then he rammed his Porsche into a wall while drunk and died in dramatic fashion in 1985. He is buried in Stockholm's famous Skogskyrkogården cemetary, where all heavy metal bands and some authors gather to take their promotional photos in front of the great monuments.

Alternative title: *The Score*

Clockwise from top left: Sven-Bertil Taube as Leo, a writer of erotic scripts, in Lejonet och Jungfrun (The Lion and the Maiden)*;*

The vicar fends off legions of female admirers with a strategically placed Bible
Courtesy of Klubb Super 8*;*

Even in days of olde, Swedes were always up to something, according to Kyrkoherden (The Vicar)
Courtesy of Klubb Super 8

LEJONET OCH JUNGFRUN
[The Lion and the Maiden]

(1975)

Director:

Lars-Magnus Lindgren

Cast:

Sven-Bertil Taube

Agneta Eckemyr

Michel Duchaussoy

Sven Lindberg

Karl-Erik Welin

Peter Lindgren

Marcelline Collard

Tor Isedal

Bibi Lindquist

While working in Paris, Swedish scriptwriter Leo (Sven-Bertil Taube) finds himself heavily criticized for his lackluster new script. His French producer demands that Leo bring out the "Swedish" more thoroughly—in other words, tells him to let loose and be more sexually daring. On his flight home to Sweden, Leo woos a stewardess and invites her to his summer getaway in the Stockholm archipelago. She accepts, and on the little island the two go skinny-dipping together and ramble about. Simultaneously, Leo tries to improve his script. The climax sees a huge crayfish party, with everyone wearing funny hats and getting totally drunk while eating tons of crayfish, as is customary in Sweden once in a while. The French producer appears as a guest at the party, where he finally witnesses firsthand the power of Sweden, full force.

Lars-Magnus Lindgren tries to revive his successful sex-and-romance recipe from such earlier movies as *Änglar, Finns Dom?* (see page 21) and *Käre John* (see page 123). This film bombed, however, and was totally panned by the critics. "Bury the movie fifty leagues under the ground. *Lejonet och Jungfrun* is all in all a movie that works its way from zero to nothing," wrote Jürgen Schildt in *Aftonbladet*.

Alternative title: *The Lion and the Virgin*

LEJONSOMMAR
[Lion Summer]

(1968)

Director:
Torbjörn Axelman
Cast:
Sven-Bertil Taube
Essy Persson
Ulf Brunnberg
Margareta Sjödin
Lasse Åberg
Ardy Strüwer
Yvonne Persson
Ann-Christine Magnusson
Annmarie Engwall
Hasse Wallbom

Notorious author Mauritz (Sven-Bertil Taube) leaves Paris to spend his summer in a little village on the Swedish island of Gotland—the perfect spot to write great things in peace and quiet. However, he has not much time left for writing, as most of his days are spent trying to woo the young ladies of the region. The local women seem more than interested in the exciting young author, which really bugs local playboy Jonas (Ulf Brunnberg), previously untouchable as the girls' favorite. Mauritz does not bother himself with these petty rivalries, though, and he unselfishly devotes himself to a glorious summer that includes a couple amorous conquests, lots of bragging about his books, and a string of other relaxing activities.

This erotic comedy is distinguished by a number of interesting appearances. Brunnberg is excellent as always in the role of the nonchalant playboy, and Essy Persson plays a glamorous actress. Though not very daring at all, the movie does offer a few memorable nude sequences, notably a scene between Taube and Margareta Sjödin in which the camerawork yields an intimate study of breasts and nipples. Overall, the film is unfortunately more crude comedy than hot eroticism. Lasse Åberg is one of Sweden's most famous actors, known universally from zany comedies such as *Sällskapsresan* (Lasse Åberg and Peter Hald, 1980), but his scenes as a corky photographer are especially trying on the nerves.

Åberg is probably also one of the most widely sold Swedish visual artists—he designed the seats that provide shelter for staggering drunks in the Stockholm subways. He also struck a deal with IKEA designing ready-made artworks for their massive line of picture frames. These paintings were essentialy abstract variations of mice, since this guy is obsessed with Mickey Mouse. Instead of doing something good or useful with all of his money, Åberg has basically spent his vast fortune obtaining the world's biggest collection of Disney memorabilia. What a jerk!

Alternative title: *Vibration*

Clockwise from top left: Ligga i Lund (Laying in Lund): *"The movie that pulls the sheets off of the students";*

The statuesque sensationsfilm *beauty Marie Forså in* Lifterskan;

Marie Forså, in Lifterskan, *prepares to get between someone else's legs for a change*

LIFTERSKAN
[The Hitchhikeress]

(1975)

Director:
Joseph W. Sarno
Cast:
Marie Forså
Harry Reems
Eric Edwards
Heidi Kappler
Irene Wendlin
Marius Aicher
Nadia Henkowa
Zoe

Young, beautiful country girl Denise (Marie Forså) tires of life on the farm, where her only entertainment is boring old ordinary sex with her corny boyfriend. She dreams of a glamorous life as a big-city fashion model, and sets off hitchhiking in the direction of happiness. After a brief encounter with a sleazy lingerie salesman who takes her into the forest and undresses her, she stumbles into the car of rich nightclub owner Frank (Harry Reems). Soon she is swept into his fancy lifestyle—jet-setting between his apartment and his club in search of cheap kicks. Before long, she realizes she is merely one drop of water in Frank's ever-flowing stream of sexual conquests. Disillusioned—as the male chauvinist slaps her face violently whenever she questions his wicked ways—Denise seeks comfort in a lesbian fling with Frank's business partner, Ruth. Eventually our heroine must hitchhike back to the farm, while Frank continues his quest for thrills, cheerfully looking into the camera and reminding us: "There'll always be another one!"

This German-Swedish coproduction by American director Joe Sarno has a lot going for it. For starters, this is the only time Marie Forså was filmed having sexual intercourse—though she denied doing so throughout her career, until the explicit version appeared in recent years, leaving no doubt. Maybe she was strapped for cash, which probably wasn't true of male star Harry Reems—the international poster boy for *New York Times*–sanctioned porn chic after appearing in *Deep Throat* (Gerard Damiano, 1972) and *The Devil in Miss Jones* (Gerard Damiano, 1973). The wild soundtrack of '70s psychedelic fuzz is as hot as the sex scenes. And for once the sex scenes really are hot. This is the place to go for believable pornography! The clothed parts of the film, however, are totally dull and hopeless, just a bunch of extremely long sequences in which nothing at all happens.

Two significantly different versions of *Lifterskan* exist. First is the almost two-hour soft-core director's cut, which is just about the most explicit soft-core film imaginable. The twenty-minute-shorter X-rated version mercifully excludes much of the nonexistent plot in favor of hard-core inserts. And anyone interested in the kicks-filled exploits of Harry Reems should read his perfectly titled autobiography, *Here Comes Harry Reems*.

Alternative titles: *Butterfly*; *Baby Tramp*; *Broken Butterfly*; *Butterfly Erotica*

LIGGA I LUND
[Laying in Lund]

(1981)

Directors:

Rune Trolleryd
Bertil Malmqvist

Cast:

Lena Andersson
Eva Ohlson
Johnny Sachs
Roland Svensson
Lea Petersen
Åke Bertilsson
Horst Sebastian
Olav Gerthel

Two students, Lena (Lena Andersson) and Eva (Eva Ohlson), lead a carefree life in summery Lund, a small town in the southern region of Skåne—Sweden's version of Texas. To secure good grades, they put out for the teachers, and they barter for nice new clothes by offering their bodies to store clerks. In their spare time, they engage in hard-hitting partying and all kinds of nonstop sexual exploits. Good for them.

Everything from the acting and dialogue to the photography and plot is lousy in this boring porn film. The sour icing on the rotten cake is the constant and consistently poor slapstick comedy. When a girl trips and somehow lands under a cow's dangling udders, she exclaims: "One at a time, boys!" The only redeeming sequence involves a guy hiring a prostitute to perform oral sex, as the she is in fact a he. This twist is highly interesting, since male homosexuality is otherwise virtually taboo in 1980s porn. Besides this odd occurrence, the main point of interest is the beautiful Lund countryside.

Ligga i Lund is based on Rune Trolleryd's successful 1966 novel, and is codirected by Bertil Malmqvist. Considering Malmqvist's track record of reasonably decent films such as *Den Ödesdigra Klockan* (see page 186), he must have sunk pretty far into decadence by this point.

Trivia fans take note! Beloved Swedish TV celebrity Bosse Larsson can be spotted participating in a carnival—perhaps by pure accident. Even if he was unaware of the mayhem around him, he couldn't have been too concerned. Before retiring in 1995, Larsson admitted to having sex with a prostitute on a boat in Africa, which apparently did nothing to diminish his appeal. "If anything, it made me popular among youngsters," he later bragged. "I reached cult status and became human. I feel so happy about it all." Can you dig it?

LOCKFÅGELN
[The Decoy]

The year is 1792, and stepsiblings Pelle (Torsten Wahlund) and Annabella (Louise Edlind) Swedenhielm travel to Stockholm after the death of their father. Their plan is to find Annabella a husband, but these simple aims are disrupted by Madame Lindstål (Siv Ericks), an old pimp who had been acquainted with their dearly departed dad. The madam plans to use the young, beautiful Annabella as bait to lure the men of the county to her whorehouse. Eventually, Annabella does gets married—to a ninety-four-year-old, who tragically dies during the wedding-night commotion. This enables the siblings to finally engage in the incestuous relationship for which they had always longed.

Probably the most expensive of all Torgny Wickman's movies, *Lockfågeln* was nicely shot by Sven Nykvist, Ingmar Bergman's cinematographer of choice. Yet despite a great deal of sleaze, foul language, heavy drinking, rumbling fights, generous doses of sex and nudity, and the oily Heinz Hopf as the sordid owner of a betting house, this film is still a bit too polished and harmless.

Even the wooden-brained critics sensed something was amiss. "I prefer to call the movie a freak," wrote Jürgen Schilt in *Aftonbladet*. "There is no logic, not one character that seems to be alive."

That the topic of incest failed to cause any commotion at the film's release might surprise foreign readers, but Swedish culture has surely taken many more bizarre and disreputable turns.

(1971)

Director:
Torgny Wickman

Cast:
Louise Edlind
Torsten Wahlund
Gunnar Björnstrand
Lauritz Falk
Siv Ericks
Rune Lindström
Ulf Palme
Heinz Hopf
Charlie Elvegård
Gunvor Pontén
Georg Årlin
Christine Gyhagen
Lars Lind
Göhte Grefbo
Holger Löwenadler
Adele Li Puma
Mona Ivarson

(1970)

Director:

Vilgot Sjöman

Cast:

Bernt Lundquist
Solveig Ternström
Tomas Bolme
Inger Liljefors
Christer Boustedt
Lars Werner
Gösta Wälivaara
Janne "Loffe" Carlsson
Bertil Norström
Olle Andersson

LYCKLIGA SKITAR
[Happy Bastards]

Truck driver Charlie (Bernt Lundquist) leads a cheerful life among friends. His existence improves further when he meets the pregnant and homeless Pia (Solveig Ternström), and the two hook up to form a mismatched but happy couple.

Another politically charged production by Vilgot Sjöman, *Lyckliga Skitar* finds the director experimenting with heartwarming comedy. The movie's approach to male nudity is completely carefree. There must surely have been more than a few Swedish families awkwardly squirming in their theater seats at the sight of all the willies. Anyone more interested in naked females need not despair, as virtually every character in the movie gets naked at some point. Otherwise, the greatest attraction of the movie is probably when Janne "Loffe" Carlsson is let loose behind the drums. What a scene-stealer!

Though Carlsson is known as an actor from a slew of silly family comedies, such as *Repmånad* (Lasse Åberg and Peter Hald, 1979) and *Göta Kanal* (Hans Iveberg, 1981), drumming was actually his true talent. He gained some attention in the prog rock outfit Hansson & Karlsson—whose fans included Jimi Hendrix— and played in Pugh Rogerfeldt's famed progressive rock band. Carlsson was also notorious during the 1970s as a party prankster; he loved to initiate wrestling challenges with uptight people at fancy restaurants.

Alternative title: *Blushing Charlie*

Clockwise from top left: One of shamefully few sensationsfilms directed by a woman, hidden gem Mackan;

An abundance of willies wag their way through Vilgot Sjöman's Lyckliga Skitar *(Happy Bastards);*

No big deal in Sweden— just a brother and sister expressing their love for each other

(1978)

Director:

*Kenneth Ahl
(Christer Dahl)*

Cast:

*Anders Lönnbro
Bodil Mårtensson
Roland Jansson
Carl-Axel Heiknert
Siv Ericks
Bo Hörnelius
Mariann Rudberg
Bernt Ström
Lena Lindgren
Anders Granström
Bo Högberg
Roland Hedlund
Gustav Kling
Sten Ljunggren*

LYFTET
[The Boost]

Kennet (Anders Lönnbro) is a petty criminal loser, constantly in and out of jail. After his latest release from prison, he decides to try and shape up his relationship with his fiancée, and fight his way back into society, away from drugs and criminality. When he ends up back in the slammer, based on false accusations, a downward spiral begins. Kennet concludes there is no way out of his destructive lifestyle. In the end, he faces a long-term sentence, just as his fiancée is about to give birth to their child.

This critical depiction of how Swedish society handles its criminals and outcasts takes the unlikely shape of a dark romantic comedy. Sometimes the film unfortunately escalates into pure slapstick, as in an early scene where Kennet and his hoodlums fumble their way through a bank robbery. The cornball humor is balanced by a couple rather sleazy sequences, notably a scene where a group of inmates with their willies dangling receive rough rectal exams from a guard wearing rubber gloves. Overall, the film is a bit too harmless, but still not too shabby. It's based on a superior book, also written by director Christer Dahl.

Alternative title: *The Score*

MACKAN

(1977)

Fourteen-year-old Mackan (Maria Andersson) is forced to move constantly, since her father works for SJ—the Swedish national railroad. After the cute girl arrives in a new small town, she soon begins dating the coolest guy around, eighteen-year-old Kenneth (Kåre Mölder). The relationship is a great boost for Mackan's social status, although Kenneth is mostly interested in having a young hot chick next to him in the car—and in bed. Mackan quickly grows tired of this insensitive clod and his knucklehead buddies. She also feels guilty for abandoning her mentally unstable social reject classmate Gudrun (Franciska von Koch). The miserable relationship with Kenneth collapses, and Mackan moves with her family to Stockholm as soon as her father gets a new post.

Birgitta Svensson nicely directs this depiction of teen anxiety and small-town boredom. She summons a magical world of '50s cars, social dances, rockabilly music, high school classrooms, misunderstanding parents, and awkward teen sex. *Mackan* was considered relatively daring in the late '70s, thanks in particular to a really nasty scene of Kenneth forcing his young, inexperienced girlfriend to give him a hand job while simultaneously yelling about how bad she is at it. Another scene shows this ultimate callous boyfriend putting a condom on his erect penis, displayed in very intimate detail—probably for educational reasons.

My movie-loving principal made all the students watch *Mackan* during my time in high school. Can you imagine the awkward moment at the school cinema when seven hundred inexperienced fourteen-year-olds viewed that erect-penis sequence? For some reason, he also treated us to a viewing of a grainy video copy of the banned *The Texas Chainsaw Massacre* (Tobe Hooper, 1974). I guess the mandatory screenings of *Stockholmsnatt* (see page 246) that same year opened the floodgates for viewing any kind of *sensationsfilms* in Swedish schools.

Otherwise, there is no other nudity at all here; not even Maria Andersson's breasts are shown. Bravo to director Svensson if she was exacting a little female revenge on the lecherous male-dominated Swedish movie industry, which had wronged so many young actresses in so many unforgettable ways. *Mackan* is a forgotten gem in Swedish film history—crowned by Kåre Mölder's highly impressive characterization of the unsympathetic douche that every teenager has hated for one reason or another.

Director:
Birgitta Svensson
Cast:
Maria Andersson
Kåre Mölder
Franciska von Koch
Hans Jonsson
Thomas Norström
Carmilla Floyd
Ulla Blomstrand
Willie Andréason
Margit Carlqvist
Marianne Aminoff

THE MAD BUNCH

Directors:
Mats Helge Olsson
Arne Mattsson

Cast:
David Carradine
Timothy Earle
Helen Arnesen
Frederick Offrein
Sam Cook
Mats Huddén
Jonas Karlzén
Harley Melin
A. R. Hellquist
Lars Lundgren

An unknown organization kidnaps a prominent and upstanding crisis negotiator, demanding that he cease his political activity. Instead of meeting their demands, the kidnapped man's daughter hires the mercenary leader of the Action Force Team to free the negotiator. The two seedy American cloak-and-dagger outfits, the CIA and the FBI, are suspected of being responsible for the kidnapping, since peace would be devastating to both organizations—the United States makes too good a profit on the balance of terror. The Action Force Team tracks down the kidnapped man, but unfortunately he is shot to death during the operation. As this tense drama continues, the dead negotiator's daughter is next to be kidnapped. A smaller war ensues, and the cornball ending reveals that nobody is exactly who her or she first seemed to be.

One of several late-'80s action movies directed by Mats Helge Olsson with almost exactly the same cast and production crew, this might very well be the worst of the bunch. Olsson seemingly strung together a couple hours of sloppily directed fistfights and gun battles, added a horrible synthesizer soundtrack, and spiked the dialogue with a few random cool English words delivered in thick Swedish accents. This is light-years away from Olsson's action fiesta *The Ninja Mission* (see page 182). No one has enough extra time in life to watch something like this. Olsson seems less adept at making up a story than a typical five-year-old playing with GI Joe dolls—which were all but banned in Sweden, anyway.

One interesting detail is the involvement of David Carradine, making him one of three actors (along with Tor Isedal and Heinz Hopf) to have worked with both Ingmar Bergman (in *The Serpent's Egg*, 1978) as well as Mats Helge Olsson during his considerably uneven career. Arne Mattsson, whose once glorious career had sunk to an all-time low, is credited as a codirector. Later that same year Olsson and Mattsson teamed up again to direct *The Hired Gun* (see page 91), which finally ended Mattsson's career for good.

MAID IN SWEDEN

(1971)

Director:
Floch Johnson
Cast:
Christina Lindberg
Krister Ekman
Monica Ekman
Leif Näslund
Per Axel Arosenius
Itela Frodi
Tina Hedström
Henrik Meyer
Vivianne Öiangen
Jim Engelau

Inga (Christina Lindberg) is an innocent little schoolgirl who shies away from smoking, drinking, and staying out late at night. When she heads to Stockholm to visit her sister Greta (Monica Ekman), a whole new world suddenly appears within her reach. Initially shocked that her older sister is secretly living with boyfriend Casten (Krister Ekman), Inga soon gets used to the free-spirited attitude of the capital city. She discovers her own erotic urges, and agrees to go on a date with Casten's friend Björn (Leif Näslund). After a couple hours of small talk, this sleazebag forces himself on her—but halfway through the assault Inga starts enjoying the rough treatment. The youngsters begin a relationship behind the backs of Casten and Greta. When Björn's attraction to Inga grows intense and possibly dangerous, Casten realizes what has been going on between his friends. Rather than assist in any way, Casten feels the sting of jealousy—it turns out he, too, is attracted to the very sexy Inga. He cannot control his desires forever, and soon he also sexually assaults the young girl. Once again, for some reason she doesn't entirely mind Casten's forceful advances. However, when Greta catches her sister and her boyfriend in the act, poor Inga is sent shuffling back to the country, burdened with shame, while the others carry on in pure Stockholm fast-lane fashion as if Inga never existed.

This is a strictly American production, but the Swedish actors and the Stockholm scenery give it a genuine Swedish atmosphere. Lindberg, before the motion picture camera for the first time, is the big attraction, and her body is exposed thoroughly throughout the entire movie. Her perfect breasts make their first appearance during the opening credits. The movie is filled with some remarkably dirty sequences, like when Inga spies on her sister having sex. The scenes of sexual assault, which hint that girls enjoy being taken by force, are particularly questionable. This is a good meat-and-potatoes *sensationsfilm*, and well worth a look.

Alternative title: *The Milkmaid*

Krister Ekman, Monika Ekman and Christina Lindberg enjoy a cup of coffee in Maid in Sweden
Courtesy of Klubb Super 8

Anna Godenius, incognito, in Män Kan Inte Våldtas (Men Cannot Be Raped)

Gösta Bredefeldt as the coldhearted assailant in Män Kan Inte Våldtas

MÄN KAN INTE VÅLDTAS
[Men Cannot Be Raped]

(1978)

Director:
Jörn Donner

Cast:
Anna Godenius
Gösta Bredefeldt
Toni Regner
Göran Schauman
Algot Böstman
Christer Björkman
Carl-Axel Heiknert
Christina Indrenius-Zalewski
Nils Brandt
Märta Laurent

While celebrating her fourtieth birthday, Eva (Anna Godenius) meets a man and accompanies him home. Oops. At his house, she is brutally raped, forced to break free and flee the site in confusion and despair. After this traumatic experience, she becomes obsessed with the man who hurt her, tracking down all information she can find in order to chart out his life. When her preparations are complete, she seeks him out in his home and avenges herself by forcing herself upon him sexually at gunpoint. Now a rapist herself, Eva decides to turn herself in to the police, but the stone-faced flatfoot turns her down, informing her with a classic retort: "Men cannot be raped."

Based on Märta Tikkanen's best-selling novel and set in grim Helsinki, Jörn Donner's politically charged contribution to the debate over sexual violence includes a powerful rape scene which leaves no one indifferent. Otherwise, this is a relatively slow-moving film that shies away from exploiting its subject. As usual when it comes to Donner, there is a sick atmosphere throughout the movie that makes the film hard to resist. Oddly, lead actress Godenius was at the height of her career at this point, having starred in the cool, lighthearted TV police series *Ärliga Blå Ögon*—the very opposite of this film in tone and outlook.

Alternative title: *Manrape*

(1977)

MÅNDAGARNA MED FANNY
[Mondays with Fanny]

Director:
*Lars Lennart
Forsberg*
Cast:
*Tommy Johnson
Maria Selbing
Ingvar Kjellson
Agneta Ekmanner
Allan Edwall*

Robert (Tommy Johnson) is a discouraged middle-aged man struggling with alcoholism, a lout who prefers to spend his miserable
days with his drinking buddies instead of his wife. Things change
all of a sudden when Robert meets happy-go-lucky Fanny (Maria
Selbing), and he sparks up a low-key affair with the free-spirited
young thing. Then she leaves him, he loses his job, and his father
dies.

Måndagarna med Fanny is a depressing drama, almost completely
detached from other *sensationsfilms* in its suffocating mood. The
loose attitude toward drinking and nudity makes up for that. One
sex scene between Tommy Johnson and Maria Selbing is quite daring, but overall the melodrama is not exceptionally interesting.

DE MÅNGA SÄNGARNA
[The Many Beds]

(1970)

Director:
Bertil Malmqvist
Cast:
Jeanette Swensson
Gudrun Brost
Åke Engfeldt
Bengt Rosén
Arne Strömgren
Christer Söderlund
Olav Gerthel
Olof Lindfors
Bengt Brunskog
Arne Dahl
Eva Nilsson
Dagny Pontén
Göran Söderström
Ronnie Lundin
Jörgen Barwe

Jeanette (Jeanette Swensson) is a young girl who finds herself locked up in youth prison after a life of debauchery. She reflects on her life, basically a litany of nothing but misery and lust. Everything started badly, as her mother was a prostitute, and she never knew her father. In high school, she befriended a bunch of sleazy characters who took full advantage of her "appetite for life." Before long, the girl was a full-fledged nymphomaniac, entangled in a world of criminality. Jeanette realizes way too late that her life has gone astray, and she find herself all alone in the world without a single friend.

After the critically slaughtered debut *Den Ödesdigra Klockan* (see page 186), few people thought that Bertil Malmqvist would ever direct again. Nevertheless, he was determined to stay in the business, and he threw himself into this confused sexual melodrama based on Lucille Borgier's 1966 biography. Several disputes arose instantly among the producers, however, and the film's premiere was delayed for years, until 1970. By then it was all over for Malmqvist, and the critics slaughtered him along with his film.

"After watching this thin porno spectacle, you wonder if the censors have already been there with their scissors, so many of the cuts in this mess are made without any talent," Ramon Fridén lamented in *Expressen*. No censors were needed—only the incompetent hands of the director.

As a final stone of shame attached to this damned production, the producers never presented the required list of the music used in the film to STIM (The Swedish Performing Rights Society). Subsequently, they never paid anybody for the music, rather strange since many of the songs were by the popular Swedish pop group the Mascots. Fortunately for the film producers, their thin necks were spared the heavy grip of the music industry, when the Mascots abruptly transformed into the heavily political prog rock orchestra Fria Proteatern, initially called NJA-Gruppen. They shunned things like money and capitalism in the name of flowers and socialism. Malmqvist, on the other hand, met a worse fate. After waiting eleven years to return to filmmaking, he emerged in 1981 with *Ligga i Lund* (see page 146), at which point he must have felt ready to look back on his own dark life.

MÅNGUDEN
[The Moon God]

(1988)

Director:
Jonas Cornell

Cast:
Agneta Ekmanner
Heinz Hopf
Per Myrberg
Thomas Laustiola
Leif Sundberg
Tord Peterson
Stig Ossian Ericson
John Harryson
Lars Hansson
Åke Lindman

Beware—a psycho killer is slaying people with a machete during full moons! He wears an ancient African moon god mask all the while, and on top of that he's filming everything. The murder-filled VHS tape ends up in the hands of washed-up inspector John Vinge (Thomas Laustiola), who takes on the case without much enthusiasm. Vinge seeks guidance from his mysterious father, a former supreme investigator who now lies hospitalized under an oxygen tent. Unable to offer much help, the fallen father instead commands our slouchy hero to seek guidance from old psychiatrist Erland (Per Myrberg). Nobody seems to find much energy to solve the case, which just drags on through several clues and characters. Eventually, someone stumbles across a missing piece of this grainy puzzle, and everything mercifully comes to an end.

Until its 2010 DVD release, Jonas Cornell's *Månguden* was considered a holy grail among Swedish film collectors. The movie had only been shown twice on television back in 1988, and it was never released on video. So what was all the fuss about? This is a slow-paced 1980s film, complete with a hideous saxophone soundtrack and ugly pumped-up hairdos. Despite the premise, the movie isn't very sensational either, with minimal bloodletting and just a bit of nudity, courtesy of Agneta Ekmanner—the only female actor with more than a minute of screen time. *Månguden*'s two redeeming qualities are the appearance of Heinz Hopf in a bit part, and the cool use of a film clip as a clue, in the style of *Cannibal Holocaust* (Ruggero Deodato, 1980).

The forces behind the DVD apparently didn't care much about this film when they finally released it, since they got the name of the main character wrong on the cover. Their lack of faith extends to the packaging, which features a hideous front cover implying that this is a modern horror film. Hilariously, the DVD marketing text claims that many families in Sweden canceled their camping holidays after this film was shown—obviously a lie, since it only aired in the fall of 1988, way after the vacation season, when it was too cold to even think about stepping outside. Note that Mikael Håfström worked as an assistant director on this stinker, before escaping to Hollywood and directing films such as *Derailed* (2005) and *1408* (2007). He escaped too easily!

MANNEKÄNG I RÖTT
[Mannequin in Red]

(1958)

Director:
Arne Mattsson
Cast:
Anita Björk
Karl-Arne Holmsten
Annalisa Ericson
Lillebil Ibsen
Bengt Brunskog
Gio Petré
Lena Granhagen
Nils Hallberg
Eivor Landström
Lennart Lindberg
Anita Lindblom
Lissi Alandh

In many ways, this film quite strikingly anticipates the Italian *giallo* pulp thriller genre by several years, weaving together motifs such as black gloves, glamorous young girls, elaborately designed murders, fluent camera work, flashing knives, dark corridors, and red velvet curtains. Sadly, much of the blunt humor that infests so many *gialli* is also present. Overall, the film is so similar to Mario Bava's pioneering *giallo* film *Blood & Black Lace* (1964) that Mattsson could likely have sued the Italian producers.

After a young girl disappears from high-class fashion house La Femme, private investigator Kajsa Hillman (Annalisa Ericson) goes undercover disguised as a model. Meanwhile, her husband, John (Karl-Arne Holmsten), teams up with the police to offer some much-needed assistance. The fashion house is run with an iron hand by Thyra (Lillebil Ibsen), a hateful ex-model who is now wheelchair-bound. She despises her foster son, Bobbie (Bengt Brunskog), favoring her sister's children, Rickard (Lennart Lindberg) and Gabriella (Gio Petré). Thyra is soon burned to death, and the power struggle within La Femme turns into a nightmare, with more deaths to come. In the bizarre and unexpected finale, everything turns upside down, and the bitter truth is finally revealed.

Arne Mattsson's second Hillman film, following *Damen i Svart* (see page 49), is in every way more exciting than its precursor, with color cinematography by Hilding Bladh, brutal deaths, and many beautiful young girls in fancy clothes courtesy of iconic Stockholm costume designer Mago. Future sleaze queen Gio Petré appears as Gabrielle. Though the film is not very extreme, it offers some striking images such as a hanged woman and the burning of a woman in wheelchair. The greatness is only impinged upon by some screwball comedy and an ill-conceived and overly obvious plot twist (something many Italian *giallo* films also suffered from). The finale is a masterful display of creepy suspense, one of the best moments of Swedish cinema history.

High on the success of this film, Mattsson quickly continued his "Swedish *giallo*" quintet of Hillman films with *Ryttare i Blått* (see page 213). Note that these five Mattsson thrillers all included a color in their titles, something that would later be typical of countless Italian *giallo* genre films.

Clockwise from top left:
A threat to Swedish tourism?
The masked murderer of
Månguden (The Moon God);

Sven Wollter and Thomas
von Brömssen in the
politically charged Mannen
från Mallorca (The Man from
Mallorca);

Arne Mattsson's
groundbreaking Mannekäng
i Rött (Mannequin in Red),
an inspiration to Alfred
Hitchcock and Mario Bava

MANNEN FRÅN MALLORCA
[The Man from Mallorca]

(1984)

Director:
Bo Widerberg

Cast:
Sven Wollter
Tomas von Brömssen
Johan Widerberg
Håkan Serner
Ernst Günther
Thomas Hellberg
Ingvar Hirdwall
Nina Gunke
Tommy Johnson
Marie Delleskog
Sten Lonnert
Niels Jensen
Gert Fylking

On St. Lucy's Day, a martyr's holiday marked in Sweden by somber processions led by young girls, a post office in central Stockholm is robbed. The villain is masked, armed, and obviously very professional. Two washed-up cops, Johansson (Thomas von Brömssen) and Jarnebring (Sven Wollter), are put on the case, and as the investigation unexpectedly grows, a little energy returns to the aging crime-fighting duo. After some mysterious deaths, and loads of lucky coincidences, the clues all point without question to someone within the police organization itself.

After some neglected films in the late '70s and early '80s, Widerberg again obtained rights to a best-selling, politically charged crime novel. Hoping to duplicate his earlier success with *Mannen på Taket* (see page 163), he employed the same central cast (except for Carl-Gustaf Lindstedt, then in poor health), another similar-sounding score by Björn J:son-Lindh, and a title that sounded connected, though the two pictures have nothing to do with each other. *Mannen från Mallorca* is a very good crime film nonetheless, although the prodigious blood-splattering of the precursor is sadly absent. Though the plot takes place in the world of prostitution, there is no nudity. Even Wollter keeps his pants on.

Most interesting is the real-life political scandal behind the film. In 1976, Swedish minister of justice Lennart Geijer and several other prominent politicians and businessmen were revealed to be regular customers of prostitutes—some as young as fourteen. Leif GW Persson was the whistle-blower who took the scandal to the media, but when the story broke, prime minister Olof Palme stood by his minister of justice. Persson was discharged from the Swedish National Police Board, though he had done nothing wrong. In the aftermath, everything was covered up, and the entire affair remains a great smear on Swedish history. Devastated, Leif GW Persson went into the forest with his rifle, planning to blow his head off. Fortunately, he got the brilliant idea instead to write everything down, and he created *Grisfesten* (The Pig Party), the novel on which *Mannen från Mallorca* is based.

Today, Persson is one of Sweden's most successful and celebrated criminologists, presiding as professor at the National Department of Police, and often appearing on dubious Fox-like TV programs along the lines of *Sweden's Most Wanted*. He is also one of his homeland's most successful novelists, so he laughs last.

(1978)

Director:
Arne Mattsson

Cast:
Helmut Griem
Slobodan Dimitrijevic
Gunnel Fred
Ivan Tchenko
Richard Warwick
John Hamill
Ivo Pajer
Zvonimir Zoricic
Igor Galo

MANNEN I SKUGGAN
[The Man in the Shadow]

During a trip to Spain, Norwegian couple Dan (John Hamill) and Siglinde (Gunnel Fred) befriend West German Willi Mohr (Helmut Griem). The idyllic vacation is shattered during a fishing trip, as a couple of rugged fishmonger brothers kill Dan, then rape Siglinde and stab her to death. Outraged, Willi sets out to crack the case, and he soon vengefully kills one of the brothers. His quest to find the other brother grows complicated, as he discovers a liberation movement involved in arms dealings. A martyr in the cause of bloody justice, Willi ends up getting gunned down by the Spanish federal police, the *Guardia Civil*.

Arne Mattsson takes on Per Wahlöö's novel *Lastbilen* (The Truck) in this Swedish-Yugoslavian coproduction. As good as the plot summary sounds, the film was released primarily in Yugoslavia, disappeared behind the Iron Curtain, and remains unfortunately impossible to track down.

Alternative title: *Black Sun*

MANNEN PÅ TAKET
[The Man on the Roof]

(1976)

Director:
Bo Widerberg
Cast:
Carl-Gustaf Lindstedt
Sven Wollter
Eva Remaeus
Thomas Hellberg
Håkan Serner
Birgitta Valberg
Harald Hamrell
Ingvar Hirdwall
Gus Dahlström
Bellan Roos
Torgny Anderberg
Folke Hjort
Carl-Axel Heiknert
Gunnel Wadner
Johan Thorén
Lennart Nordlund

Police inspectors Beck (Carl-Gustaf Lindstedt) and Rönn (Håkan Serner) have been assigned a red-hot case—one of their fellow officers has been stabbed to death by a bayonet at Sabbatsbergs Hospital. The twist: He was already terminally ill. As the investigation progresses, an uncomfortable series of interrogations behind the blue line reveal that the culprit is an ex-cop. As they close in on the killer, the cold-blooded maniac barricades himself in a tall building and starts gunning people down from the rooftop. With some help from the public, the police finally manage to nail the murderer.

Bo Widerberg's crime flick starts with a jolt, then builds slowly and methodically until reaching an intense conclusion. The grisly opening sequence required eight liters of pigs' blood, and still the director required seven takes. Each required a full day to complete. The ending sequence is famously spectacular, with several police officers pierced by bullets, and a helicopter crashing in downtown Stockholm in the middle of Odenplan Square. No less a spectacle is the scene that reveals Sven Wollter's penis dangling beneath his minimal T-shirt. Being dressed only on the torso is truly the champion kind of nudity. Which brings to mind an interesting detail: Harsh sleaze king Bo A. Vibenius (*Thriller – En Grym Film*, see page 258; *Breaking Point*, see page 42) worked as a production manager on this film, as did *Mods Trilogy* (see pages 26 and 51) director Stefan Jarl.

Wollter's penis aside, the movie is great and uniquely Swedish in temperament, based on the best-seller *Den Verdervärdige Mannen från Säffle* (The Vile Man from Säffle—a much better title), written by married couple Per Wahlöö and Maj Sjöwall, who together initiated the modern era of Swedish crime thrillers. Although no match for Arne Mattsson's movies, *Mannen På Taket* is leagues ahead of a rash of films based on the Inspector Wallander character during the 1990s and 2000s. Even a couple of British films about Wallander have been made, with Kenneth Branagh as the doughy yet sharp-witted inspector. The world must be mad.

(1985) MASK OF MURDER

Director:
Arne Mattsson
Cast:
Rod Taylor
Christopher Lee
Valerie Perrine
Sam Cook
Heinz Hopf

After a number of women fall victim to a masked murderer armed with a razor, the police track down the slasher and kill him in a gun battle in which the chief of police (Christopher Lee) is wounded. However, just as the police are finishing up their paperwork on the sensational case, a couple new murders are committed that demand their attention. The only clue—witnesses speak of a man in a white mask.

This Arne Mattsson thriller from late in his career is mostly subpar. Granted, a masked killer slicing up young women with a razor sounds plenty interesting, but instead of a stylized thriller we get apathetic, tedious police work. Not even the arrival of nudity and murder can sustain interest—you almost pity the cops for their workload more than the unfortunate victims. Wooden Rod Taylor has free rein as the main character, while the ingenious Heinz Hopf is wasted in a small part as a barber. (The fact that Heinz Hopf appears as a victim of torture rather than the villain is a sure sign of insanity or stupidity.) Even the legendary Christopher Lee's role is quickly diminished when the script sends him to the hospital. The casting director should be keelhauled.

Alternative title: *The Investigator*

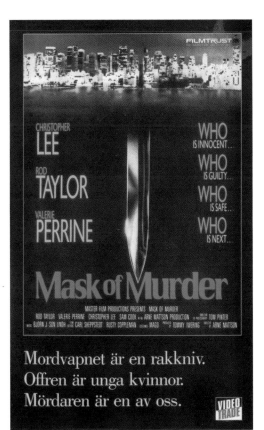

Clockwise from top left:
"The murder weapon is a razor.
The victims are young women. The
murderer is one of us." Overstylized
video cover for Mask of Murder;

Circa 1976 French poster for
Mannen på Taket, *eerily foreboding*
the 9/11 attacks as planes smash
into skyscrapers that look far more
like the World Trade Center than
anything in Stockholm;

Mannen på Taket *video box*

(1970)

Director:

Torgny Wickman

Cast:

Maj-Brith Bergström-Walan

Inge Hegeler

Sten Hegeler

Bertil Hansson

Johan Wallin

Bengt Lindkvist

Bruno Kaplan

Tommy Hedlund

Anna Berggren

Mirjam Israel

MERA UR KÄRLEKENS SPRÅK
[More from the Language of Love]

In this somewhat more twisted sequel to the highly successful *Kärlekens Språk* (see page 126), we enjoy learning about lesbianism, transvestitism, useful pornography, sex after childbirth, venereal diseases, and—last but not least—the sex lives of the handicapped. The increasingly lurid sex expert Maj-Brith Bergström-Wahlan tries in vain to uphold some kind of scientific aura, but this is pure sensationalism, more of a mondo-style "shockumentary" than the documentary it pretends to be.

Kerstin Vinterhed at *Dagens Nyheter* saw through the scientific guise: "The message of this movie is simple: Fuck and get free!"

Alternative titles: *More About the Language of Love*; *Spör Inge och Sten*

MIDSOMMARDANSEN
[The Midsummer Dance]

Set at a dance party during the Swedish *midsommar* holiday, this film follows a number of partiers and their exploits during the night. Heavy drinking leads to nudity; drunken conversations provoke jealousy; anxiety serves as foreplay to sex; and eventually fights and drunken driving bring a tragic and abrupt end to the celebrations. When a bus and a car collide, many of the partygoers die in the crash.

Arne Stivell's adaptation of Hannu Salama's short story revels in the typical events of a regular Swedish midsummer celebration. An abundance of drinking mostly hard liquor straight from the bottle leads to fights, sex, incoherent rambling, and flaming collisions—more or less in that order. Just another night in Sweden. Couples copulate left and right, in cars, buses, shrubs, and thickets. The most memorable sex scene presents all-purpose actor Tor Isedal hard at work with two sisters. Another remarkable sequence shows someone killing a bird, and toward the end there is even some gore in the aftermath of the violent bus accident. Overall, it's a top-notch movie for everyone to enjoy!

Alternative title: *Midsummer Sex*

Director:
Arne Stivell

Cast:
Stefan Ekman
Hans Ernback
Monica Ekman
Lissi Alandh
Tor Isedal
Tommy Johnson
Bengt Eld
Christer Söderlund
Bernt Lundquist
Kim Anderzon
Rolf Demander
Bo Persson
Christer Rahm
Rose-Marie Nordenbring
Sven Erik Vikström

SWEDISH *SENSATIONSFILMS* A–Z   167

(1969) MISS AND MRS. SWEDEN

Director:
Göran Gentele

Cast:
Jarl Kulle
Sven Lindberg
Gunn Wållgren
Wivian Öiangen
John Harrysson
Meg Westergren
Per Oscarsson
Claire Wikholm
Cia Löwgren

Greedy editor in chief Leif Mix (Jarl Kulle) of weekly magazine *Vecko-Hatten* (The Weekly Hat) arranges a grand Miss Sweden pageant in order to boost sales. A group of hippies protests the sexist arrangement and tries to sabotage the competition by employing a girl from their group as a spy—which all leads to wild tumult.

In this light-handed satire of the cynical world of the weekly press, Kulle sparkles with uncompromising overacting. Any kind of plot is hard to find, and the creators compensate with the simple sensation of a few exposed female breasts. Overall, this distant ancestor of *Miss Congeniality* (Donald Petrie, 2000) was a failed project that falls flat in the satire genre, and also lacks the sensual atmosphere of the many *sensationsfilms* which were pumped full of far more nudity.

Marie Forså sneaks a peek in Molly –
Familjeflickan (Molly, the Family Girl
Courtesy of Klubb Super 8

Miss and Mrs. Sweden—
"Festive farce in COLOR!"

The simple message of Mera ur Kärlekens Språk (More from the Language of Love)
about to be spelled out for audiences **Courtesy of Klubb Super 8**

(1977) MOLLY – FAMILJEFLICKAN
[Molly, the Family Girl]

Director:

Bert Torn
(Mac Ahlberg)

Cast:

Maria Lynn
(Marie Forså)

Charles Canyon
(Chris Chittell)

Eva Axén

Peter Loury

Darby Lloyd Rains

Kim Pope

Eric Edwards

Jack Frank

André Chazel

Anita Andersson

Molly (Marie Forså) is unhappily in love with Peter (Chris Chittell), an upper-class playboy who leads a dangerous and depraved life where out-of-control parties are the norm. Peter's brother Robin (Peter Loury) is in love with Molly, and out of desperation she agrees to marry him. They immediately realize the marriage is a mistake, and Molly somehow lands Peter, who promises to change his wild lifestyle.

Based on a novel by Daniel Defoe (believe it or not!), this Mac Ahlberg-directed gibberish places boring porn sequences at a much higher priority than plot. In a misguided attempt to liven things up, the film consistently hints at incestuous relations, and adoptive siblings have sex with one another. Otherwise the stupid dialogue and wild disco music do not rescue the movie, which is a shame as Ahlberg should be above this. He can actually make great movies, like *Jag – En Kvinna 2. Äktenskapet* (see page 108), which probably explains why he is credited here under a false name.

After this French-Swedish coproduction, Ahlberg ceased making films in Sweden. He went to Italy, where he directed one film, *Gangsters* (see page 76). He then fled to America, where he became a cinematographer on films such as *Re-Animator* (Stuart Gordon, 1985), *House II* (Ethan Wiley, 1987), and *Beverly Hills Cop III* (John Landis, 1994).

Alternative titles: *Molly*; *Sex in Sweden*

MONAS HEMLIGA SEXDRÖMMAR
[Mona's Secret Sex Dreams]

Mona (Monique Cardin) spends her vacation with her husband in a cottage. They are bored and tired of each other, and flee the monotony by fantasizing about erotic adventures.

This predictably tiresome movie is loosely held together by various pornographic dream sequences. The only sequences imaginative enough to mention are a scene involving masturbation with a screwdriver, and another in which a nymph wears two erect penises on his head in place of horns. Otherwise this poorly-circulated film is just plain annoying, and, like the protagonists, viewers will find their thoughts starting to wander. The Swedish board of censors should have mandated warning labels for embarrassing slapstick!

Alternative titles: *Sextasy*; *The Secret Dreams of Mona Q*

(1979)

Director:
Charles Kaufman
Cast:
Monique Cardin
Marilyn Anders
Sandy Reynolds
Rose Taft
Sharon Mitchell
Wade Nichols
Tom Baker
Uschi Inger
Swen Kringel
Inga Bjorg
Bob Astyr
Michael Shea
Helga Unster
Reneé Verlaine

MONTENEGRO ELLER PÄRLOR OCH SVIN
[Montenegro, or Pearls and Pigs]

(1981)

Director:
Dušan Makavejev

Cast:
Susan Anspach
Erland Josephson
Per Oscarsson
Bora Todorovic
Marianne Jacobi
Jamie Marsh
John Zacharias
Svetozar Cvetkovic
Patricia Gélin
Lisbeth Zachrisson
Marina Lindahl
Nicola Janic
Lasse Åberg
Dragan Ilic
Milo Petrovic
John Parkinson
Jan Nygren

American woman Marilyn (Susan Anspach) marries a Swede and lives a quiet pampered family life in posh Stockholm suburb Lidingö. After missing an airplane flight to Brazil, she accepts a ride back to town from the airport with jolly Yugoslavian Alex (Bora Todorovic). Stepping sideways into his world—a shady realm she never knew existed in Sweden—Marilyn passes the next few days in an illegal liquor factory, finding herself in a bender of fights, drunken dancing, and passionate, alcohol-fueled sex. Her husband, Martin (Erland Josephson), believes she has been kidnapped, and she plays along with that misconception in order to spend a couple more days with the life-loving Yugoslavian gang. After a night of hot sex, she returns to her family.

Dusan Makavejev's story of culture shock in Sweden is part confusion, part delight. Every character comes across as a total nutcase: The trigger-happy grandfather, the peculiar upper-class kids, and the drunken liquormongers—all are equally insane! The cast, except that annoyance Lasse Åberg, is great. The movie's nudity is daring, and the standard quota of female breasts is spiced with powerful close-ups of male genitalia. This leads to sex scenes that reek of smut, as people on the outskirts of society (and possibly even civilization altogether) fuck the hell out of each other. In all this, one scene stands in a league of its own: A stripper dances around a remote-controlled tank whose gun turret has been outfitted with a dildo. After several minutes of carefree dancing, the "warhead" connects with its target, and the girl is hit by the remote-controlled gadget—a clear violation of the Geneva convention even if the Swedish censors allowed it to pass. This scene alone would recommend any movie, but in a good movie like *Montenegro* it's just extra credit.

This film represented Sweden at the 1981 Cannes Film Festival. Though it won no prizes, distribution rights were sold in over fifty countries. The world premiere was held in New York City, leading to a consensus of approval from critics and also the nice people of 42nd Street.

Alternative title: *Montenegro*

MÖRDAREN – EN HELT VANLIG PERSON
[The Murderer: A Completely Normal Person]

(1967)

Director:

Arne Mattsson

Cast:

Allan Edwall

Lars Ekborg

Britta Pettersson

Karl-Arne Holmsten

Erik Hell

Heinz Hopf

Elsa Prawitz

Nils Hallberg

Curt Masreliez

Björn Gustafson

Tore Bengtsson

Frej Lindqvist

Ewa Strömberg

Christina Carlwind

Mördaren – En Helt Vanlig Person begins on a train, introducing the various travelers. We meet a sex-crazed young couple, a stressed-out conductor, a group of grumpy old men, and a CEO who abuses a girl during the journey. When one of the travelers disappears, things turn ugly. The train breaks down, and the passengers take shelter in a small nearby hostel. Paranoia grips the party, as the players suspect and accuse one another of having murdered the missing person. And just when the mystery finally seems clear—it is further deepened in a strange surprise ending.

This tense murder mystery by Arne Mattsson delivers brilliant acting, especially by Allan Edwall and Heinz Hopf, the latter sporting a bowl haircut that makes him look creepier than usual. The train milieu is fantastic, and a sharper script would have made this film the equal of its subway-based American contemporary, *The Incident* (Larry Peerce, 1967).

Unfortunately, the great sleaze—complete with sexual abuse and murder—is restrained by boring slapstick. For comic relief, an uptight soldier kvetches about the lack of traditional *midsommar* fare like smoked salmon or chicken; the train only offers Swedish veal jelly and bad beetroot. His wife also packed the whiskey too deep in his suitcase, poor guy. But why should we suffer listening to his petty complaints? A little more backbone from Mattsson, and *Mördaren* could have been amazing, but it is still very good.

A completely normal person doing his thing in Mördaren – En Helt Vanlig Person
(The Murderer: A Completely Normal Person)

Courtesy of Klubb Super 8

A lover's quarrel in Mördaren – En Helt Vanlig Person*;*
good thing the sadist remembered to pack his whip

Courtesy of Klubb Super 8

Morianerna (The Moors), *a thriller clearly promoted as plain smut in America. By this point, the concept of Swedish sin had really caught on*

Death and anxiety in Arne Mattsson's Morianerna
Courtesy of Klubb Super 8

(1965)

Director:
Arne Mattsson

Cast:
Anders Henrikson
Eva Dahlbeck
Heinz Hopf
Elsa Prawitz
Olle Andersson
Erik Hell
Ove Tjernberg
Tor Isedal
Ella Henrikson
Walter Norman
Elisabeth Odén

MORIANERNA
[The Moors]

Vicious CEO Verner Vade (Anders Henrikson) is an evil, demanding patriarch who drives his whole family insane by creating an atmosphere of anxiety and hatred. The Vade household is pretty decadent overall, and depression and adultery run rampant. Suddenly, the hideous Verner is assaulted, and if that isn't bad enough, later the same evening he is murdered. The police launch an investigation, and all members of the hapless family are suspected.

Arne Mattsson's adaptation of Jan Ekström's novel is a dazzling display of evil and eerie atmosphere. The perversions are many, beginning with a child burning a doll on a stake, and including an obligatory "fiddling with the nipple" scene—those seemed to surface in every mid-1960s Swedish movie, for some reason. Already in the opening sequence, the beautiful young housekeeper exposes herself to eighty-year-old CEO Vade. As always, the best actor of the bunch is Heinz Hopf, playing the mentally unstable son who loves rats, cuddling them with creepy affection.

Jürgen Schildt of *Aftonbladet* got worked up by the relentless approach to moviemaking: "If Mattsson has set out to break down the so-called sexual barrier, he does it with the grace of a bison." If only Sweden had been lucky enough to have a stampeding herd of bison like Mattsson, all the little bleating sheep in the national movie industry would have been wiped away completely!

Alternative titles: *I, the Body*; *Morianna*

...ove in the short Swedish summer in
...Som Havets Nakna Vind

ANITA
-ur en tonårsflickas dagbo...

CHRISTINA LINDBERG · STELLAN SKARSGÅRD
PER MATTSSON · EWERT GRANHOLM · ARNE RAGNEBORN

Foto: Hans Dittmer · Musik: Lennart Fors · Manus och regi: TORGNY WICKMAN · Prod.: Swedish Film Production

Färg

DISTRIBUTION **pallas fi...**

DAMEN i SVART

EFTER FOLKE MELLVIGS HILLMAN-SERIE
Regi: ARNE MATTSSON

"Den första svenska
thrillern i Hitchcocks
toppklass. Pittutar av
trivsel och sjuder av
spänning."

"Sällan har det skrikits till
så ofta, sällan har chocker-
na tagits så glatt. Kanske
den bästa thriller som
gjorts här i landet."

ANITA BJÖRK
KARL-ARNE HOLMSTEN
ANNA-LISA ERICSON
SVEN LINDBERG
NILS HALLBERG
LENA GRANHAGEN · ISA QUENSEL
SIF RUUD · LENNART LINDBERG

"En pålitlig s.k. rysare.
Absolut SPÄNNANDE.
Förskräckta skrik och
belåtna flabb, allt efter-
som de kalla kårarna
ilar utefter ryggraden."

"Fasan dallrar i salongen och
huden knottrar sig på åskådaren.
Kort sagt OVANLIGT BRA
SVENSK THRILLER-FILM."

"I särklass, i skräckklass
och i skrattklass."

SANDREWS

Dirch Passer and Carl-Gustaf Lindstedt as
the hapless Viking berserkers o...
Här Kommer Bärsärkarna

Just when you thought you'd seen it all...

GIO PETRE and MARIE LILJEDAHL

ANN AND EVE

The love animals of
"INGA"
and
"I, A WOMAN,
PART 2"
trade secrets.

with Francisco Rabal, Julian Mateos, Olivera Vuco.
Directed by ARNE MATTSSON
Released by CHEVRON PICTURES a division of Cinecom Corp.
Color Prints by Movielab

(X) NO ONE UNDER 17 ADMITTED

ULLA JACOBSSON
FOLKE SUNDQUIST

EDVIN ADOLPHSON JOHN ELFSTRÖM
IRMA CHRISTENSSON ERIK HELL
REGI: ARNE MATTSSON

Hon dansade en sommar

NORDISK TONEFILM

Above: Christina Lindberg in Exponerad **Courtesy of Klubb Super 8**

Left: Stellan Skarsård caught conquering women in the erotic summer saga Strandhugg i Somras

BLOOD TRACKS

CANDICE DALY HARDING MICHAEL FITZPATRICK
NAOMI KANEDA BRAD POWELL PETER MERRILL HARRIET ROBINSON
TINA SHAW FRANCES KELLY KARINA LEE HELENA JACKS
Production manager: BRUNO JOHANSON Director of photography: HANS VON DITTMER F.S.F
Special effects: MIKE JACKSON Stunt coordinator: TOMMY ELLGREN Special make-up effects:
DICK LJUNGGREN Music by: DAG UNENGE Title song by: EASY ACTION Editor: DAVID GILBERT
Written by: MIKE JACKSON & ANNA WOLF Executive producer: GEORGE ZECEVIC Produced by:
TOM SJOBERG Associate director: DEREK FORD Directed by: MIKE JACKSON

BENGT ERLANDSSON OCH MATS-HELGE OLSSON
Presenterar
CARL-GUSTAF
LINDSTEDT

JUBEL I
VÄSTERN-
BUSKEN.

I DÖD MANS SPÅR

SUNE MANGS · STEN ARDENSTAM · TOR ISEDAL
ISABELLA KALIFF · SOLVEIG ANDERSSON
INSPELAD I FÄRG PÅ HIGH CHAPARRAL

Violent Sweden (clockwise from upper left): Glam rockers, lingonberry cowboys, bleeder vikings, and Dennis Hopper

Se upp för honom-innan han
får syn på dej...

SVERIGES FÖRSTA VIDEO RYSARE
BLÖDAREN

Åke Eriksson · Danne Strähed · Mia Hansson · Sussi Ax · Agneta Ölund
Eva Pettersson · Maria Landberg · Tony di Ponziano · Eva Danielsson

Han levde för utmaningen.
Slogs gärna. Hårt.
Nu blev han utmanad.
Av en okänd, livsfarlig fiende...

SLAGSKÄMPEN

THE INSIDE MAN

EN FILM AV HRAFN GUNNLAUGSSON

KORPEN FLYGER

French literature gets the Swedish sensationsfilms treatment in Mac Ahlberg's Nana

Marie Forså hiking up her skirt to hitch a ride in Lifterskan

Another Swedish summer, more love in Kyrkoherden

Diana Kjaer and her (surprisingly clean-shaven) Danish lover in Fanny Hill

Anna Godenius, with her eye set on revenge, in Jörn Donner's Män Kan Inte Våldtas

Left: Diana Kjaer shows off her womanhood to a rather mature boy in Vindingevals

The ever-popular Deep Throat *of Sweden:* Fäbodjäntan

Below: "Count Porrno and his Women," a superior alternative title for Jag en Markis – Med Uppdrag att Älska

En helsexig svensk porrkomedi

Harry Reems
Christa Linder
Maria Lynn
och massor av
läckra brudar!

BelAmi

En EROTISK KOMEDI med SKOJ – SEX – SADISM

GABRIEL AXEL
ELSA PRAVITZ
LOTTE TARP
HANS LINDGREN
CARL AXEL ELFVING

**GREVE PORRNO
och hans
KVINNOR**

NÅGON ATT ÄLSKA
[Someone to Love]

(1971)

Director:
Joseph W. Sarno
Cast:
Marie Liljedahl
Tommy Blom
Lennart Lindberg
Inger Sundh
Harriet Ayres
Lennart Norbäck
Lissi Alandh
Lasse Svensson
Göran Lagerberg
Maria Wersäll
Jeanette Swensson
Liliane Malmquist

After Inga (Marie Liljedahl) is abandoned by her boyfriend, she sits alone and out of work in her drab apartment in central Stockholm. She takes work as secretary for aging writer Stig (Lennart Lindberg), and the two fall in love. When Stig must later travel out of town for a job, Inga turns to musician Rolf (Tommy Blom) for comfort. The young woman is torn between her two lovers, yet the situation reaches new heights of confusion when Inga also finds herself attracted to Stig's former mistress Greta (Inger Sundh). After Stig dies in a car crash, Inga consoles herself with her first lesbian encounter with Greta, but she eventually leaves town with Rolf.

This is a sequel to *Jag, en Oskuld* (see page 112), but dirtier and way sleazier. The bewitching Marie Liljedahl again takes the lead, now opposite former pop sensation Tommy Blom from Tages—a genuine relic of the 1960s Swedish rock 'n' roll explosion, still handsome enough to be in a sleazy movie. Unlike its predecessor, which was relatively innocent, this sequel wastes no time building up to the sleaze, as wild nightclubs and sex are now a daily routine for Inga. The movie is elevated by unsavory details, such as Inga's landlord running a brothel, and Stig keeping his stepdaughter as a mistress—by this point, director Joe Sarno must have realized he could get away with anything at all in Sweden, for he was truly running wild. The lesbian encounter between the two girls is outstanding, especially when Sundh holds a broken bottle to Liljedahl's naked body.

Needless to say, the Swedish press hated the movie. They must have been forced to review every single Swedish film, but they didn't have to like them. "The intelligence level of this movie is so low that you have to dig up the whole region in order to find anything resembling water," wrote Jürgen Schildt in *Aftonbladet*. Regardless of the low intellect, the sleaze level is very, very high. But please, American directors, including Joe Sarno and John Waters, take note: "Inga" is actually a very rare name in Sweden.

Alternative titles: *Inga Two*; *Inga and Greta*; *The Seduction of Inga*

It's More
Inga...
More
Daringly
Delicious...
More
Daringly
Erotic!

THE SUBMISSION!   THE PROPOSITION!   THE THREAT!

ALL NEW AND IN COLOR

The Seduction of
Inga

(X)

HER NEWEST MISADVENTURE!

Jerry Gross presents a Vernon P. Becker production

starring MARIE LILJEDAHL · Introducing TOMMY BLOM · Produced by VERNON P. BECKER · Written and Directed by JOSEPH W. SARNO
A UNICORN ENTERPRISES PRODUCTION · A CINEMATION INDUSTRIES RELEASE · COLOR BY DELUXE

*Clockwise from top left: Anna Gaël lets it
all hang out in* Nana
Courtesy of Klubb Super 8

The US Någon att Älska (Someone to Love)
poster looks awfully familiar;

Tommy Blom and Marie Liljedahl in
Någon att Älska

Inger Sundh in Någon att Älska

NANA

(1970)

Nana (Anna Gaël) makes a hugely successful debut as a performer at Bonds nightclub, and the celebration party escalates into an orgy. She swiftly attracts a troop of devoted admirers, and an important businessman even gives her a house on the coast. Nana's wild lifestyle backfires on her, however, when an article appears in the press, gossiping about her scandalous ways. Her artistic downfall soon follows. Suddenly, Nana finds herself living in a cramped apartment with nightclub singer Rikki (Rikki Septimus), far away from gala premieres and coastal houses. Things pick up, and a movie offer catapults her back into the spotlight and a new wave of erotic adventures. In the end, everyone who has ever been in contact with Nana sees his or her life turn to misery. The girl herself is excluded from the collective bad luck, though, and sees a bright future as a celebrated actress.

Curious as it may sound, this is director Mac Ahlberg's (admittedly very free) interpretation of Emile Zola's classic novel *Nana*. The movie met with minor legal issues after its release, as Gaël claimed she had not expected the movie would be so highly erotic. Go figure.

As usual, the critics annihilated Ahlberg. "Photographer and pornmonger Mac Ahlberg has transformed the heroine of *Nana* into a high-end modern-day prostitute," complained Hans-Erik Hjertén in *Dagens Nyheter*. "Where exactly she is whoring, I could not tell you—I only know the camera locked me in a claustrophobic plastic-wrapped hell until I could not breathe. Do not go see this movie, and spare yourself the trouble of running away from it."

Alternative titles: *Tag Mig – Älska Mig; Nana 70; Poupée d'Amour; Take Me, Love Me*

Director:
Mac Ahlberg
Cast:
Anna Gaël
Gillian Hills
Lars Lunøe
Keve Hjelm
Gérard Berner
Rikki Septimus
Hans Ernback
Peter Bonke
Keith Bradfield
Poul Glargaard
Fritz Ruzicka
Erik Holme
Simon Rosenbaum
Willy Peters
Elsa Jackson
Yvonne Ekman
Helli Louise
Bonnie Ewan

(1966)

Director:

Mai Zetterling

Cast:

Ingrid Thulin
Keve Hjelm
Jörgen Lindström
Lena Brundin
Naima Wifstrand
Monica Zetterlund
Lauritz Falk
Rune Lindström
Christian Bratt
Lissi Alandh
Axel Fritz
Willy Koblanck
George Årlin

NATTLEK
[Night Games]

Thirty-five-year-old John (Keve Hjelm) returns to the castle where he grew up. Wandering through the deserted and silent corridors with his girlfriend, he reminiscences about a number of episodes from his childhood, most involving his relationship with his eccentric mother. As the slew of memories wears him down, he decides to settle the score with his past in a very drastic way.

Mai Zetterling's second movie is surreal and bizarre. More artistic than exploitative, it boasts plenty of sleazy details that draw it closer to the brink of sensation. Several incestuous insinuations pave the way for a perverse atmosphere. Other visual shocks include some incredible vomiting from John, and some breasts and butts. Otherwise that the movie could almost be PG-rated. Maybe there are titillating scenes left on the cutting room floor, but as it is, the movie drags a bit compared to the best *sensationsfilms*.

The graphic poster for this film—a detailed cross-section of sexual intercouse, originally drawn by genius and sleazebag Leonardo da Vinci—stirred up quite a commotion at the 1966 Cannes Film Festival. The head of the festival couldn't take the heat, and the film's public screening was canceled. Only some critics and the jury were allowed to see it, which created quite a mystique back home in Sweden. An entire police squad had to be called in to keep order at the Stockholm premiere, but afterwards the film was hardly ever mentioned again.

Alternative title: *Längtan*

Love in its most graphic form on the original Nattlek (Night Games) *poster*

Mats Helge Olsson's superb The Ninja Mission, *the prolific director's finest hour by far*

(1984)

THE NINJA MISSON

Director:
Mats Helge Olsson

Cast:
Christopher Kohlberg
Curt Broberg
Hanna Pola
Matthew Jacobs
Bo F. Munthe
Hans Rosteen
John Qvantz
Sirka Sander
Wolf Linder
Leo Adolfson
Mark Davies
Mats Helge Olsson
Brett Barber

Tough mercenary Mason (Christopher Kohlberg) and his ninja commando are sent to save scientist and defector Karl Markov (Curt Broberg), who has been captured by the Russians. Markov has developed some kind of program for nuclear energy, and world peace would be threatened if the Russians got their hands on it. To make sure things run smoothly and ensure the old man's co-operation, the Reds also kidnap Markov's daughter (Hanna Pola). Mason and his ninjas have no choice but to storm the fortress where Markov is being kept, and bring him back safely to Sweden.

Produced by Charles Aperia, the man behind legendary Swedish videocassette label VTC (Video Tape Center), *The Ninja Mission* is one of Mats Helge Olsson's most expensive productions. For the director, this was an uncharacteristic success from both a production and a creative standpoint, as it is well crafted and highly entertaining. The action scenes are without a doubt some of the best ever in Swedish cinema, filled with lots of blood and slow motion. In what must be the most spectacular death scene in all of Scandinavian film, a man suffocates on his own vomit. The downside is the sometimes dissatisfactory acting—although Olsson's cameo as evil Ivan is unforgettable.

Both *The Ninja Mission* and its unofficial sequel, *Eagle Island* (see page 53), are distinct products of their time, with the haunting Cold War serving as background for cinematic conflict. The ninjas themselves are very typical of the early '80s, armed exotically with samurai swords, throwing stars, etc. Internationally, *The Ninja Mission* was a huge success—but take with a grain of salt the claim on the Swedish DVD box that the film has held the number one position on US video rental charts for decades. Olsson himself has boasted that the film made millions of dollars in theaters. Also according to the director, a special version with a parallel love story was sold in Asia, but Sweden was never treated to a shred of evidence of any of these claims.

The press hated the movie, of course, and could not even credit the well-crafted action scenes. "If you try to disregard everything else and only focus on the action sequences, *The Ninja Mission* still remains close to indescribably bad," said Mårten Blomkvist to readers of *Dagens Nyheter*. Coincidentally, this was the last of Mats Helge Olsson's films to get theatrical distribution in Sweden.

NORDEXPRESSEN
[The Northern Express]

(1992)

Director:
Mats Helge Olsson
Cast:
Robert Aschberg
Elisabeth Granneman
Gert Fylking
Taggen Axelsson
Johan Widerberg
Peter Ahlm
Lennart Jähkel
Lars Lundgren
Hasse Aro
Thorsten Flinck
Karl-Johan Fröjd
Johan Kekonius
Dan Lindhe

Even by the scattershot standards of Mats Helge Olsson, the plot of *Nordexpressen* is really confusing. Johan (Robert Aschberg) is a journalist in Stockholm. Fed up with hard city life, he leaves for Nordbyn in the north. "I was overworked and sick of the city," he says. "You know how it is, too much whiskey and too little sleep."

But NATO is running a secret lab in Nordbyn, full of hordes of kicking terrorists led by the vicious Wolfgang Mueller (Gert Fylking). Of course, Johan sees it as his business to take care of this, and he transforms into an action hero. After many armed battles and traditional fistfights, the hero journalist finally relaxes in his camouflage fatigues, his M16 resting safely by his side. But Mueller soon captures him. In the final scene, the terrorist, laughing hysterically, is about to destroy our hero in a garbage compactor. Suddenly, the screen halts and a dreaded title appears: TO BE CONTINUED.

In the early '90s, Mats Helge Olsson was suddenly unable to find funding for his movies. Fortunately, the kingpins of brand-new TV Channel 3 wanted to turn late-night talk show host Robert Aschberg into an action hero, and they made the mistake of allowing Mats Helge to direct a TV pilot. Apart from a lot of Channel 3 faces (Gert Fylking, Hasse Aro) and a few fairly big actors (Lennart Jähkel, Thorsten Flinck), Olsson unwisely cast the film himself, so the rest of the actors are basically lousy amateurs.

The demon director shot tons of crazy fight sequences in Stockholm's Lunda industrial area. Since he lacked talent and a proper script, the results turned out like most of his other films—a disaster. When the financial backers saw the tests, they stamped on the brakes in terror, hastily converting what they had into this confusing TV movie. After the broadcast, Aschberg invited viewers to vote whether there should a continuation as promised. The "no" side won by a landslide. Mats Helge Olsson was never allowed to direct again. Shortly after, he left Sweden in a hurry, chased by tax officials, to whom he owed more than a million dollars. This dispute is why we won't see any official Swedish DVD releases of his films.

In 2001, Olsson made a fleeting comeback in Canada, as coproducer of the awful Leslie Nielsen action comedy *Kevin of the North*. He occasionally appears in Sweden, secretly lecturing at film schools. Mats Helge Olsson will be remembered as a true maverick of Swedish filmmaking, and he is really missed, for better or worse.

NYCKELHÅLET
[The Keyhole]

(1974)

Director:

Paul Gerber
(Gerhard Poulsen)

Cast:

Marie Ekorre

Torben Larsen

Max Horn

Bent Warburg

Dorte Jensen

Pia Larsen

Lene Andersen

Director and nude photographer Sören (Torben Larsen) is commissioned to write a script for a new pornographic movie. The producers, Per (Max Horn) and Jens (Bent Warburg), require the script to be realistic in order to differentiate their movie from all the other lowbrow smut out there. With the help of Per's daughter Mette (Marie Ekorre), with whom our hero is having an affair, Sören gets to work spying on friends and acquaintances in order to write a script reflecting their sexual escapades. The investigations reveal that Jens has sex with his secretary, and that Per frequently visits a massage parlor to get satisfaction. However, Sören gets stuck trying to find a little something extra to really spice up the script, so the thrifty Mette comes up with a solution—she sleeps with her father's colleague, and soon the script is finalized. Sören shows his masterpiece script to the producers, but it is rejected—they find all the antics too unbelievable!

Nyckelhålet is high-quality Danish-Swedish sleaze directed by Gerhard Poulsen, a movie which seemingly cannot get enough eroticism. The whole palette is here, from sweet make-out sessions to no-nonsense graphic sex. A few of the more spectacular shenanigans include an orgasmic photo session in Sören's studio, and a blunt hand job at the corner massage parlor. The camera has a free-spirited attitude toward nudity, and all genitalia are equally laid bare. Marie Ekorre once again proves that apart from being sinfully sexy, she also is a decent actress. As usual, she keeps away from the more lurid porn scenes. The plot itself drowns in all the sex, and *Nyckelhålet* does not really reach the same level as Poulsen's following movie, *I Lust och Nöd* (see page 97). Nevertheless, this over-the-top sex comedy is worth seeking out. It must be the most sinful movie ever to hold its world premiere in the moral stronghold of Norway, where stern Christian values still reign supreme.

Alternative titles: *Noeglehullet*; *My Teenage Daughter*

Den Ödesdigra Klockan
(The Fateful Bell) *poster
does not skimp on sex and
violent beatdowns*

*Marie Ekorre and a bearded
Dane in* Nyckelhålet
(The Keyhole)
Courtesy of Klubb Super 8

(1966) DEN ÖDESDIGRA KLOCKAN
[The Fateful Bell]

Director:

Bertil Malmqvist

Cast:

Lars Passgård
Yvonne Norrman
Marianne Nilsson
Owe Stefansson
Bengt Rosén
Roy Fjärstad
Gustaf Färingborg
Charlotte Dittmer
Nils Bäckström
Emy Storm
Ragnar Landerholm
Oscar Karlsson
Gunilla Ohlsson

Following the death of his father, young Sven (Lars Passgård) remains tormented by an anxious childhood memory of hitting his head on a church bell. As his unsettling thoughts grow worse, Sven is institutionalized. He soon escapes the nuthouse, however, and becomes a member of a criminal gang. After pulling off a post office heist, Sven is assaulted by his new friends and thrown out of the gang. Hellbent on revenge, Sven becomes fixated on seeking out and killing the leader of the gang. Following this twisted path, he finds himself barricaded in the very church tower where his misfortune began. As the police break down the doors to get him, the poor soul leaps to his death.

This is a reasonably rough gangster story by first-time director Bertil Malmqvist. Not too much nudity on display here; instead, Malmqvist offers plenty of scenes with tough guys sweating it out in gyms, hanging around boxing clubs, planning nightclub break-ins, and beating people up in alleys.

"To be honest, *Den Ödesdigra Klockan* is little more than a pretty horrible variation on the questionable thug movies that Arne Ragneborn tormented us with during the '50s," wrote the washed-up and weary critic Jonas Sima in *Expressen*. Soon after, the fateful bell rang for the director, and his career sank to the extreme lows of worthless pornography.

DEN ONDA CIRKELN
[The Vicious Circle]

(1967)

Director:

Arne Mattsson

Cast:

Gunnel Lindblom

Erik Hell

Gio Petré

Mathias Henrikson

Marie-Louise Håkansson

Heinz Hopf

Karl-Arne Bergman

Eva Larsson

Young Maria (Gunnel Lindblom) returns to the traumatic place where she was raped as a little girl—a little inn where everyone's behavior is more or less peculiar. When yet another little girl is sexually abused, Maria hastily departs the terrible little community, bringing the girl with her.

Arne Mattsson created a somewhat unique movie using a very small ensemble. The cast of characters acts as a solemn parade of the morbid and broken in this masterful portrayal of dismal atmosphere and depression. Heinz Hopf is seemingly wasted in a small part, but his brief stint on the silver screen leaves a lingering impression. He really takes his time sexually assaulting a child, and then laughs it off afterward. Another memorable sequence portrays costar Gio Petré masturbating while two men peep through her window.

A suggestive and odd movie, this should not be easily dismissed as "one of the more severe breakdowns in recent Swedish cinema"—as *Aftonbladet*'s resident charmer Jürgen Schildt described it. Yet this became the turning point of Mattsson's career, as critics across Sweden abandoned him like rats from a sinking ship. The veteran director died, unsung and forgotten, in 1995. For shame, lousy critics!

ONDSKANS VÄRDSHUS
[The Guesthouse of Evil]

(1981)

Director:
Calvin Floyd

Cast:
Curd Jürgens
Patrick Magee
Per Oscarsson
Marilù Tolo
Brendan Price
Niall Toibin
Barry Cassins

The year is 1815, and young nobleman Robert (Brendan Price) is bored with his life in an English castle. He lusts for young girls and adventures. So after his father's death, Robert sets off to France, where he becomes entangled with a beautiful young girl who cruises around doing mysterious things in a black carriage painted with a dragon. After some mishaps, Robert checks into a strange guesthouse named The Flying Dragon. Odd things begin to happen, and he hears stories about vampires in the village. Death and confusion reign, but all the while, things might not be what they seem.

This was the last of five films Irish director Calvin Floyd made in Sweden, and definitely one of the most interesting. Based on Irish novelist Sheridan LeFanu's 1872 book *The Room in the Dragon Volant*, this film revels in gothic horror, complete with imposing castles, dark corridors, moonlit cemeteries, howling wolves, magic potions, tarot cards, vampires, and even the old stake-through-the-heart routine. This is not traditional horror, though, as the film stays away from the slasher/splatter tendencies that ruled the early '80s. Instead, this is more like psychological drama, a disorienting attack on the senses.

The lack of a clear logic seemed to offend critics of the time, like *Svenska Dagbladet*'s Hans Schiller. "The failure is almost complete," he huffed. Enraged by such murderous critiques, Calvin Floyd left Sweden for good, claiming the country had misunderstood his genius. In hindsight, Floyd probably should have put more blood and guts into his films, but he wouldn't listen to reason and remained the grumpy victim. In any case, he never directed again.

Alternative title: *The Sleep of Death*

ORMEN
[The Snake]

(1966)

Director:
Hans Abramson

Cast:
Christina Schollin
Harriet Andersson
Hans Ernback
Tor Isedal
Gudrun Brost
Brita Öberg
Eddie Axberg
Lars Passgård
Björn Gustafson
Tommy Nilson
Morgan Andersson
Lars Edström
Margareta Sjödin
Signe Stade
Hans Bendrik

Billed prophetically as "the Swedish film that has made a sensation," *Ormen* is set in the '40s, and based around a Swedish military camp and a brigade of soldiers who are more inclined toward partying than staying in a state of alert. Young Irène (Christina Schollin) works near the camp, and her story is tragic. Things start nicely enough when she begins dating a boy, but he cheats on her since she will not put out. Then she accidentally shoves her mother off a train, and finally she is raped and beaten. In the end, Irène gets hammered at a party and wakes up the next day in utter anguish.

This story might sound nice in summary, but in reality the movie is a harsher version of a regular old Swedish *pilsnerfilm*—a lightweight, watered-down zany comedy genre that ruled the 1940s, in which fat men drink beer and sing much of the time. In summary, *Ormen* is a melodrama with some nudity, some drunkenness, and a pretty rough rape as added minor attractions. According to Schollin, she turned down an Elvis Presley picture to do this film. At least she won a Guldbagge prize for best actress at Sweden's film industry awards. Initially, Vilgot Sjöman was lined up to direct *Ormen*, but he got tied up doing *Syskonbädd 1782* (see page 254). He would have done a better job.

Alternative title: *The Serpent*

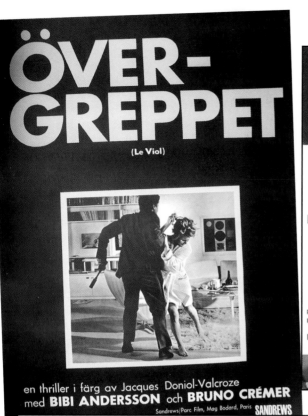

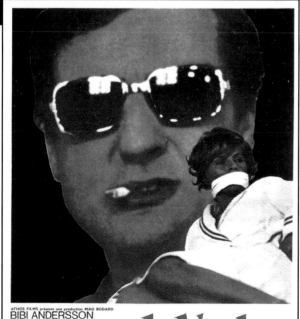

Clockwise from top left: Swedish poster for Övergreppet (The Violation);

Poster for the glorified pilsnerfilm Ormen (The Snake);

Sweden makes, and Europe takes—as this considerably more sinister French poster for Övergreppet proves

ORMENS VÄG PÅ HÄLLEBERGET
[The Snake's Path on the Rock]

(1986)

Director:
Bo Widerberg
Cast:
Stina Ekblad
Stellan Skarsgård
Reine Brynolfsson
Pernilla Östergren
Tomas von Brömssen
Pernilla Wahlgren
Ernst Günther
Birgitta Ulfsson
Johan Widerberg
Melinda Kinnaman
Åsa Göransson
Michael Kallaanvaara
Carl Carlswärd
Amelia Glas-Drake
Gun Fors

This tragedy takes place in the late nineteenth century, and its story deals with inherited family shame and debt. A creep named Ol Karlsa (Ernst Günther) forces a suffering family to repay the sums they owe in sexual favors. The obligation is passed down to the children, and when mother Tea (Stina Ekblad) is too old to satisfy Karsla's son Karl's (Stellan Skarsgård) perverse urges, he turns to daughter Eva (Pernilla Östergren) instead. In a desperate attempt to end the family's humiliation, son Jani (Reine Brynolfsson) finally castrates the tormentor and throws his genitals into the fireplace.

Make no mistake—despite a hefty budget and impressive cast, this is very sensationalized fare. The serious undertones take the edge off the well-directed nude scenes, while the mostly restrained direction by master of pacing Bo Widerberg creates a believable foundation for this gloomy story.

The movie received largely good reviews. "It is a powerful and cruel story, and Widerberg portrays it with a rhythm and imagery unprecedented in modern Swedish cinema," applauded Jan Aghed in *Sydsvenska Dagbladet Snällposten*.

(1968)

Director:

*Jaques Doniol-
Valcroze*

Cast:

Bibi Andersson

Bruno Crémer

*Frédérick de
Pasquale*

Katarina Larsson

ÖVERGREPPET
[The Violation]

A stranger (Bruno Crémer) rings the bell at the home of Mr. Severin (Frédérick de Pasquale) while the man of the house is out hunting. His wife, Marianne (Bibi Andersson), is home alone. When she opens the door, the nasty stranger attacks her and ties her up. Next follows a long period of degradation, during which time Marianne is physically abused and forced to undress. Despite the harsh treatment, Marianne finds herself relating to the intruder somehow. His name is Walter, and he turns out to be well-mannered and educated. Even so, when Marianne tries to use the telephone, Walter fires a warning shot with his gun and threatens to kill her. The death threat only drives Marianne mad with desire, and she manages to lure Walter into bed. After their lovemaking, he leaves the apartment, only to return later that same night—this time invited by Marianne's husband! In the end, it seems that disturbed lovers Marianne and Walter will continue their erotic role-playing for as long as movie audiences can stand to watch.

Övergreppet is the first Swedish-French movie made after the ultra-serious "Film Co-Production Agreement of 1965," which mandated in the most important-sounding language imaginable the terms of a new cooperation between the Swedish Film Institute and France's Centre National de la Cinématographie. Of course they kicked off this enterprise with a sadistic film about degradation—and it's unclear whether any other films were ever made under the agreement. The result is a powerful erotic drama that crosses the line and becomes more than a traditional thriller. This is a very provocative movie, suggesting that women enjoy sexual abuse—a common approach in southern European films— yet it still managed to capture the respect of critics, and unbelievably earned an "11" rating in Sweden, allowing children eleven and up to view the perversity. That aside, the film is refined and elegant, with a sadomasochistic theme that could have been explored a little more deeply.

Alternative titles: *A Question of Rape*; *Le Viol*

P. S. SISTA SOMMAREN
[P. S. Last Summer]

(1988)

Director:
Thomas Samuelsson
Cast:
Lena Nilsson
John Patrick Stenman
Roberto Jelinek
Pia Green
Peder Falk
Göran Stangertz
Örjan Ramberg
Susanne Alfvengren
Ulf Larsson
Tommy Wahlgren
Hans Bendrik
Kjell Höglund
Mona Seilitz

Matte (Johan Patrick Stenman) and Kranken (Roberto Jelinek) are two carefree seventeen-year-old guys roaming the streets of Stockholm in search of summer kicks. While Kranken dabbles in petty crime, Matte picks up upper-class girl Lisa (Lena Nilsson). The trio decides to go to the island of Gotland together, and a love triangle introduces new drama. The rich Lisa naturally is attracted to the wilder Kranken, and before long she is sexually entangled with both of the guys. The situation gets more tense when the police come around looking for the bad boy. Worse yet, a dirty motorcycle gang spies on the trio as they bathe naked, and a terrible confrontation with the gang ends with death and disaster.

P. S. Sista Sommaren has a lot in common with Staffan Hildebrand's *Ingen Kan Älska som Vi* (see page 98). Both movies start with youngsters leaving Stockholm, followed by a lot of nothing for over an hour, and then end explosively in a scene of total sensationalism. But whereas Hildebrand's film just leads up to later Bond girl Izabella Scorupco showing her tits, Thomas Samuelsson really comes up with something nasty. The final scene involves group rape and stabbing and is genuinely disturbing—this movie shocked a generation of Swedish teens. Just a few more violent moments, and this film could have been a sleaze classic.

The rest of the film offers a few sex scenes and some nudity, and even great actors such as Örjan Ramberg are let down by the non-existent direction and bland dialogue. Critics rightly slaughtered the film, as it was mercilessly obvious that Samuelsson was not director material. Though he clearly had little talent and even less to say, the director came back in 1993 with the thriller *Tryggare Kan Ingen Vara...* (see page 264).

(1982)

Director:

*Andrew Whyte
(Andrei Feher)*

Cast:

*Barbi Andersson
Ingdrid Lindgren
Jean L. Laporte
Isabelle Dior
Silvano Di Roma*

PILSKA JULIA PÅ BRÖLLOPSRESA
[Bawdy Julia on Her Honeymoon]

Romeo (Jean L. Laporte) and Julia (Barbi Andersson) spend their honeymoon on the French Riviera, cruising around on a motorcycle and dressed in their wedding outfits the entire time! Normal marital urges demand their constant attention, and whenever the couple cannot restrain themselves they stop by the edge of the road and make hot love until falling asleep. When they wake up to find someone has stolen both their motorcycle and their luggage, they throw caution to the wind and head out for a scandalous journey through France, drinking and fucking with abandon. During their adventures, they end up at a sleazy porn club, where they cause a big commotion putting on a show as a newlywed Swedish couple. Loads of sex and complications follow, until they wake up to discover—everything was but a dream!

Yet another peculiar porn flick directed under a pseudonym by Andrei Feher, this is definitely one of his most entertaining and outrageous efforts. Oddly, he chose to colorize certain scenes with a red filter. The dialogue is shamelessly stupid, and Barbi Andersson's dubbing makes her sound like a ten-year-old girl.

During production, the sex scenes were filmed for both hard-core and soft-core versions to be released. In the hard version of the film, both takes are included, which creates a weird sense of déjà vu. It's idiotic, insane, and wonderfully entertaining for viewers in the right mood! This is apparently the only Swedish hard-core sex production of 1982, and in a way marks the end of the great unique era of Swedish erotica.

POJKDRÖMMAR
[Boyhood Dreams]

(1993)

Director:
Hrafn Gunnlaugsson
Cast:
Steinthor Matthiasson
Edda Björgvinsdóttir
Alda Sigurðardóttir
Tinna Finnbogadóttir
Agneta Prytz
Helgi Skúlason

Seven-year-old Gestur (Steinthor Matthiasson) is sent to the Icelandic countryside to spend the summer with some relatives. Living at the farm is a teenage girl, Helga (Alda Sigurðardóttir), who captivates Gestur with her feminine charms. Together, they spend an intoxicating summer, filled with fantasies and discoveries.

This Icelandic-Swedish drama deals with a young man getting in touch for the first time with his sexuality. To be frank, director Gunnlaugsson should have stuck with the violence and lust of his *Korpen Flyger* (see page 134) and *Bödeln och Skökan* (see page 41). The most sensational element of the production is the generous exposure of young Alda Sigurðardóttir's naked body, something which surely was more tempting for the audience than the movie's other qualities. When the creators of a typical drama like this throw the dice and decide to bet it all on using the naked body of a young beautiful girl to sell a movie—bingo, you are comfortably in the territory of a Swedish *sensationsfilm*.

Alternative title: *The Sacred Mound*

(1985) THE PORNO RACE

Director:

Andrew Whyte
(Andrei Feher)

Cast:

Barbi Andersson
Marilyn Lamour
Betty Davis
Gun Friberg
Nelly Bergman
Christina Andersson
Lars Sandgren
Tina Carmelton

Photo model Tina Carmelton is some kind of master of ceremonies during an international sex contest between the US, Sweden, France, Germany, and Italy. Somehow, the whole event will be broadcast on TV. From the starting shot, the contest becomes a giant worldwide sex fest, with contestants and audience giving it their best in the sexual activities, all in the name of national pride.

Another of Romanian-born Andrei Feher's Swedish-produced sex movies, this one features a plot that is even more of an after-thought than usual. One sex sequence follows another, at which point the interesting balance is lost. All in all, it's a monotonous mess for everyone to avoid.

After the equally disappointing *Dreams of Love* (see page 52) the same year, Feher finally called it quits, and Swedish pornographic film died with him. For this director at his best, seek out *Pilska Julia på Bröllopsresa* (see page 194) or *Kärleksvirveln* (see page 130) instead.

Alternative titles: *Marathon Love; World Sex Festival*

It's a sleazy world, after all—the nations compete in a race to the bottom in The Porno Race

"She is naughty, sensual, crazy. She accepts every indecent proposal!" The film known in English as Bawdy Julia on Her Honeymoon

(1973)

Director:

Joseph W. Sarno

Cast:

Nadia Henkowa

Anke Syring

Marie Forså

Nico Wolf

Ulrike Butz

Flavia Keyt

Alon D'Armand

Irina Rant

Natasha Michnowa

Eric Mancy

Christa Jaeger

Heidrun Hankammer

DEN PORNOGRAFISKA JUNGFRUN
[The Pornographic Maiden]

Mysterious sexual rites are being conducted by a sect in a medieval castle. These acts are dedicated to Baroness Varga, an accused vampiress who was executed numerous years ago. Lo and behold, down in the crypts the baroness is somehow still alive, and in fact she still fully controls the deviant sect. But her immortal luck comes at a price: In order to seek revenge and remain alive, she must continually drink the blood of the descendants of those who once tried to kill her. Her pursuit for blood mostly seems to lead to an abundance of rites and lesbian sex. When she finally does get her hands on some suitable blood, she suddenly meets her grisly demise and ends up impaled on a pole. The baroness at last goes to her eternal sleep, the sect members are freed from her curse, and everyone is happy.

This questionable Swedish-Swiss coproduction is all about vampires, rites, sex, and nudity. The ritual scenes with naked girls, wild drumming, obscure symbols, burning fires, and big dildos make the movie worth watching. A young and very beautiful Marie Forså in her undressed state is the acting highlight. On the other hand, the story suffers from a total lack of narrative logic. Why the guests never just leave the morbid castle remains a mystery, as this sample of silly dialogue proves:

> Q: "Why are we here?"
> A: "I really don't know!"

But who cares about such trivialities as a painfully low budget and poor production values when we are served a raging, no-holds-barred trash fest? Despite the title, there is no hard-core sex at all, but director Joseph W. Sarno fully made up for that oversight a few years later by delivering the classic pornographic spectacle *Fäbodjäntan* (see page 58).

Unlike most Swedish sex films, this movie was never reviewed in the mainstream newspapers. It would have disappeared entirely without mention, until Monika Tunbäck-Hanson decided to write an article in *Göteborgs-Posten* arguing that *Den Pornografiska Jungfrun* should never be given any exposure in the media. What an idiot.

Alternative titles: *Vampire Ecstasy*; *Veil of Blood*; *Veil of Lust*

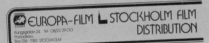
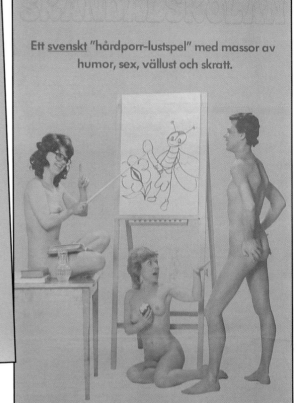

Clockwise from top left: Promo sheet for Porr i Skandalskolan (Porn in the Scandal School)*;*

Educational Porr i Skandalskolan *poster;*

Peeping in the school of "Bo Goldendick" from Porr i Skandalskolan

Courtesy of Klubb Super 8

(1974)

Director:

*Bert Torn
(Mac Ahlberg)*

Cast:

Peter Berg

Jack Frank

Jim Styf

Kim Frank

Teresa Svensson

Agda Dahl

Bridget Mayers

Suzy Andersson

Monica Anders

Nickan Harding

Romeo

Julia

PORR I SKANDALSKOLAN
[Porn in the Scandal School]

Bo Gyllenstake (Peter Berg)—a man full of so full of lust that his name literally means "golden dick"—finds himself sole heir to a fortune after rich Uncle Joakim kicks the bucket. But wait, there's a catch: The will stipulates that Bo must prove he leads a life of virtue. So to improve his banged-up reputation, Bo starts a school at his estate for the moral and ethical enlightenment of girls. Before long, upper-class families are sending their problematic daughters by the busload to get educated. Naturally, the school is nothing but a sham; within its walls, wild orgies rage around the clock.

Suspicious relatives send lawyer Elliot (Jack Frank) to the school to find out the truth, hoping to get their hands on the inheritance. Their plan backfires, however, as Elliot himself is drawn into the indecent games almost immediately. When the relatives finally go to the school to check things out themselves, not even they can control their carnal urges. The secrets of the school are kept secret, and the well-bred orgies continue, with dead Uncle Joakim no wiser.

This early Swedish porn by the amicable Mac Ahlberg mixes nudity, lust, and laughter in a curious soup. The plot is pretty refined for a sex film, and the movie would work fine as a sexy comedy even if the graphic sex were cut. One scene that would not make an R-rated edition shows Elliot being roughly raped by ten sex-starved girls. If the roles had been reversed, the sequence would never have gotten through the Swedish censors, even in the X-rated version! Overall, it's a classic pornographic spectacle from a different era, when it was acceptable for a young girl to have hair between her legs, and under her arms, too.

Alternative titles: *Skandal i Skolan*; *Second Coming of Eva*

PUNKMORDET
[The Punk Murder]

(1981)

Director:
Staffan Hildebrand
Cast:
Dominik Henzel
Joakim Schröder
Micha Koivunen
Sebastian Håkansson

Three gangs spend their days training in martial arts, watching violent movies, and playing punk rock music. The story follows a week in their lives. They shamble around acting tough until they accidentally bump into rivals in a subway station, and a fight leaves one of the punk rockers mortally stabbed.

This documentary-style drama is based on what the media at the time dubbed "The Punk Murder," a real incident in which sixteen-year-old Roger Johansson was killed inside the Gamla Stan subway station in Stockholm. Dramatic reenactments are intertwined with an interview with Roger's real-life brother Rickard, and scenes from Roger's actual funeral. It's a serious and deserving project indeed, which unfortunately fell into the hands of director Staffan Hildebrand. The embarrassing amateur acting and oversimplification of everything are packaged with production values that seem low even considering that this is a made-for-TV movie. Hildebrand recruited the same crappy actors again a few years later for the enormously successful coming-of-age movie *G* (see page 73). His career reached an untoppable crescendo of kicker kitsch with the hilarious *Stockholmsnatt* (see page 246).

The real perpetrator of the punk murder, Johnny "Wanker" Munksjö, played guitar in the bands Ur Funktion and Brilliant Boys. The latter included Bosse Stagman, later known as Zinny Zan, vocalist of Easy Action, the Swedish band in Mats Helge Olsson's hideous horror film *Blood Tracks* (see page 40). Zinny Zan never found his real name again—fortunately for him, he did make it back to TV in 2002, serving as a tour manager for rap metal band Tribal Ink on the Swedish reality TV show *Wannabe*. Munksjö himself died somewhere along the way.

Alternative title: *Veckan Då Roger Dödades* (The Week Roger Got Killed)

(1959) RAGGARE!

Director:
Olle Hellbom

Cast:
Bill Magnusson
Hans Wahlgren
Christina Schollin
Anita Wall
Svenerik Perzon
Inga Botorp
Tommy Johnson
Thor Hartman
Lars Amble
Sven Almgren

Bibban (Christina Schollin) is a beautiful young girl from a wealthy family. She enjoys life to the max, which means hanging out with both scruffy *raggare* and rich older men. Her free spirit catches the attention of *raggare* leader Roffe (Bill Magnusson), but his interest in her soon crosses the line into obsessed jealousy. Bibban finds herself living on the edge, as hazardous car rides, violent fights, and narcotic usage become natural elements of her everyday life. The complexity of the situation deepens when she falls in love with Lasse (Hans Wahlgren), a *raggare* lower down in the hierarchy. The spurned Roffe does not take their love lightly, and the ensuing bitter struggle leads to a sad death.

This is the first of a trio of Swedish *raggare* movies, followed by Ragnar Frisk's *Raggargänget* (see page 203) and Gunnar Hellström's *Chans* (see page 46), all inspired by such wild American youth movies as Nicholas Ray's *Rebel Without a Cause* (1955). Though these juvenile delinquents appear like US greasers in this film, the *raggare* scene continues in Sweden to this day, pretty much unchanged. They are like motorcycle gangs without organization—or motorcycles.

Raggare are hell-bent on violence, but unlike the members of 1980s kicker subculture depicted in *Stockholmsnatt* (see page 246), *raggare* are undisciplined slobs. Two kickers could easily subdue a hundred *raggare*. In the late 1970s, however, *raggare* went on the warpath, and saw it as their civic duty to purge Sweden of punks, even laying siege to the Sex Pistols' hotel during the UK band's first Scandinavian sojourn. The acrimony survives to this day, as explained by Sweden's first true punk band, Rude Kids, in the anti-*raggare* anthem (covered by Turbonegro), "Raggare Is a Bunch of Motherfuckers."

The ingredients for this lowbrow film genre (as well as the *raggare* subculture) were juvenile delinquency, car and motorcycle fetishism, violence, drinking, and liberal sexuality. This movie depicts all those elements pretty innocently, though it received a lot of scandalized attention at its premiere. The most powerful sequence depicts a young girl being used by a drug addict after he tricks her into taking a bunch of pills. Definitely a recommended film, though it came well before the truly crazy stuff that defines *sensationsfilms*.

Alternative title: *Blackjackets*

RAGGARGÄNGET
[The Raggare Gang]

(1962)

Director:
Ragnar Frisk

Cast:
Ernst-Hugo Järegård
Jan-Olof Strandberg
Carli Tornehave
Maud Adelson
Britt Damberg
Sigge Fürst
Edith "Morsan" Jansson
Arne Källerud
Morgan Andersson
Artur Fischer
Maud Nygren
Laila Westersund
Ingrid Olofsson
Mona Andersson
Solveig Ternström

Berra (Ernst-Hugo Järegård) and Kritan (Jan Olof Strandberg) are two ruthless *raggare* who terrorize everyone and everything around them. Also in the *raggare* gang is promising boxer Svenne (Morgan Andersson), who has fallen in love with upper-class girl Kristina—portrayed by *schlager* star Carli Tornehave, popular in the late 1950s. Kristina loathes the lowlife *raggare* ruffians but cannot help falling for Svenne. The illusion of happiness shatters when Kristina is beat up and raped by Berra during an out-of-control party. Reality does catch up with Berra, but only after he assaults an innocent man and is forced to flee from the police. In an act of desperation, Berra kidnaps Kristina and takes refuge in an old house. When he realizes the game is over, he leaps to his death.

After the box office success of Olle Hellbom's *Raggare!* (see page 202) a few years before, Ragnar Frisk decided to try out the *raggare* genre himself. The result is an unbelievable turkey. Starting with the positives, Ernst-Hugo Järegård is upliftingly unpleasant in his portrayal of bad seed Berra. The scene where he forces himself on Kristina especially brings out his creepiness. Otherwise, any kind of tension or atmosphere is unfortunately wrecked by the cheery musical interludes that recur with annoying frequency. As far as *sensations* goes, there is not much apart from the rape, just a few naked breasts of swimming girls. Despite the drawbacks, this movie is one of the better showings by *Åsa-Nisse* brain-dead comedy veteran Ragnar Frisk—but that says more about the director than about the quality of *Raggargänget*.

Swedish raggare of the late 1970s must have been horrified and disgusted by the alternative title *Swedish Punks*, as it referred to their arch enemies, the safety-pin infested punks.

Alternative titles: *Raggen går...*; *Swedish Punks*

"Exposes all! Shows all!" Landmarks and ladies of the night come together in Rapport från Stockholms Sexträsk (Report from Stockholm's Sex Scene), *a mondo documentary of the back alleys of Sweden's capital city*

Courtesy of Klubb Super 8

Early ad for Raggare!: *"An honest and topical film that definitely concerns all of us!"*

RAPPORT FRÅN STOCKHOLMS SEXTRÄSK
[Report from Stockholm's Sex Scene]

(1974)

Director:

Arne Brandhild

Here's a documentary, very questionable in authenticity, about the legal sex market in Stockholm during the 1970s. Some obviously staged scenes from "nightclubs" and "live sex shows" are mixed with authentic enough interviews with prostitutes and nude models, and the movie inventories the porno stores, sex trade, and swinger clubs of the era. This might sound pretty daring, but the movie really is quite tame. The sex is pretty toned down, apart from some insane dildo masturbation in the final scene. Though Brandhild's movie is tactless in many ways, it is still highly recommendable—it's especially fun is to see all the long-lost seedy Stockholm locations where the old immoralities took place, now buried beneath the gloss and polish of fashionable high-end boutiques and important modern offices.

Arne Brandhild worked on a variety of questionable Swedish films, serving as editor on *I Död Mans Spår* (see page 95), cinematographer on *Ta Mej i Dalen* (see page 256), and producer of *AWOL – Avhopparen* (see page 29). The only thing he directed apart from *Rapport från...* was a short film called *Girlography*. I don't even want to think about the contents of that one—but I would bet it involves a collage of his own sexual encounters.

RES ALDRIG PÅ ENKEL BIUETT
[Never Travel on a One-Way Ticket]

(1987)

Director:

Håkan Alexandersson

Cast:

Mikael Samuelson
Thomas Lundqvist
Gert Fylking
Mats Flink
Peter Kneip
Ylva Törnlund

In a not-too-distant dystopian future, most humans live in the sewers underground. An illusionist, the Great Hassan (Thomas Lundqvist), proclaims that he has the power to teleport people to a divine place—an artificial paradise on earth. A private eye called the Investigator (Mikael Samuelson) is dispatched on a shady quest to discover the truth about the teleportation. Violent encounters follow, until the Investigator is eventually transported himself, at which point he realizes that the so-called paradise appears to be a an elaborate hoax. Things go from bad to worse when the paradise is fully revealed to be a human slaughterhouse.

This film from the infamous duo of director Håkan Alexandersson and writer Carl Johan de Geer (based on his novel *Kyss mej Dödligt* [Kiss me Deadly]) is a slow-paced and sinister art film dealing with many themes, from quasi-philosophical issues to pornography. The uneven acting is wooden, to say the least, and the female lead, Ylva Törnlund, especially leaves a poor impression—although she volunteers for blow jobs like there's no tomorrow. What the film lacks in pace and coherence, it makes up for with gore and nudity. The filmmakers have a lot of strange ideas. Notably, the Investigator tries to collect some evidence using psychoactive microdots transferred to him during intercourse, via magnetic material painted onto his dick. Trust me, it really works!

This esoteric film never found an audience in Sweden, and passed unnoticed after just a few screenings in art house theaters in Scandinavia. In fact, the film is not even mentioned in de Geer's 2008 autobiography.

However, actor Gert Fylking is a well-known radio and TV personality in Sweden, and a front-runner for the most uncouth cad in the country. Clad perpetually in a pink jogging suit, every year the wizened old party-crasher ruins the Nobel Prize announcements by screaming: "Finally!" when the prize for literature is announced. Likewise, he trashed a Clint Eastwood press conference by arriving dressed in Indian garb, demanding repayments. He can usually be found chasing the King of Sweden, shouting: "Hurray for the king!" I don't know how much Gert Fylking the world can take. Carl Johan de Geer, on the other hand, is a respected artist.

THE RETURN OF JESÚS, PART II

(1993)

The lingonberry western rides again! This romp in the Swedish sagebrush and deserts was made around 1993 by the small record label Birdnest, which suddenly made millions of dollars when the previously obscure punk band Dia Psalma skyrocketed to popularity and sold about 100,000 albums just in Sweden. With all the money, they covered their entire hometown of Köping in sand and shot a western including their friends and fellow musicians, from bands like No Fun at All, Millencolin, and Merciless.

This fair-weather windfall was shown once in 1996 in a rented theater, and then nothing was ever heard about it again. There is a soundtrack CD available as well, featuring bands like Charta 77, Stukas, Rövsvett, and Motorpsycho, they got that part right.

Director:
Mikael Katzeff
Cast:
Adam Alsing
Alice Bah
Carl Johan de Geer
Lena Endre
Johan Johansson
Micke Olsson

(1970)	# RÖTMÅNAD
Director:	## [Dog Days]

Director:

Jan Halldoff

Cast:

Ulla Sjöblom

Carl-Gustaf Lindstedt

Christina Lindberg

Ernst Günther

Eddie Axberg

Ulf Palme

Jan Blomberg

Curt L. Malmsten

Frej Lindqvist

Carl-Axel Elfving

Bo Halldoff

Ludde

Assar (Carl-Gustaf Lindstedt) is a kind, middle-aged man who enjoys a quiet life with his daughter (Christina Lindberg) in the Stockholm archipelago. Everything changes when his long-estranged wife suddenly shows up to put an end to the calm island life. The awful woman quickly turns the boathouse on the edge of the water into a sail-through brothel, where the daughter is sold to nasty old seafaring men. After Assar cannot take it anymore, he draws up a scheme to be rid of the wife. Unfortunately, he is not a very good murderer, and he ends up blowing the whole family to bits!

Jan Halldoff's daring *sensationsfilm* surely must have had more than a few audience members choking on their popcorn in 1970. Though *Maid in Sweden* (see page 153) was produced first, that film was not released until 1971, making this Christina Lindberg's silver screen debut after achieving notoriety as a pinup model. Though she only has a few lines, she is exposed throughout—it must have been very easy to cast male actors for this film. The photographer in one scene cannot help but gasp when he sees her perfect body. As we all know, Lindberg soon became queen of Swedish *sensationsfilms*. *Rötmånad* is high-quality Swedish sexploitation, complete with stupid humor and excruciating pacing punctuated by crazy misunderstandings. Starring Ludde as Ludde the dog.

Alternative title: *What Are You Doing After the Orgy?*

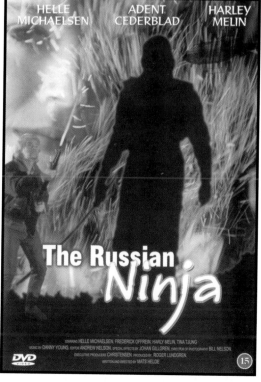

Clockwise from top left: Rötmånad
(Dog Days) *video box*
(not pictured: Ludde the Dog);

Rötmånad *promotional sheet;*

Frederick Offrein listlessly firing
into the air on the DVD cover
of Mats Helge Olsson's hopeless
Russian Terminator, aka The
Russian Ninja

(1990) # RUSSIAN TERMINATOR

Director:
Mats Helge Olsson
Cast:
Helle Michaelsen
Timothy Earle
Magnus Cederblad
Harley Merlin
Mats Huddén
Tina Ljung
Frederick Offrein
Ramon Sylvan

This lifeless combination of ninja action and some kind of James Bond spy affair is insanely boring, consisting of nothing but monotonous gunfights. Mats Helge Olsson had completely lost it by this point, and *Russian Terminator* would be one of his last efforts before retiring from a long career in ambitious low-budget moviemaking. However, he will always be remembered as a daredevil rebel who never followed the constricting conventions that still rule the Swedish film industry.

While other directors fell to their knees, pleading for funds for their projects, Olsson just threw himself into the action, and made movies totally detatched from any official cultural institution. This is why he remains—at least on an honorary basis—just as he describes himself: "Sweden's only 'professional' filmmaker."

Alternative title: *The Russian Ninja*

RYMDINVASION I LAPPLAND
[Space Invasion in Lapland]

(1959)

Director:
Virgil W. Vogel

Cast:
Sten Gester
Barbara Wilson
Robert Burton
Åke Grönberg
Bengt Blomgren
Gösta Prüzelius
Doreen Denning
Göran Asserlind
Ittala Frodi
Lars Åhrén
Brita Borg

"A curious thing lands among the mountains up by the National Border. This must be examined, and so the confusion begins with the discovery of a tall coarse-furred monster at least five meters tall who causes all kinds of trouble."—*Norrköpings Tidningar-Östergötlands Dagblad*

So the morning newspaper summarized events in this Swedish 1950s sci-fi flick. The movie is not all that sensational, but we do get a scene where a naked woman's body can be glimpsed through a shower curtain. The terrifying monster is actually an abominable snowman rather than some alien, and its appearance and actions were probably scariest to the filmmakers whose reputations were on the line.

In fact, a hairy giant would fit probably right in in Lapland. That area is kind of the Swedish equivalent of Alaska, a big piece of land in the freezing north where nobody ever wants to go. The very small population—roughly 80 percent male—spends its time drinking moonshine and threatening anyone who says anything nice at all about Stockholm.

Yet *Rymdinvasion i Lappland* remains one of very few Swedish sci-fi movies, remarkable for its boring dialogue and endless skiing. Charitably, this almost deserves to be be called a Swedish version of Ed Wood's classic *Plan 9 from Outer Space* (1959). Voice narration by the venerable John Carradine was inserted for a re-cut American version of the film.

Alternative titles: *Horror in the Midnight Sun*; *The Invasion of the Animal People*; *Space Invasion from Lapland*; *Space Invasion of Lapland*; *Terror in the Midnight Sun*

*The abdominable alien
snowman, unique to*
Rymdinvasion i Lappland
Courtesy of Klubb Super 8

*In the vast frostbitten north,
there is only one fool-proof
way to keep warm... From*
Rymdinvasion i Lappland
Courtesy of Klubb Super 8

RYTTARE I BLÅTT
[Rider in Blue]

(1959)

Director:
Arne Mattsson
Cast:
Annalisa Ericson
Gunnel Broström
Nils Hallberg
Gio Petré
Erik Hell
Lena Granhagen
Lennart Lindberg
Karl-Arne Holmsten
Mona Malm

At the Swedish Army's school of horse riding, a local legend named "the Blue Rider" mysteriously disappears. The combined forces of the army and the police can't seem to make much progress with the case, but by fortunate coincidence private investigator Kajsa Hillman (Annalisa Ericson) is attending a class at the school. (Her husband, John [Karl-Arne Holmsten], the main character of the Hillman series, is away on business for the entire length of the film, for some stupid reason.) She soon finds the body of the missing horseman, and unwinds threads of jealousy and envy among the soldiers. Things get confusing when someone dressed as the Blue Rider begins galloping around the premises. After a long, long while, another body turns up, and in the end Hillman solves the case—sort of.

The third installment in Arne Mattsson's five-part Hillman series is a slow-moving and unengaging letdown compared to its predecessors. The film contains far too little suspense, and way too much farcical comedy. Once again, Nils Hallberg is totally grating as Freddy. Even the murders pass with little fanfare, and thrills are hard to locate. The most daring sequence portrays a group of women sitting around in 1950s-style bathing suits—a sensation far less titillating than Mattsson's own films from a decade earlier. The saving grace is wonderful Gio Petré as the icy Git, and it's worth mentioning that this was the only Hillman film shot in Cinemascope. Nevertheless, *Ryttare i Blått* cemented Mattsson's enormous popularity, and before long he returned with *Vita Frun* (see page 276) to take full advantage of the public and critical acclaim.

SAMS
[In Agreement]

Director:

Calvin Floyd

Cast:

Christina Carlwind

Stig Törnblom

Jean-Jacques Lapeyronnie

Kent-Arne Dahlgren

Louise Tillberg

Gunilla Thunberg

Erik Hammar

Sara Gillborg

Mats Bergström

Gunilla Bergström

Lars Lennartsson

Lars Amble

Nine people—three couples, a single mom, and two kids—rent a house in the archipelago in order to start a big collective family and change their boring suburban lives. What starts as a new beginning with wine, singing, freedom, and sexual experimentation, soon morphs into a new kind of boredom. Frustration emerges in the intense intimacy, and great arguments erupt when cooperation and understanding break down. One of the girls runs away to Paris with one of the men, and the other relationships find themself ground down by jealousy and resentment. In the end, the players return to the collective, and some kind of reconciliation seems imminent.

This is a reasonably pleasant film wallowing in flowered wallpapers, colorful clothing, and tuneless acoustic prog music in the glorious 1970s. A number of corny sequences about guys who cannot cook and so on are mixed with semi-exploitative elements of sex, drinking, and nude shots of males and females alike. Even though the active ingredients are all set up for sensation, the film comes across as cozy rather than socially or creatively daring. A long, very boring sequence in Paris really kills the movie, however—surely it only exists in order to please the French coproducers.

The French were not pleased at all with the finished film, however, it was not the juicy sex film they had in mind. Without permission, they heavily reedited *Sams*, added several dirty porn sequences (allegedly shot by Torgny Wickman), and released the film as *The Voyeurs*. When the Swedish actors realized what had happened, they successfully sued producer Alvar Domeij for damages.

Alternative title: *The Voyeurs*

DEN NYA HILLMAN-THRILLERN

RYTTARE i BLÅTT

REGI: ARNE MATTSSON

ANNALISA ERICSON · BENGT BRUNSKOG · GUNNEL BROSTRÖM
NILS HALLBERG · MONA MALM · BJÖRN BJELVENSTAM
GIO PETRÉ · LENA GRANHAGEN · ERIK HELL · LAURITZ FALK
KOTTI CHAVE · LENNART LINDBERG samt KARL-ARNE HOLMSTEN

Sandrews

MANUS: FOLKE MELLVIG och LASSE WIDDING
FÄRGFILM – AGASCOPE

KENT-ARNE DAHLGREN · GUNILLA O. LARSSON
SOLVEIG ANDERSSON · CHRISTINA LINDBERG
TOR ISEDAL · ÅKE FRIDELL

Sängkamrater

Regi: GUSTAV WIKLUND · Foto: MAX WILÉN · Musik: BJÖRN ISFÄLT
Prod.: GUSTAV WIKLUND och CONCORDE FILM AB

FÄRG   pallas film

Clockwise from top left: The third of Arne Mattsson's Hillman movies, Ryttare i Blått (Rider in Blue)*;*

A movie of seemingly endless possibilities: Sängkamrater (Bedfellows)
Courtesy of Klubb Super 8*;*

Cozy, down-to-earth sensations in Sams (In Agreement)
Courtesy of Klubb Super 8

(1975)

SÄNGKAMRATER
[Bedfellows]

Director:
Gustav Wiklund
Cast:
Kent-Arne Dahlgren
Gunilla Ohlsson-Larsson
Solveig Andersson
Christina Lindberg
Tor Isedal
Åke Fridell
Leif Ahrle
Jan Sjödin
Jan-Olof Rydqvist
Per-Axel Arosenius
Karin Miller

Taxi driver Paul (Kent-Arne Dahlgren) is forced to bring his plastered dad home to live in the apartment he shares with girlfriend Marianne (Solveig Andersson). Their life together is a tangle of sex and madness, made worse when Marianne's baby sister Beryl (Gunilla Ohlsson-Larsson) also moves in with the chaotic gang. Photo sessions, odd parties, and lavish dinners are on the agenda, until one drunken night Beryl is picked up by a rich, dirty old man (Jan-Olof Rydqvist), who amuses himself by whipping her in his luxurious house. The young woman manages to flee but accidentally grabs a bundle of drugs on the way out the door. The owners of the drugs are hot on her trail, and after a number of close scrapes somebody sends the cops after the bad guys.

Sängkamrater takes place in a sleazy dream world of seemingly endless possibilities. The plot is hard to follow with all the abundant distractions in the form of half-naked girls, whip-crazed sleazebags (Rydqvist excels), and dirty photographers. The high points all feature Christina Lindberg, as she has sex in a stable and basically plays herself, exposing herself generously during a photo session. Veteran Tor Isedal is unfortunately wasted, mainly used for cheap comic relief in his role as a manservant. Slapstick elements stain the production a little, but overall the film is nicely paced.

The ungrateful press did not seem to enjoy the movie at all, not even an experienced sex film expert like Roland Klintberg. "I now understand what a poor actor has to go through when unemployment knocks. There is no other explanation for being involved with a production like this. Friends of hard-core porn do not need to bother, this stage on the porn barometer has passed long ago," he wrote in the daily paper *Skånska Dagbladet*.

Alternative title: *Wide Open*

SCORCHED HEAT

(1987)

When they were children, Erik (Martin Brandquist) and Steve (Harald Treutiger) accidentally burned their sadistic teacher Mr. Andersson to death when a practical joke got out of hand. Now an adult, Erik is tormented by visions of Mr. Andersson, and he grows more and more convinced that the old monster has been brought back to life. Erik seeks out Steve so they can join forces and uncover what is going on. Steve and his girlfriend arrive at Erik's house, only to find that Erik is but a shadow of his old self. Soon the dark forces around them start taking a toll on the couple, too. Everything comes to a ghoulish head during a lethal encounter with Mr. Andersson's burnt corpse.

One of very few attempts at a Swedish horror movie, and unbelievably inadequate at that, *Scorched Heat* does shake loose a few scares. Though not as spine-chilling as the dark, fateful chords that play whenever anything happens, there are a number of repulsive scenes with decaying zombies, messy puke, crawling worms, and other disgusting elements. All of these horrors are almost unprecedented in Swedish film history. Apart from the vulgarities, a couple things worth mentioning are the demonic voice-harmonizer effect, which seems duplicated from Sam Raimi's *Evil Dead* (1982), and the appearance of prominent TV host Harald Treutiger as one of the leading men. This film trained Treutiger well for his future role as the original host of *Robinson*, the Swedish reality show that was sold to America as *Survivor*.

Though *Scorched Heat* is far from a masterpiece, it is a delight in comparison to the ungodly work Treutiger has mustered since. For better or for worse, this film is a groundbreaking catastrophe.

Director:
Peter Borg

Cast:
Martin Brandquist
Harald Treutiger
Babs Brinklund
Johnny Harborg
Peter Borg
Dennis Castillo
Eric Elmerson
Michael Flanigan
Tony Ellis
Demba Conta
Anders Jönsson
Max Fredriksson

(1987) SILENT CHASE

Director:
Mats Helge Olsson
Cast:
Frederick Offrein

This is one of the lost gems of Swedish *sensationsfilms*, since no known copy exists, and not a single screening has ever been confirmed. Hardly any information can be found about the film, and I haven't heard of anyone who has actually seen it.

That said, *Silent Chase* is supposedly a Mats Helge Olsson thriller with a script by Anders Nilsson and music by Dough Anderzon, shot in the US and starring Frederick Offrein. Offrein himself reportedly can't remember the film, though, so consensus has grown that this is indeed just a trailer which has evolved into a film over the years, purely through the telling of its myth.

Olsson's career is filled with such controversy and mystery. Appearing on the Swedish TV program *Rekordmagasinet* in 1986, he talked about working on a film called *Fruktan i Skymningen* ("Fear of Dawn," according to the reporter, though the literal translation is "Fear at Twilight"). The script allegedly consisted of just two lines: "Two girls in a car. One madman in a forest." Based on that premise and on short clips that aired with the interview, the film sounds like a horror film in the slasher vein. Yet curiously, the film has never been mentioned outside that program—it might even be the production that later turned into *Silent Chase*.

The restless Mats Helge Olsson was known for reportedly starting to shoot new films whenever there was a coffee break in a production—script, instructions, real actors, or any direction at all could be damned. When he had real time off, Olsson shot many generic action scenes, which he later incorporated into his future efforts. In this way, he also spewed out promo films and trailers for films that never got made, hoping to secure overseas funding without really having anything to sell. Some of the scenes from such trailers eventually ended up in his other productions (particularly *Animal Protector,* see page 22).

The clouds of riddles lingers thick over the eternal maze that is the life's work of Mats Helge Olsson. The director himself sums up his method best: "I shoot mainly at night, because then you can't tell where you are."

SILVERHAWK

(1987)

"They Call Him SilverHawk. He's A Hunter... A Hero... A Heartbreaker."

After working as a cameraman on *The Ninja Mission* (see page 182), an actor and an editor on *Eagle Island* (see page 53), and a producer/cinematographer/editor on *War Dog* (see page 279), Anders Nilsson decided stop messing around and just direct a movie himself. The result was *Silverhawk*, which was apparently such a terrible mess that none of the Mats Helge Olsson regulars involved wants to remember it anymore. They probably burned the master.

Since *Silverhawk* reportedly turned out worse than even the most haphazard Mats Helge Olsson production, Nilsson had no other career choice but to go back to work as his mentor's right hand, serving on every single Mats Helge film after 1987. When Olsson was ousted from the movie industry in 1992, Nilsson's career naturally came to a complete halt.

Surprisingly, Nilsson made a comeback as a director in 1999 with the lousy but rather accomplished police thriller *Noll Tolerans*, first in a series of films about inspector Johan Falk. Nilsson has been in business ever since. Watch out for the pseudonyms Andrew Nelson, Anthony Newton, and Andy Nelson—they all most likely refer to this hack director.

Director:
Anders Nilsson

Cast:
Frederick Offrein
Taggen Axelsson
Jonas Karlzén
Timothy Earle
Karl-Johan Fröjd
Mats Huddén
Victoria Johansson
Tina Ljung
Ramon Sylvan

DET SISTA ÄVENTYRET
[The Last Adventure]

(1974)

Director:

Jan Halldoff

Cast:

Göran Stangertz
Ann Zacharias
Marianne Aminoff
Thomas Bolme
Åke Lindström
Birger Malmsten
Margit Carlqvist
Berto Marklund
Nils Hallberg
Ann-Sofie Nielsen

Off the hook from mandatory Swedish military service thanks to his odd behavior, young Jimmy (Göran Stangertz) takes a job as a substitute teacher of biology. During a school dance, he is seduced by sixteen-year-old student Helfrid (Ann Zacharias). They commence a blissful relationship, but the happiness doesn't last long. Jimmy's escalating jealousy leads to fits of rage. He slips further and further into full-blown psychosis, and eventually he is institutionalized.

This is an early Jan Halldoff production starring a very young Göran Stangertz. The even-younger Ann Zacharias walks away with the movie as the female protagonist. She has never looked more sensual than in the hands of this director, who gladly displays his ingenue's voluptuous physique. As far as sex scenes, one in particular where Stangertz takes Zacharias from behind over a kitchen sink is enormously sleazy. Otherwise, this only loosely qualifies as a *sensationsfilm*, but Zacharias's mere presence merits a recommendation.

Although Finland put a "16" rating on the movie, Swedish censors approved *Det Sista Äventyret* for viewing by everyone, the equivalent of a "G" rating. Take that, Walt Disney.

Alternative title: *The Last Adventure*

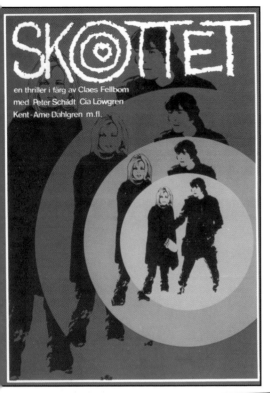

COBRA PRODUCTIONS presents SCORCHED HEAT
Starring MARTIN BRANDQVIST HAROLD TREUTIGER BABS BRINKLUND
and JOHNNY HARBORG as Mr Andersson
Special appearance by TONY ELLIS and MICHAEL FLANIGAN
Co-producer STEFAN PEGREUS
Director of Photography MATS HALLESJOE
Production Manager JOHAN A. DERNELIUS
Production assistent LEIF ALDERKMAN
Music by MARTIN BRANDQVIST
Mode designed by KAJ GROENBERG
Sound Director LARS HALLESJOE
Property Master ANDERS JOENSSON
Based on a story by SAM MANSFIELD and STEFAN SILVERGRUND
Screenplay by PETER BORG JOHAN A. DERNELIUS
and ANDERS JOENSSON
Mixed at FILMMIXARNA Laboratory FILMTEKNIK
Produced by KJELL LARSSON
Directed by PETER BORG
Copyright © MCMLXXXVII COBRA PRODUCTIONS INC.

DOLBY STEREO
IN SELECTED THEATRES

Det sista äventyret.

Efter en serie egendomliga episoder erhåller befälseleven Jimmy Mattson, 23, frisedel från militärtjänsten med den uttalade motiveringen:
— Ni är helt enkelt inte klok!

När Jimmy kommer hem försöker han slå sig fri från de två kvinnor som hittills dominerat hans liv.

Han får jobb som extralärare i biologi. På en skoldans blir han uppbjuden av Helfrid, 16, elev i första ring.

Hans förhållande med Helfrid utvecklas dramatiskt. Situationen blir ohållbar när rektorn ger honom rådet att "ta sitt förnuft tillfånga". Samtidigt får Jimmy veta att Helfrid varit otrogen.

Jimmys psyke spänns allt hårdare...

Filmen är baserad på Per Gunnar Evanders uppmärksammade roman "Det sista äventyret". Jan Halldoff har skrivit manus och regisserat. Producent är Hasse Seiden som också svarar för filmfotot. Jimmy spelas av Göran Stangertz. Helfrid av Ann Zacharias. Distribueras av Europa Film/Stockholm film.

Clockwise from top left: Skottet (The Shot) *video box;*

" ...hunted by a horrific evil that is stronger than death itself...," Scorched Heat *pulls no punches and pours it on thick;*

Highly informative Det Sista Äventyret (the Last Adventure) *poster*

SIV, ANNE & SVEN

Director:
Joseph W. Sarno
Cast:
Bosse Carlsson
Liliane Malmquist
Britt Marie Engström
Marie-Louise Fors
Eva Rönnklint
Britten Larsson
Peggy Holm

"The first film of its kind...*from Stockholm*," promised the marketing tagline to this film. "Make no mistake, what goes on is strictly 'No Holds Barred'!"

Of course, this is just another of American director Joe Sarno's dirty films about Sweden. Here we follow photographer Siv (Liliane Malmquist), who spends her days screwing her model Sven (Bosse Carlsson) and seducing her assistant Anne (Britt Marie Engström). Not much else happens—the two female protagonists play with each other's breasts while a slew of topless models parade through the workplace.

The actors, if you want to call them that, have a very hard time saying their lines. None of them seems to know English, but that doesn't detract much, since the film is basically plotless. After an hour and a half, everything just ends abruptly, as if the team simply ran out of film stock. Joe Sarno didn't run out of steam though — he continued to churn out these US/Swedish productions for years to come.

Alternative title: *Love in the Third Position*

SKÖNA JUVELER
[Nice Jewels]

(1984)

Director:
Hans Iveberg
Cast:
Lena Nyman
Kim Anderzon
Lars "Brasse" Brännström
Johannes Brost
David Wilson
Ernst Günther
Örjan Ramberg
Kent Andersson
Janne Carlsson
Carl-Gustaf Lindstedt
Margaretha Krook

This is one of the worst films ever to come from Sweden. No need to bother recounting the pathetic storyline. The only excuse for mentioning this at all is the novelty of a Swedish futuristic film noir. The producers probably saw *Blade Runner* (1982) and thought they could match Ridley Scott's masterpiece using a couple of surplus cardboard boxes and a bunch of comedy actors. Trust that this is exactly what they did, and also trust that it could never fucking work. What morons!

Director Hans Iveberg's career is one of the most mysterious of Swedish film history. His first film, *Göta Kanal* (1981), was a family comedy that remains to this day one of the most successful Swedish films ever. Then he made *Gräsänklingar* (see page 77), which is only memorable as Christina Lindberg's last film appearance. Next he made this abysmal mess, and finally he ended it all with *Enkel Resa* (1988), a film that hardly anyone saw. He should have quit while he was ahead—and how the hell did he get ahead in the first place?

SKOTTET
[The Shot]

(1969)

Director:
Claes Fellbom

Cast:
Peter Schildt
Cia Löwgren
Kent-Arne Dahlgren
Halvar Björk
Solveig Ternström
Harry Ahlin
Leif Ahrle
Tord Peterson
Hans Strååt
Gunel Wadner
Diana Kjaer

Young criminals Ronny (Peter Schildt) and Bertie (Kent-Arne Dahlgren) rob a weapons warehouse. Understandably, they can't wait to try out the booty. As they play around with the guns, however, Ronny accidentally shoots and kills Bernie, and an intense flight from the police commences. With his fourteen-year-old girlfriend Len (Cia Löwgren) by his side, Ronny flees the long arm of the law. The outlaws try hiding in a summer cottage, while they forge false passports in order to leave the country. Unfortunately, they continue digging themselves deeper into trouble, pulling off a number of clumsy robberies while the heroin-addicted Ronny suffers severe withdrawal symptoms. In the end, the couple hides at an old man's house in the countryside. The upstanding citizen notifies the police, and the couple surrender without resisting—their first smart impulse.

This late-'60s Swedish thriller is surprisingly high-quality. Constant unpleasant tension throughout is relieved not with gratuitous nudity, for once, but by a few relatively intense acts of violence. The harsh scene in which Len is sexually abused by a sweaty truck driver is especially nasty and raw. Also remarkable, and uncharacteristic of Swedish cinema at that point, is the movie's open depiction of narcotic use. The acting is good overall—most of the police are actual Swedish homicide cops who improvised their lines using standard police phrases. A heavily made-up Diana Kjaer, a familiar face in *sensationsfilms*, plays a roughed-up doper. The wonderfully young-looking Cia Löwgren is great in her starring role.

SKRÄCKEN HAR 1000 ÖGON
[Horror Has 1,000 Eyes]

(1970)

Director:
Torgny Wickman
Cast:
Solveig Andersson
Anita Sanders
Hans Wahlgren
Barbro Hiort af Ornäs
Willy Peters
Gösta Prüzelius
Suzanne Hovinder
Karin Miller
Bertil Norström
Maud Hyttenberg
Per-Axel Arosenius

After vacationing in the Canary Islands, preacher-man Sven (Hans Wahlgren) and his pregnant wife, Anna (Anita Sanders), return to the vicarage they call home in northern Sweden. Also living at their house is Anna's friend Hedvig (Solveig Andersson), who works as the maid. Strange events start to happen, as Anna sees visions and has problems sleeping. It appears Hedvig is involved with something mysterious as she performs strange rituals, groping Anna in her sleep and eventually seducing the parson's wife in an erotic encounter. The plot and the horror thicken with a couple of inexplicable deaths. As only the most wise old fortune-tellers could imagine, everything escalates into an erotic satanic mass. The spellbound preacher and his wife are forced to participate in an orgy with Hedvig, who has sworn herself to Satan.

This daring foray into the horror genre by sex film authority Torgny Wickman hides its thrilling elements among a bloody torrent of poorly executed clichés: close-ups of knives, impaled dolls, a car with no driver, and so on. When Hedvig cuts her and Anna's thumbs in order to seal a union in blood, the slicing actually comes across as authentic, and really seems to hurt! Naturally, in the following scene Hedvig slices Anna's breasts. Leaving the horror behind, the sex and eroticism are highly interesting. Wickman's other productions offer more nudity, but there is still plenty of naked skin on display. In honor of all things sensual, the girls parade around in short-shorts despite loads of snow outside and an obviously freezing environment!

The erotic high point is the lesbian meeting between the female protagonists, which almost becomes hypnotic in all its satanic ardor. Perhaps it is the dull first hour that makes the end seem so orgasmic, but it works. The score is stolen outright from the Italian thriller *The Strange Vice of Mrs. Wardh* (Sergio Martino, 1970), an added bonus to what is certainly the oddest film Torgny Wickman ever made. Reportedly the story is based on Wickman's own childhood, which explains a few things.

The critics hated it. "What purports to be a study in sex, horror, and magic turns out to be a study in incompetence," wrote Hans Schiller in *Svenska Dagbladet*.

Alternative titles: *Fear Has 1,000 Eyes*; *Natten Har 1000 Ögon*

"A study in horror, sex and magic!" summoned by Skräcken Har 1000 Ögon (Horror Has 1,000 Eyes)

Solveig Andersson exercises one of her less impressive witch powers on Hans Wahlgren and Anita Sanders in Skräcken Har 1000 Ögon

Courtesy of Klubb Super 8

SLAGSKÄMPEN
[The Inside Man]

(1984)

Director:
Tom Clegg

Cast:
Dennis Hopper
Hardy Krüger
Gösta Ekman
Cory Molder
(Kåre Mölder)
Celia Gregory
Lena Endre
Per Mattsson
Leif Ahrle
Torsten Wahlund
János Herskó
Lill Lindfors
Charlie Elvegard
Sven Melander

In 1984, with the Cold War at its absolute freezing point, the seas around Sweden are violated constantly by foreign submarines looking for military secrets. Swedish scientist Mandell (Hardy Krüger) invents a ridiculous submarine-seeking laser. He invites the minister of defense and some other suits to see his toy, including scene-stealing Dennis Hopper as CIA agent Miller. Unfortunately, Mandell's discovery is too successful. Thieves steal his laser and blow up his factory. The espionage case is assigned to Stig Larsson (Gösta Ekman), head of Swedish military intelligence, who quickly spots the telltale signs of an inside job. Larsson hires former boxer and ex-marine Thomas Kallin (Kåre Mölder) to infiltrate Mandell's group. The inspector entices Kallin with the promise of regaining his elite military job, which he lost in the first place for fist-fighting naked in the sauna. (Hey, it's Sweden!) Meanwhile, Hopper's CIA character wastes no time before ranting about how Sweden does everything wrong.

This loose adaption of Harry Kullman's novel was doomed from the start, as the staggering budget of two million Swedish kronor guaranteed that no profit could ever be made. Several initial backers realized this and stepped away. This brought a lawsuit from original leading man Bo Svenson—known from Italian B movies such as *The Inglorious Bastards* (Enzo G. Castellari, 1978), and dusted off by Quentin Tarantino for *Kill Bill: Vol 2* (2004). He received $25,000 for his trouble. When the project was resurrected without Svenson in 1983, he stepped up and sued again, this time for $1.5 million, of which he received nothing. While Svenson's lawyers were busy, the lead role went to Kåre Mölder, whose only previous part was as a horny teenager in *Mackan* (see page 151). The beleaguered film backers decided they would rename him Corey Molder to remake him as an international star. Well, that scheme failed.

Instead of a tense political thriller, this goofball story becomes a bumbled search for a stupid laser. The costly action sequences look as cheap as anything from Mats Helge Olsson. The dialogue is terrible—it must have been hard in educated Sweden to find so many actors unfamiliar with English. How Larsson could be head of military intelligence is a mystery. In one scene, he loudly discusses sensitive details of the case while buying wine at the government-run liquor store, surrounded by thirsty drunks. Evidently, the producers of *Slagskämpen* realized they were in trouble, and they stirred things up with some exposed breasts. Producer Calvin Floyd was a prolific director of *sensationsfilms*, who left Sweden in a rage after his *Ondskans Värdshus* (see page 188) recieved bad press. The self-proclaimed misunderstood genius probably saw the waste of valuable Swedish taxes on this pointless production as his minor revenge.

(1971) SMOKE

Director:
Torbjörn Axelman

Cast:

Lee Hazlewood

Cia Löwgren

Frank Sundström

Ulf Brunnberg

Christina Lindberg

Lena Edling

Miel Saan

Björn Lindberg

Gunnar Naeslund

Herman Howell

Håkan Serner

Jan Naliwajko

Badou Kasse

Axelle Axell

Monika Karlberg

Johannes Brost

Lindgren (Frank Sundström) is a ruthless CEO with a penchant for beating up cheeky employees and squeezing perky teen breasts. His nemesis among the workers is Smoke (Lee Hazlewood), the leader of some sort of hippie collective where a group of employees live. When the workforce goes on strike, Lindgren is forced to soften up, and he even allows his daughter to hang out with the hippies. At this point, the communal gang inexplicably buys a big batch of guns, which soon leads to a totally pointless killing. While battling with guns, a member of the collective is shot and taken to the emergency room. The rest of the crew steals a milk truck and storms the hospital, armed to the teeth, in order to free their companion. Meanwhile, a straggler gang member back at the homestead kills Lindgren's daughter, and in turn is killed by Smoke himself. The hippies, the cops, and boss Lindgren and his goons finally assemble for a bloody confrontation.

From its title to its endless communal bull sessions, this odd lethargic effort might as well have been directed by a bag of pot, but Torbjörn Axelman takes the credit. Acts of violence seem to occur totally randomly, while the dialogue mixes Swedish and English, further confusing the already confused audience. Apart from the violence, a refreshing and dirty exploitative scene depicts Lindgren groping his young mistress's perfect bosom while muttering angrily about his business. Abruptly, he finishes the scene by throwing the poor used girl out—all of a sudden she disgusts him! Among the actors, giants such as Ulf Brunnberg and fully-clothed-and-then-some Christina Lindberg stick out, as does young Johannes Brost as an arms dealer. Looming over the others with a giant square bandage plastered to his face the entire time, Lee Hazlewood plays the male lead. He is also credited as scriptwriter, and he performs the theme song. He is not only a sex symbol, but the only songwriter the world will ever need. "*Smoke* is a movie which lacks everything," wrote Hans Schiller in *Svenska Dagbladet*. What planet was Schiller from?

As if living out the scenario of this film, in 2008 at the age of seventy-six, director Axelman was involved in standoff against six guys who came to collect a debt. Still in command, Axelman shot one of the young bucks and trapped three others. He then barricaded himself in his house, threatening to set everything on fire. A violent confrontation with police followed, during which he was shot in the chest and the leg, but he was never jailed. Sweden just doesn't have the heart to treat a nice old guy that way.

SMUTSIGA FINGRAR
[Dirty Fingers]

(1973)

Director:
Arne Mattsson
Cast:
Peder Kinberg
Isabella Kaliff
Ulf Brunnberg
Heinz Hopf
Frank Sundström
Barbro Hiort af Ornäs
Lena Bergqvist
Jim Steffe
Ulf Palme
Claude Kazi-Tani
Jan-Olof Rydqvist

After drug addict Lotta (Lena Bergqvist) has a bad trip, she commits suicide by jumping out a window. Her brother Stefan (Peder Kindberg) is devastated, and together with his friend Jonas (Ulf Brunnberg), he looks closer into his sister's life. The two sleuths are soon on the tracks of a narcotics syndicate, and they quickly are in deeper trouble than they can handle. The syndicate stops at nothing when dealing with its enemies, sending henchmen to kill them and kidnap Stefan's girlfriend Tina (Isabella Kaliff). Against even the wishes of the crime bosses, she is drugged and raped by the dirtiest of the rugged gangsters. As the pursuit for the mobsters grows bloodier, an escalating number of people are killed, and the truth only seems to lead straight to society's elites. When the whole affair is finally revealed, Sweden's crime and corruption problems turn out to be even more frightening than anyone feared.

Director Arne Mattsson delivers this brutal and ruthless thriller. He claims to have taken inspiration and elements of the story from authentic police reports, and if that's true, Stockholm must have been a very unpleasant city during the early '70s. This is a merciless story of drugs, kidnapping, torture, perversion, prostitution, abuse, violence, and needless death. The violence in particular must have come across as highly extreme at the time—after all, the extreme sexuality in so many other Swedish films was like compensation for the repressed violence in the country's films, a total reversal of the situation in the US. The sequences where a man's face is torn to pieces by a razor-covered glove, and when a retarded gangster sexually abuses the drugged-out Tina, are just jarring. The movie is also daring regarding nudity, as when a prostitute pinches her nipples to get them stiff and perky.

The cast is overflowing with the crème de la crème of Swedish exploitation, notably the impressive Heinz Hopf and Ulf Brunnberg. *Smutsiga Fingrar* was initially blocked by the censors, but was later released on behalf of the Movie Reviewing Council. Mattsson later claimed that producer Inge Ivarsson had taken the liberty of deleting a few scenes, but what could he possibly have removed?

Mattsson's masterpiece was of course slaughtered by the press: "Even if you completely disregard artistic, moral, and other qualities, it is unreasonable that someone with the most basic knowledge in moviemaking can create something as sloppy and depressingly moronic as *Smutsiga Fingrar*," cried Maria Ortman in *Sydsvenska Dagbladet Snällposten*. Wrong again.

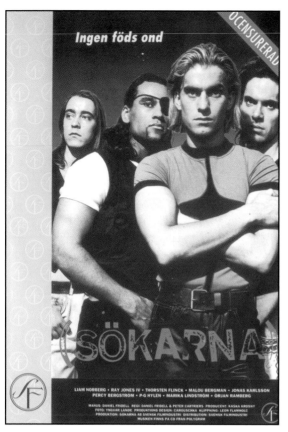

*Clockwise from top left:
Swedish scowls decorate the
uncensored home video release
of* Sökarna (The Seekers);

*Suicide, guns, needles, cocaine-
dipped pacifiers, black gloves,
strangulations, and Heinz
Hopf—1970s classic* Smutsiga
Fingrar (Dirty Fingers) *gets the
1980s video box cover treatment;*

Wacky Snacka Går Ju... (It's
Easy to Talk...) *poster*

SNACKA GÅR JU...
[It's Easy to Talk...]

(1981)

Director:
Ulf Andrée

Cast:
Carl-Gustaf Lindstedt
Håkan Serner
Margaretha Krook
Mona Seilitz
Bernt Lundquist
Kerstin Tidelius
Anna Godenius
Rolf Björkholm
Sten Johan Hedman
Per Matsson
Viveca Dahlén
Svante Odqvist

SG (Carl-Gustaf Lindstedt) and Acke (Håkan Serner) are two aging photographers, who, despite a lot of setbacks, still dream of the big scoop. The dream remains just a fantasy, though, as their life is a slow mixture of chess, whiskey, and idle chat. When the two accidentally get their hands on a couple of inappropriate photos of a female CEO, they are suddenly injected with energy. SG and Acke commence blackmailing the stressed-out CEO in order to earn a buck or two—they finally made the big time!

Snacka Går Ju... is totally based around Carl-Gustaf Lindstedt's acting talent, but fans should watch *Rötmånad* (see page 208) or *Mannen på Taket* (see page 163) instead. Lindstedt's portrayal of a photographer turning dirty in his elder years is far from exhilarating. The movie flashes a few penises at a Turkish bath to keep the audience awake, and offers a scene with a young and reasonably cute Mona Seilitz showing off her breasts for purely sensational reasons.

Mona Seilitz is famed for looking worn-out and drunk all the time, yet she is sexually potent. The superfluousness of the nude sequences are a perfect example of how sensationalism is used to increase the drawing power of an otherwise harmless and mundane movie. However, Mona's admirable effort does not completely shine up the dullness around her here.

(1993)

Directors:

Daniel Fridell

Peter Cartriers

Cast:

Liam Norberg

Ray Jones IV

Malou Bergman

Thorsten Flinck

Nina Lindén

Musse Hasselvall

Jonas Karlsson

Percy Bergström

Yvonne Schaloske

Marika Lindström

Örjan Ramberg

Jan Nygren

SÖKARNA
[The Seekers]

Appearing in 1993, *Sökarna* is one of the last Swedish exploitation movies of importance. Here's the "captivating" story of a young man who gets off on the wrong foot with society and drifts into the dangerous side of big-city life. The logic is simple: Bad conditions at home breed violent outbursts, which lead to a trip to the slammer, which introduces the lad to bad company, bringing drugs and weapons into the picture, which spawn more violence. Eventually, death comes knocking.

Sort of an unrelated follow-up to *Stockholmsnatt* (see page 246) with everything pushed to the limit, Daniel Fridell's feature film debut is an uncompromising and wild display of violence, drugs, filth, murder, and misery. A more dystopian portrayal of Stockholm has likely never been made. The movie hovers between two modes: fairly disturbing, and unbelievably laughable. This duality is reinforced by a cast that throws together ingenious actors (Jonas Karlsson, Örjan Ramberg) with lousy ones (Liam Norberg). All of them are in their twenties, playing teenagers. Best of all is nutcase Thorsten Flinck, an Ingmar Bergman favorite, as a sleazy lunatic jailbird. *Sökarna* often comes across as a giant ego trip for Norberg, who gets to run around and act out his bad-boy fantasies throughout the entire production.

It is baffling, considering the excess of insane shenanigans on display here, why the Swedish Film Institute agreed to back this production. The National Board of Film Classification—an institution that preapproves movies before release—demanded four minutes of cuts before the premiere, including a forced blow job (now restored in consumer releases). The film earned an extra dimension of credibility, as it turned out to be partially financed by Liam Norberg's involvement in the so-called 930 million coup, Sweden's largest-ever cash robbery. I saw this film for the first time the day before I moved to Stockholm, and I almost stayed in the beautiful country, safe from Sweden's roving gangs of violent criminals.

Alternative title: *The Searchers*

...SOM HAVETS NAKNA VIND
[...As the Naked Wind of the Sea]

(1968)

Directors:
Gunnar Höglund
Ulf Palme
Cast:
Hans Gustafsson
Lillemor Ohlson
Anne Nord
Barbro Hedström
Gio Petré
Ingrid Swedin
Barbro Hiort af Ornäs
Gudrun Brost
Siw Mattson
Stephan Karlsén
Charlie Elvegård

Leander (Hans Gustafsson) drops out of a Swiss music school and returns to Sweden. Upon his arrival, he is instantly trampled by a horde of love-thirsty women, all easily seduced by his charm and virtuoso violin playing. After he covers every girl in the surrounding area, he crowns his era of conquest by having sex with his own half sister. All's well that ends well.

This wholesome-seeming movie includes many daring depictions of sexual fantasies and real encounters, and serves up vast amounts of nudity and sex scenes. Many of the erotic episodes come in the form of delirious dreams and flashbacks—and a couple of these are considerably sleazy, as when Leander has sex with his half sister. Leander tearing a virgin's clothes off before taking her is another heated moment. More dirty than hot, however, is a flashback of another virgin being ravaged by a mentally retarded farm boy, eagerly cheered on by his mother and a maid. Adding to the madness, a couple of copulating cows indolently watch the couple, and the girl at the center of all the attention ends up enjoying the rough treatment—sensational, to say the least!

Aftonbladet's reviewer Jürgen Schildt did not appreciate the smudge on Sweden's pristine silver screen: "To find anything of use in Gunnar Höglund's movie, you have to rummage like a pig looking for truffles." Banned in Finland and X-rated in the US, this was just another family flick in Sweden, rated "15" for kids fifteen and up.

Alternative title: *One Swedish Summer*

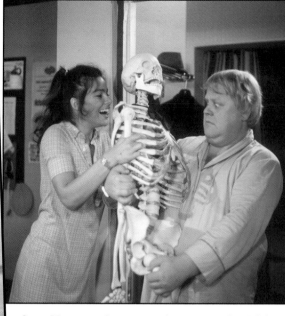

Harriet Andersson in Sommaren med Monika (The Summer with Monika)

Sune Mangs as the nervous doorman at the girls' dorm in Som Hon Bäddar Får Han Ligga (As She Makes the Bed, He Lies in It)
Courtesy of Klubb Super 8

Working on his thesis. Bed made quite comfortably for Harald Leipnitz in Som Hon Bäddar Får han Ligga
Courtesy of Klubb Super 8

Hans Gustafsson wooing girl in ...Som Havets Nakna Vind (...As the Naked Wind of the Sea)
Courtesy of Klubb Super 8

SOM HON BÄDDAR FÅR HAN LIGGA
[As She Makes the Bed, He Lies in It]

German sociologist Hans Praterweiss (Harald Leipnitz) arrives in Stockholm in order to perform studies that will dispel the myth of Sweden as a stronghold of sex and sin. Why? Nobody will ever know. Maybe the German sense of national pride was upset, and they wanted to claim the dubious title of sleaziest nation in Europe?

In any case, most of Hans's field research takes place at a dormitory—probably a bad idea. Letting his guard down like so many others after inhaling the cold, gray Swedish atmosphere, the social scientist becomes more interested in getting it on with young girls than in trying to support his thesis. (In fact, that was probably the idea of this German-Swedish coproduction all along—getting down with some crazy blonde girls.)

This sex and slapstick *sensationsfilm* features a cast of semi-big actors, a couple of daring scenes, and some female eye candy. Overall the movie is too repetitive and best forgotten. Gunnar Höglund proved he could do better with movies such as ...*Som Havets Nakna Vind* (see page 233).

Alternative titles: *Svensk Synd – Finns Den?*; *Do You Believe in Swedish Sin?*; *Swedish Sin*

(1970)

Director:
Gunnar Höglund
Cast:
Harald Leipnitz
Diana Kjaer
Vera Tschechowa
Lil Terselius
Helena Mäkelä
Annabella Munther
Sune Mangs
Lissi Alandh
Cia Löwgren
Jarl Borssén
Håkan Westergren
Sten Ardenstam
Börje Mellvig
Lars Lennartsson
Bert-Åke Varg

(1953)

Director:

Ingmar Bergman

Cast:

Harriet Andersson

Lars Ekborg

Dagmar Ebbesen

Åke Fridell

Naemi Briese

Georg Skarstedt

John Harryson

Åke Grönberg

Gösta Ericsson

Gösta Gustafson

Sigge Fürst

Gösta Prüzelius

SOMMAREN MED MONIKA
[The Summer with Monika]

Two working-class youths (Harriet Andersson and Lars Ekborg) flee the city in a rowboat and soon experience an intense and dazed summer full of erotic adventures.

Along with Arne Mattsson's *Hon Dansade en Sommar* (see page 92), this Bergman movie is one of the pioneer works of Swedish *sensationsfilms*. In the early '50s, the straightforward sexuality was considered shocking, and the Swedish film censors shortened the running time a bit, cutting some scenes of sex and violence. Today, the film comes across as very innocent. "It was not violent porn—it was not rabid porn," actress Harriet Andersson correctly declared in later days.

Attracted by the film's groundbreaking use of nudity, American distributor Kroger Babb snapped up the film, sight unseen, marketing it along the lines of a Russ Meyer picture. Not impressed with Bergman's talents as a director, they cut nearly forty minutes to create an hour-long drive-in film. The heathens further punched up Bergman's efforts with some nude inserts by hack director Jerald Intrator, and added a jazzy score by Les Baxter that really does makes the film sound like a porno movie!

Alternative titles: *Monika*; *Monika, the Story of a Bad Girl*

SOMMAREN MED VANJA
[The Summer with Vanja]

(1980)

Director:
Heinz Arland
Cast:
*Yvonne Jonsson
(Oili Viirta)*
Mona Jörgensson
*Bertil Svensson
(Sven Olof Eriksson)*
Harry Andersson
Steven Collins
Kurre Levin
Ulla Leinonen
Kerstin Williamsson
Orvar Pederson
Inger Olsson

This lovely story involves young Vanja (Oili Viirta) and her summer romance with married man Börje (Bertil Svensson). Along the way she has time for several other sex adventures—like a romp with some guys on a road trip. The car they do it in is so small that one of them has to stick his head up through sunroof hatch as he humps! Vanja also sleeps with Bertil's son. After a whole string of sexual events, the great summer ends with a decadent group sex party.

Against all odds, this classic Swedish porn became a huge success after its premiere. In reality, the movie is just an assortment of eternally boring sex scenes performed by less-than-attractive actors. The highlights are the jazzy soundtrack, some nice late-1970s settings, and (on most versions) an unbelievably listless dubbing that must be heard to be believed! Although she wasn't deemed attractive enough to appear on the video box, Oili Viirta rose to some kind of porn stardom in Sweden at the time. Sadly, she later demolished that image by gaining several pounds and starring in a variety of dirty amateur productions.

While Viirta passes her august years scrounging for beers in Stockholm dive bars, the producers probably fared better. *Sommaren med Vanja* reportedly remains Swedish cinema's most successful sex film ever. It was certainly the last to play in sold-out theaters, as videocassettes soon arrived, bringing a new fortress of solitude for masturbation professionals and amateurs alike.

SOMMARENS TOLV MÅNADER
[The Twelve Months of Summer]

(1988)

Director:

Richard Hobert

Cast:

Hans Mosesson
Göran Stangertz
Halvar Björk
Pierre Lindstedt
Eddie Axberg
Pär Ericson
Bernt Ström
Bergljót Árnadóttir
Kajsa Reingardt
Sven Lindberg
Jan Tiselius

Somewhere in Sweden, a secret government experiment is underway. Personnel surrounding the project lose their minds, and the entire area is evacuated. Desperate to protect their ill-conceived project, the unscrupulous scientists summon six veteran construction specialists away from long-term projects in dangerous and distant places. All they are told is that they will be away for twelve months, and they will be paid ten years' salary for their efforts. The workers arrive blindfolded in a summery location, although the rest of Sweden is in the grip of total winter. The assignment makes no sense, but regardless, they begin building bogus constructions with no purpose whatsoever. Slowly but surely, the workers' mental health is tested by hallucinations and panic attacks. When one of the men disappears in the middle of the night, the others realize the weird climate isn't the only cause for alarm.

Though not altogether sensational, this unusual Swedish attempt at science fiction has a dark and tense atmosphere. The film does not rely on visual excess, but does offer a fair share of nudity. Unfortunately, it is the 1980s. Forget about teenage girls bouncing around like the 1970s—this era was ruled by overweight old men running around with their willies out. The best of the willy-flashers is Pierre Lindstedt as Bryggarn, a sleazy but jovial character who only cares about drinking, porno magazines, and bragging about hookers. In one mad scene, the scientists treat the workers to a sinful *Lucia* procession of Asian prostitutes in order to boost their morale. So what is the secret experiment, anyway?

The most sensational thing about this made-for-TV movie is that utterly talentless director Richard Hobert was involved in something decent for once. The rest of his career was catastrophic to any rational person. However, the Swedish Film Institute snubbed common sense and granted the bastard millions and millions of dollars taken from the pockets of hardworking taxpayers, enabling Hobert to direct a slew of films no one ever cared about. The zenith of his rotten career was the 2004 movie *Tre Solar*, a mediocre crap fest of bad wigs and abysmal acting that famously left people laughing in the theater aisles. Any other director would have quit, but Hobert continued as if nothing had happened. Discussing the problems of the Swedish film industry in 2004, Lady Gaga/Metallica video director (and ex-drummer of Bathory) Jonas Åkerlund urged everyone to lay off Hobert: "It's not his fault he is allowed to direct movies." He hit the nail on the head.

SOUND OF NÄVERLUR
[The Sound of the Birch Trumpet]

(1971)

Director:
Torbjörn Lindqvist
Cast:
Sten Ardenstam
Eva Rydberg
Mayny Mikaelsson
Rolf Andersson
Rebecca Pawlo
George Thunstedt
Rune Halvarsson

When a famous American astronaut arrives in Rättvik in the rustic province of Dalarna, he is greeted by an awaiting delegation of *dalmasar* and *dalkullor*—local men and women dressed in traditional costumes. After throwing some money around and chasing all the most beautiful girls in the area, the American gets into trouble. Before long, he is forced to flee the police on skis in the classic fashion of Gustav Vasa—the sixteenth-century founder of modern Sweden. Gustav is mythified for, among numerous other adventures, having skiied across Dalarna to escape the henchmen of the mythologized Christian the Tyrant of Denmark.

This movie is extremely corny slapstick that exploits such *dala* customs as midsummer dance, folk music, folk costumes, and full-on *raggare* boozing. The most provocative scene has Eva Rydberg stripping down to her bra, panties, and funny accent, and if that does not sound exhilarating, well . . . it is not. The soundtrack is pretty decent, filled with Hammond organ, sitar, and fuzz guitars. With this mud puddle of a movie as well as the catastrophic *Grossisten* (see page 80) on his résumé, Torbjörn Lindqvist remains in the running for the worst Swedish director of all time. Even the *raggare* couldn't save him.

However, nothing can take away from the the beauty of Dalarna, arguably the most Swedish region in all Sweden, with its many folk traditions, its funny accents, very old history, lovely nature, wonderful *dalkullor* girls, and top-quality moonshine. For those interested in fast music and very short songs, Dalarna is also the birthplace of grindcore, as genre godfathers Asocial recorded their 1981 demo tape "How Could Hardcore Be Any Worse?" there in the town of Hedemora.

Alternative titles: *Kalla Mig Kulla*; *Den Vilda Jakten på Astronauten*

Clockwise from top left: *No-frills early* Sound of Näverlur (The Sound of the Birch Trumpet) *video box boasts, "Sten Ardenstam is the Louis de Funes of Swedish cinema";*

Johnny Harborg and a ghost kid haunt the US video release of Sounds of Silence;

Someone more attractive than Oili Viirta fills in for her on the cover of Sommaren med Vanja (The Summer with Vanja)

SOUNDS OF SILENCE

(1989)

After Los Angeles resident Peter Mitchell (Peter Nelson) unexpectedly inherits a house from an unknown Swedish aunt, he heads across the Atlantic with wife Sarah (Kristen Jensen) and her son Dennis (Dennis Castillo) to check out the new property. Upon arrival to Sweden, chilling things start to happen—for starters, the car breaks down near an old orphanage. Dennis hears strange noises, despite the fact that he is deaf. When the family finally finds the house, they discover not a humble Swedish cabin but a big mansion, maintained by housekeeper Margareth (Vanja Rodefeldt). She relates the tragic story of Peter's late aunt Annie (Elsa Gåstrin), who as a young girl birthed a son out of wedlock, Bill. Times were hard, and she had to move to the big city, leaving baby Billy at the sad local orphanage. All the children there died from a mysterious disease, and Annie never recovered from the guilt. Unmoved by this tragic tale, the Americans try to enjoy some fresh country air. Dennis sees mysterious figures lurking around in the forest and the house. He realizes that all the dead children from the orphanage need his help. Will the old tormentors win again, or will the orphans finally get their revenge?

Director:
Peter Borg

Cast:
Peter Nelson
Kristen Jensen
Dennis Castillo
Rico Rönnbäck
Gunnar Öhlund
Vanja Rodefeldt
Troy Donahue
Johnny Harborg
Elsa Gåstrin
Jonas Ivarsson
Peter Borg
Bruno Desire
Hasse Andersson

This pretty obscure piece of Swedish horror comes from the same people that gave us *Scorched Heat* (see page 217). Aiming for pure scares, they were overeager and showed the ghost children in the very first scene, breaking the old rule of not revealing the monster too soon. The sad orphans reappear every five minutes, until they become more familiar than most of the wooden characters. Far more disturbing than these demonic children is hilariously overacting Johnny Harborg as creepy plumber Frank. When not attending to the malfunctioning kitchen sink, this sleazy lunatic spends his time trying to rape Sarah and kill Annie's attorney with a sledgehammer to the head. Old American heartthrob Troy Donahue appears in a minor role as Peter's attorney—lots of lawyers in this horror film. He must have owed a lot of alimony. All in all, *Sounds of Silence* is a hidden gem in Swedish film history. The crew ekes a lot from a small budget, making a very cheap movie look just kind of cheap. The charming photography employs plenty of zooms and pans as the camera rushes through long, dark corridors. Periodically, a dark, tense atmosphere descends over the movie. Sadly, the overblown score is as loud and thrilling as humanly possible. Almost immediately, this film fell into obscurity, and Borg never directed again. It is probably the last watchable Swedish horror movie until the wonderful *Låt den Rätte Komma In* (Tomas Alfredson, 2008) came out almost two decades later.

(1987)

Director:

Mats Helge Olsson

Cast:

Mats Huddén

Sune Mangs

Bert-Åke Varg

Linda Olsson

Rebecca Olsson

Rasmus Kronqvist

Melker Jadenberg

Eva Friberg

Heinz Fritsche

Mats Helge Olsson

SPÖKLIGAN
[The Ghost League]

After the dreadful *Eagle Island* (see page 53), Mats Helge Olsson hooked up with a fellow maverick director, Finland's Renny Harlin, starring as a priest in Harlin's *Born American* (1986). But whereas Harlin soon escaped to America to marry Geena Davis and direct such hits as *Die Hard 2* (1990), *Cliffhanger* (1993), and *Deep Blue Sea* (1999), Mats Helge Olsson was shipped straight back to Sweden.

Seeming to be at a creative loss—a usual situation for this ultra-productive director—Olsson very unwisely decided to make a scary movie for children using the regular faces from his action films, plus a few bigger names like Sune Mangs and Bert-Åke Varg. The result is, of course, awful—far worse than Bo A. Vibenius's attempt at entertaining kids almost two decades earlier. Instead of getting his foot into the legitimate Swedish film business, Mats Helge effectively alienated himself for good with this mess. The film was never granted a theatrical release, and he soon returned to making senseless action films. The mighty Mats Helge Olsson himself can be spotted here in the role of Böna. Apart from that, there is nothing too see in this film except a bunch of kids running around screaming.

It doesn't help matters at all that the title itself is basically a crass attempt to cash in on *Ghostbusters* (Ivan Reitman, 1984). If that seems like a stretch, please consider that the full Swedish title of that blockbuster was *Ghostbusters – Spökligan*. Case closed.

STENANSIKTET
[The Stone Face]

(1973)

Director:
Jan Halldoff
Cast:
Jan Blomberg
Ann-Mari Adamsson-Eklund
Annika Levin
Per Eklöv
Leif Möller
Ted Gärdestad
Mats Robbert
Bo Halldoff
Mari Lundin
Evert Granholm
Bert-Åke Varg

Harry Eriksson (Jan Blomberg) becomes involved in local politics after his son dies and his wife is committed to a mental institution. Disgusted by the cynicism he sees in the corridors of bureaucracy, he sets out on a personal vendetta against ruthless politicians. To do his deadly bidding he hires a gang of disillusioned youths, who otherwise mostly kill time by beating up alcoholics, harassing senior citizens, popping pills, and overturning cars. In fact, that's how they meet—the youths overturn his car one afternoon because he runs over a beer can they were kicking around.

Under Harry's command, the gang turns into a merciless killing platoon that efficiently wipes out his political antagonists. As it turns out, Harry's power over the gang is not as strong as he thought, and the eerie mob of perfect blonde Swedish pubescents ends up stabbing him to death after an argument over money. They flock, expressionless, toward violence, like a nihilistic and modern version of the spawn of Midwich from classic Hammer horror film *Village of the Damned* (Wolf Rilla, 1960). As final credits roll, we see that the suburb is now completely deserted, as all the inhabitants have fled their inhospitable environment.

Stenansiktet is an astoundingly dirty movie, in which alienation and boredom are displayed in unpolished, brutal form. The indifferent kids who kill people without remorse are depicted with frightening accuracy, and the dystopian mood is genuinely chilling. Such a twisted atmosphere reinforces already bizarre scenes like one where a small crying kid is pelted with beer cans, or the unforgiving murder scene early in the film where a man is drowned in a tub. The most heartless scene, however, has a very young girl being violently undressed in the empty lot of a demolished building. Before she is even fully stripped, the gang yells at her and abandons her. Add a script full of dialogue that is hard as nails and grim, plus some exceedingly cold locations in the Stockholm suburb Skärholmen (birthplace of death metal band Entombed) while it was still mostly under construction, and you have yourself a masterpiece. This is Halldoff's most interesting, and best, movie.

(1969)

Director:

Tor-Ivan Odulf

Cast:

Anders Petersen
Lena Madsén
Nina Kajtorp
Christina Stenius
Hasse Andersson
Mårten Moberg
Janine Söderhjelm
Anita Lönn
Susanne Valentin
Miriam Julin
Linda Julin

STOCKHOLMSSOMMAR
[Stockholm Summer]

A young, insecure Stockholm man reflects on his life—or at least his lousy sex life. He gets laid sometimes, but all he can think about is whether he really does satisfy the women. To clear his mind, he leaves for the Canary Islands and gets it on with tanned beauties. Even in the lap of paradise, the miserable ingrate still cannot clear his mind of girls he has known in the past.

Swedish beat author Tor-Ivan Odulf's only feature film is a curious visual meditation on sexuality with voice-over narration. This directorial debut (and swan song) was smashed to pieces by the critics of the day: "The movie is a catastrophe from beginning to end," warned Rune Struck in *Aftonbladet*. "There are no extenuating circumstances."

Director Odulf had only worked in the cinema world once before, playing the bit role of "angry man" in the boring film *Mirage* (1959). He died in 1980.

*Paolo Roberto's mug
on the DVD cover
of* Stockholmsnatt
(Stockholm Night). *Note
the policeman learning
a lesson in kicker rage*

*Jan Halldoff's ruthless
masterpiece* Stenansiktet
(The Stone Face)

STOCKHOLMSNATT
[Stockholm Night]

(1987)

Director:
*Staffan
Hildebrand*

Cast:
*Paolo Roberto
Vincenzo Roberto
Ellen Roberto
Ian Roberto
Quincy Jones III
Camilla Lundén
Jonas Rasmusson
Niklas Dahlqvist
Liam Norberg
Lena Sjögren
Karl Dyall*

Paolo Roberto, considered one of the most dangerous youths in Sweden, plays himself in this dramatization of real events in the teen gang underworld of late-'80s Stockholm. Paolo and his buddies sleep all day, practice martial arts in the evening, and then fight, rob, and vandalize all night long. They kick old people and phone booths—nothing is safe. As the violence escalates, Paolo meets a girl. After she throws his gift of ill-gained jewelry into a bowl of soup, he realizes he should start a new life and end his destructive ways. He manages to woo the girl, and everybody is happy when all scores are settled with a friendly dance-off between kickers at a youth discotheque.

In 1986, the telephone company Televerket initiated the Stoppa Sabbet (Stop the Vandalism) campaign to counteract attacks on pay phones. Swedish schoolkids were ordered to draw pictures portraying their feelings about the pointless destruction. (I did it—this was as universal and mandatory as Swedish military service.) The best drawings appeared on the covers of local phone books. The campaign also spawned this movie, which was shown in schools to every single child in Sweden. Instead of inspiring respect for private property, this social engineering experiment backfired badly, starting an aggravating breakout of brawls nationwide. Everyone suddenly wanted to wreak havoc and fight. Entire auditoriums of Swedish kids jumped to their feet cheering when the movie kickers assault the police.

History aside, *Stockholmsnatt* is an embarrassing story acted out by lousy amateurs, in which fighting kids are portrayed more like heroes than villains. Since Paolo Roberto's immigrant background is constantly referenced (his family migrated from Italy), the movie also fueled the fires of xenophobia. I have a hard time imagining a public awareness campaign going more wrong. Even the Swedish capital recieved a black eye, as people around the country witnessed this ruthless depiction of Stockholm and stayed home in fear.

The movie made no difference—violence today is much worse. Director Hildebrand's career was all but finished. Far from abandoning violence, star Paolo Roberto became a successful boxer, then tried politics. He still turns up on TV, spouting off meaningless opinions. He also has a cameo in *The Girl Who Played with Fire* (Daniel Alfredsson, 2009), the sequel to *The Girl with the Dragon Tattoo* (Niels Arden Oplev, 2009). If he seems like a terrible actor, he is not acting; he is just himself, having trouble speaking even the simplest of sentences. Liam Norberg, who portrayed antagonist Mange, starred in the similar *Sökarna* (see page 232), funded by bank robberies he pulled off himself. As for the poor phone booths —who the hell remembers them today?

Alternative title: *The King of Kungsan*

STRANDHUGG I SOMRAS
[Shore Raid Last Summer]

(1972)

Director:
Mikael Ekman

Cast:
Annie Birgit Garde
Stellan Skarsgård
Siv-Inger Svensson
Börje Nyberg
Monica Ekman
Kent-Arne Dahlgren
Linda Lidbrink
Britt Åkesson
Gun Åkesson
Kerstin Kull

Young photographer Erik (Stellan Skarsgård) heads out to the beautiful archipelago of thousands of islands spreading out from Stockholm to enjoy the few short weeks of sunny Swedish summer. He finds himself on an island, where he meets the mature Gudrun (Annie-Birgit Garde), and together they enjoy an erotic adventure. Right after meeting Gudrun, Erik saves young Sonja (Siv-Inger Svensson) from drowning, and they fall in love. Difficulties occur when our hero realizes that Sonja is the daughter of Gudrun—not to mention that Erik's sister is having an affair with Sonja's father. Erik is forced to abandon his newfound love, but when all parties bumps into one another the following winter, they emerge from the confusion in triumphant love.

Like *Sommaren med Vanja* (see page 237) after it, this is a typical Swedish summer saga where naked butts are the strongest selling point. Young Stellan Skarsgård's ego must have recieved a considerable boost after the actor got the chance to fool around at length with Annie Birgit Garde as well as Siv-Inger Svensson. Director Mikael Ekman's totally carefree attitude toward male nudity extends to several inspections of Skarsgård's nude body. "Stellan Skarsgård mostly runs around and shows off his willy," *Expressen*'s Jonas Sima subtly put it. Prepare for a bird's-eye view of the point of origin of Skarsgård's son—*True Blood* actor Alexander Skarsgård.

Wonderful music by Charles Dieden and Anders Henrikson sets the relaxed mood perfectly, and the only drawbacks are the reoccurring bits of broad comedy and the sometimes confusing narrative. Despite those minor details, Ekman's erotic summer flirt is definitely worth a roll in the hay.

Alternative title: *Raid in the Summer*

Early, innocent sensations in Susanne
Courtesy of Klubb Super 8

Stellan Skarsgård, running around showing off his willy in Strandhugg i Somras (Shore Raid Last Summer)
Courtesy of Klubb Super 8

SUSANNE

(1960)

Beautiful but shy teenager Susanne (Susanne Ulfsäter) explores adult life during a hot Swedish summer. Her friend Bibbi (Rosalie Börjesson) takes her dancing, and Susanne meets slightly older boy Olle (Arnold Stackelberg) and falls in love. The couple's lifestyle is pretty wild, and Susanne ends up seriously hurt in a car accident. During a long period of unconsciousness, she experiences several odd hallucinations; when she wakes up, her personality is totally changed. Gone is the shy girl, and taking her place is a cocky and self-assured rebel who takes orders from no one. The sweet life ends when Susanne gets pregnant, and she and Olle are forced to marry. As time passes, the more worldly Susanne appreciates her new life, as she finally understands what responsibility is all about.

This is an awkward portrayal of a young blonde learning about life pretty quickly, moving from heavy petting, cool cars, drunken fights, and dances straight to marriage and childbirth. The film shows off one of Susanne Ulfsäter's breasts, but gets more graphic and uncomfortable with a bloody surgery scene. In one of Susanne's dream sequences, she and her parents witness Olle raping her. The acting and direction are pretty weak, and the narrative is oddly constructed—a big part of the movie is devoted to the aftermath of the accident, a period when nothing happens. As a harmless movie about youth gone wild and immediately suffering permanent consequences, *Susanne* definately has its moments.

Director:
Elsa Colfach
Cast:
Susanne Ulfsäter
Arnold Stackelberg
Rosalie Börjesson
Catrin Westerlund
(voice-over only)
Kristina Adolphson
(voice-over only)
Björn Bjelvenstam
(voice-over only)
Ellika Mann
Torsten Lilliecrona
Bengt Blomgren

(1992)

Director:

Rumle Hammerich

Cast:

*Tova Magnusson-
Norling*

Figge Norling

Björn Kjellman

Liv Alsterlund

Malin Berghagen

Niklas Hjulström

Lars Green

Agneta Ekmanner

Marie Göranzon

Reine Brynolfsson

Björn Granath

Thomas Roos

Gunnel Fred

SVART LUCIA
[Black Lucia]

Mikaela (Tova Magnusson-Norling) is a young, beautiful student who happens to be in love with one of her teachers. She starts writing wildly erotic essays for him, and he responds by living out her fantasies with other women. Soon the relationship becomes more obsessive, as Mikaela dreams up more dangerous stuff and starts spying on her teacher. At the same time, nasty events start to happen around the school—before long Mikaela finds herself living within a nightmare.

Svart Lucia was advertised aggressively at the time of its release, winning lots of local attention due to the rarity of something as unusual as a homegrown Swedish horror thriller. The film revels in Euro-horror clichés such as fluent camera work, vivid colors, clanging sound effects, dark hallways, and even black gloves. But that doesn't translate to any real suspense here. The compulsive sexual part of the story is more successful, although apart from a shot of a naked guy the eroticism is pretty restrained. Overall this is a flawed film that doesn't tremendously shock, excite, or arouse. However, one particularly startling moment involving a mutilated cat would have made the late Italian horror maestro Lucio Fulci proud.

On the whole, since this film is primarily meant to be a mainstream drama rather than sheerly a vehicle for shocks and sensations, it clearly anticipates the end of the *sensationsfilms* era.

Clockwise from top left: Tuva Magnusson-Norling on the poster of Svart Lucia (Black Lucia)*;*

Diana Dors exploiting someone else's body for a change, on the American poster for Swedish Wildcats*;*

Swedish Wildcats, *too sexy even by Swedish standards*

(1980)

SVERIGE ÅT SVENSKARNA
[Sweden for the Swedes]

Director:

Per Oscarsson

Cast:

Per Oscarsson
Ernst Günther
Georg Adelly
John Ahlgren
Lissi Alandh
Jörgen Andersson
Kent Andersson
Willie Andréason
Wanja Basel
Jan Bjelkelöv
Olle Björling
Jarl Borssén
Janne Carlsson
José Castro
Lars Edin
Allan Edwall
Margaretha Krook
Christina Lindberg
Lena Nyman

By popular demand, here's a movie about the saga of the battle for Sweden during the fifteenth century. A Swede, a German, an Englishman, and a Frenchman all make claims for the Swedish throne. After a series of adventures and complications, the yarn unravels into some kind of confused battle between warlords.

Per Oscarsson's ego trip (he is credited as director and producer, and plays several parts) is nothing more than a bunch of slapstick scenes, one after the other. A couple morbid shots of hanging victims, boiling cauldrons, rituals involving nuns, and a "monster" in a cage make the movie bearable. At very best, this is a Swedish attempt at something like Pasolini's *Il Decameron* (1971), a success that spawned a short-lived southern-Europe film genre portraying sexual adventure during medieval times.

Without the blood-colored glasses, the view is much harsher. Lars Lönroth wrote in *Sydsvenska Dagbladet Snällposten*: "Per Oscarsson's comedy is a poorly thought-out whim that lacks any kind of structure." The cast overflows with famous names, the most interesting belonging to coproducer Mats Helge Olsson and actress Christina Lindberg.

This film is reportedly the biggest box-office bomb of all time in Sweden, and it is impossible to understand how Oscarsson secured funding for this immensely expensive project. An even bigger mystery is how the hell he managed to get about a hundred of Sweden's best actors to appear in it—most of them without payment. For many of these actors, this film was the only stain on an otherwise respectable career.

Alternative titles: *Battle of Sweden*; *The Drinking Man's War*

SWEDISH WILDCATS

Brothel madame Margaretha (Diana Dors) in Copenhagen specializes in supplying young girls for private upper-class parties. For the dirtiest assignments, she uses her poor nieces, Karen (Solveig Andersson) and Susanna (Cia Löwgren). As the jobs get worse and worse, the young girls start detesting their existence; Karen soon runs astray with a man. Susanna has also started seeing a man, Peter (Peder Kinberg), and plans to use him as a ticket out of her miserable life. But Peter's boss, Gerhard (Ib Mossin), is unfortunately a drug-dealing sadist. He recognizes Susanna from the brothel, and thereby tries to ruin the relationship. However, Gerhard is arrested in a police raid, leaving Peter and Susanna to finally get some peace.

Swedish Wildcats is a sexy drama set in a brothel, directed by our friend Joseph W. Sarno, and filmed in bearded Denmark. The perversions Margaretha dreams up are creative: A woman is violently whipped by two young girls; old men chase body-painted "wildcats" with landing nets; and young female quarry are "sold" to rich guests via a mock auction. The character Gerhard is wonderfully slippery, with his worn-out tattoos and his love of biting and beating girls. The stunning Christina Lindberg's talent is unfortunately wasted with her very limited screen time. Overall, the film is a turkey if ever there was one—and, failing to meet the standards for a "15" rating, it was banned in Sweden.

Alternative title: *Every Afternoon*

Director:
Joseph W. Sarno
Cast:
Diana Dors
Cia Löwgren
Peder Kinberg
Solveig Andersson
Ib Mossin
John Harryson
Christina Lindberg
Urban Standar
Egil Holmsen
Claes Thelander
Alan Lake
Sven Olof Erikson
Jan Rohde
Poul Glargaard

(1966)

Director:

Vilgot Sjöman

Cast:

Bibi Andersson

Per Oscarsson

Jarl Kulle

Tina Hedström

Gunnar Björnstrand

SYSKONBÄDD 1782
[Sibling Bed 1782]

In 1782, Jacob (Per Oscarsson) returns home after spending several years away. He reunites with his sister (Bibi Andersson), and it becomes clear that the feelings between the two are not suitable for siblings. The charged atmosphere intensifies under the pressure of the impending marriage between the sister and the unpleasant Baron Carl-Ulrik (Jarl Kulle). A carousel of jealousy, desire, and guilt is set in motion, inevitably spinning out of control and landing all players in the lap of tragedy.

Flirting heavily with incest, this somewhat sleazy drama was directed by Vilgot Sjöman. Oscarsson and Andersson share several spicy moments, and one scene depicts Jacob reveling with two naked girls in a shabby hotel room. Overall, *Syskonbädd* is more like a historical drama than a *sensationsfilm*, though, thanks to some really hurting long-winded dialogue. Anyone born after 1979 will probably fall asleep after a few minutes, but they won't miss very much.

Alternative title: *My Sister My Love*

TA' MEJ DOKTORN
[Take Me, Doctor]

(1981)

Director:

*Andrew Whyte
(Andrei Feher)*

Cast:

Gabriel Rivera

Christina Andersson

Marina Delesbac

Marilyn Jé

Marie Laffont

Chris Regan

Brigitte Latosu

Eva Bestucci

A young doctor runs a private practice outside Paris. He gladly sees beautiful ladies, while his female assistants cure their impotent husbands. The doctor also keeps himself busy outside the office, and his home is in constant commotion—as a matter of fact, everyone in this movie is exceptionally gung ho! However, along with his professional and amorous commitments, the doctor engages in the dreadful side project of driving around in his sports car and killing hitchhiking girls. After a number of murders and sexual adventures, reality catches up with the psychotic physician.

The sex scenes just keep piling up in this pornographic mess directed by the always energetic Andrei Feher. The production finds its own little niche in Swedish movie history thanks to the questionable combination of frenetic hard-core porn and a wildcat murder spree, usually a taboo combo. This daring blend automatically gives the entire operation a perverted foundation; not surprisingly, *Ta' Mej Doktorn* is overall a pretty interesting escapade.

Alternative titles: *Ecstasy, Inc.*; *Heat and Lust: Diary of a Sex Therapist*; *Swedish Sex Clinic*

(1977)

TA MEJ I DALEN
[Take Me in the Valley]

Director:
Torgny Wickman
Cast:
Madeleine Laforet
Charles Canyon
Eric Edwards
Knud Jörgensen
Darby Lloyd Rains
Kim Pope
Anita Chris
Anne Magle

Shy and impotent George (Eric Edwards) is shipped off to his chauvinist cousin Richard's (Charles Canyon) estate to learn how to conquer women. The lessons mostly consist of him watching his cousin have sex with a string of cute girls, including the mechanic, the stable girl, and the chef. Meanwhile, Richard's wife, consumed by jealousy, is planning to kill her immoral husband. Instead of becoming a sexual predator, George ends up falling for the equally shy Ester, a teacher. In the end, good old predictable true love ends up being the remedy for his romantic problems. Even Richard's wife ends up satisfied, as she finally gets to spend some quality time roughhousing in bed with her husband.

Exploitation authority Torgny Wickman delivers one of his few purely pornographic movies. The title can also be translated as "Take Me in the Ass," and that tasteless pun was probably the sole original idea for this whole damned production. The film mostly consists of a number of tiring sex sequences, put into context by some slow-moving rural imagery of grazing cows and mud-loving pigs. Keeping audiences in good spirits is the swanky, slightly jazzy soundtrack of bass, guitars, organs, and drums. In case a sharp agent in Hollywood is planning on remaking this doozy, it's worth mentioning that the very dirty scene where a farmhand inserts objects into the privates of a sleeping girl is highly questionable!

Alternative titles: *Country Life*; *Practice Makes Perfect*

TABU
[Taboo]

(1977)

Director:
Vilgot Sjöman
Cast:
Kjell Bergqvist
Lickå Sjöman
Halvar Björk
Gunnar Björnstrand
Viveca Lindfors
Frank Sundström
Heinz Hopf
Lars Amble
Olle Björling
Stig Ossian Ericson
Mona Andersson
Axel Düberg
Toivo Pawlo
Gerd Hagman
Peter Ahlm
Stellan Skarsgård

Kristoffer Lohman (Kjell Bergqvist) is a controversial attorney fighting for the rights of sexual minorities. Young Sara (Lickå Sjöman) is fascinated by his commitment, and the two become romantically involved. Sara soon enters a whole new world, full of transvestite parties, masochism, sadists, slippery orgies, adultery, and general wild abandon. Lohman's plan to gather all sexual minorities for a collective demonstration of strength backfires, and his hopes for solidarity never rise above a spate of internal power struggles. Crushed by this defeat, the attorney watches his life fall apart, but not before he manages to seduce yet another girl. In the final moments, he describes his next book to his timid new conquest: It will be a mighty critique of the sexual revolution!

This eccentric paean to unleashed sexuality was directed by Vilgot Sjöman, and features an impressive all-star cast including Gunnar Björnstrand, Stellan Skarsgård, Viveca Lindfors, and even the great Heinz Hopf as a snotty sadomasochist (and necrophiliac!). The movie is built entirely on tons of sex and nudity—the coolest scene depicts Kjell Bergqvist doing the helicopter dance by flinging his semi-erect member around. All the sleaze might have had something to do with the presence of Bo A. Vibenius of *Thriller – En Grym Film* (see page 258) and *Breaking Point* (see page 42) infamy on the production crew.

Tabu seems to be trying to get some kind of political or religious message through to the audience, but it's lost in the sweaty confusion and buried in pretentious dialogue. Though Sjöman is usually considered a serious filmmaker, this movie confirms that deep inside he is a dirty old man, after all—and he's good at it!

(1974)

Director:
Alex Fridolinsky
(Bo A. Vibenius)

Cast:
Christina Lindberg
Heinz Hopf
Despina Tomazani
Per-Axel Arosenius
Solveig Andersson

THRILLER – EN GRYM FILM
[Thriller: A Cruel Picture]

Thriller – En Grym Film is likely the most prominent Swedish *sensationsfilm*, still enjoying international success and notoriety. Quentin Tarantino based much of *Kill Bill* on the film, and called *Thriller* "definitely the roughest revenge movie ever made."

Enchantingly beautiful Madeleine (Christina Lindberg) leads a quiet life with her stepparents in the countryside. She is mute after being sexually assaulted as a child, but has learned to deal with the trauma and lives in humble happiness on a farm. Everything changes when Madeleine is kidnapped by pimp Jerry (Heinz Hopf), who drugs her and forces her into prostitution. Her clients, an endless stream of perverted scum, all stem from society's highest income bracket and prominent social spheres. Broken down with sorrow, thinking their little girl has abandoned them, the stepparents soon kill themselves, and Madeleine swears to avenge their deaths. She secretly studies martial arts, learns how to shoot, and figures out how to drive. After mastering these skills, Madeleine methodically kills off her tormentors. In the big finale, she employs a horse to strangle Jerry in brutal fashion.

Vibenius's creation is a grade-A rape and revenge movie, made all the more disturbing by the insertion of several incongruous hardcore sex scenes. It remains unclear whether Christina Lindberg knew the sex scenes would be edited this way, as the strong impression is that the actress is having sex for real! According to legend, Vibenius filmed the close-ups on the cheap at a Stockholm live sex show. Regardless, Lindberg was heavily exploited during the production. Among other anomalies, the film's producers took out a huge life insurance policy on her, as real ammunition was used in the action sequences. She was also asked to inject saline solution during the drug scenes. Supposedly, an authentic corpse was used as a stand-in when Lindberg's eye is cut out.

This movie is explosive by any standard. The honorable Heinz Hopf is absolutely fantastic as Jerry. Seldom has a bigger creep been spotted anywhere. In typical Swedish fashion, the pacing gets a bit slow, and tighter editing could have lifted the movie a little—the grim introduction is totally incomprehensible on first viewing. Nevertheless, this is the crown jewel of Swedish *sensationsfilms*, and Christina Lindberg has never been put to better use. The movie was banned nearly everywhere in 1972, but was later released with a whopping twenty-six minutes cut.

Alternative titles: *Hooker's Revenge*; *They Call Her One Eye*

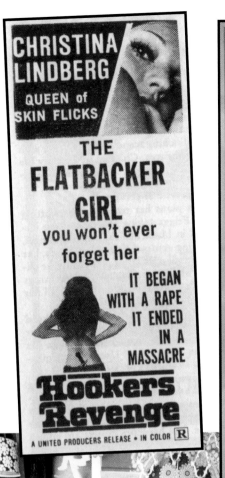

CHRISTINA LINDBERG
QUEEN of SKIN FLICKS

THE FLATBACKER GIRL
you won't ever forget her

IT BEGAN WITH A RAPE
IT ENDED IN A MASSACRE

Hookers Revenge

A UNITED PRODUCERS RELEASE • IN COLOR **R**

Den första svenska film som någonsin blivit totalförbjuden av censuren.
Nu i amerikansk version.

Bo A Vibenius presenterar

THRILLER
—en grym film—

CHRISTINA LINDBERG • HEINZ HOPF

FÄRG

Clockwise from top left:
Sensationalistic US newspaper ad for Thriller – En Grym Film *(Thriller: A Cruel Picture, aka Hooker's Revenge)*;

Classic Thriller *poster reads: "The first Swedish movie ever to be banned by the censors. Now in American version"*;

Director Bo A. Vibenius, star Christina Lindberg, and composer Ralph Lundsten
Courtesy of Ralph Lundsten

(1965)

Director:

Lars Görling

Cast:

Sven-Bertil Taube

Helena Brodin

Tina Hedström

Marrit Ohlsson

Inga-Lill Åhström

Bjarne Næess

TILLS. MED GUNILLA MÅND. KVÄLL O. TISD.
[With Gunilla Mond. Eve and Tues.]

Hans (Sven-Bertil Taube) and Gunilla (Helena Brodin) are a young couple driving a custom 1960s Volvo Amazon car around the roads of Sörmland, near Stockholm. Their carefree existence is shattered when they hit and kill an unknown person by mistake. At first they roam the countryside aimlessly, trying to make sense of the horrible situation. Soon, the emotional turmoil of the accident creates violent turbulence in their relationship.

This psychedelic experimental movie was totally misunderstood at the time of its premiere. The few sequences featuring nudity and sex put audiences in a state of shock, and the reaction internationally was one of total disgust. Even though the discussion was heated, the movie got away with no cuts from Sweden's censors. It's good they kept their scissors sharp for everything that was soon to arrive in the years ahead.

Director Lars Görling had earlier written the landmark book *491*, which was made into a movie by Vilgot Sjöman in 1964 (see page 17). Sadly, the talented young Görling ended his own life in 1966.

Alternative title: *Guilt*

TONÅRSFLICKOR PÅ DRIVEN
[Teen Girls Roaming Aimlessly]

(1982)

Director:

Mai Zetterling

Cast:

Amanda York

Chrissie Cotterill

Elisabeth Edmonds

Kate Ingram

Amanda Symonds

Imogen Bain

Honey Bane

Bebby Bishop

Kathy Burke

Steve Adler

This is the dark tale of two young girls living in a reform school. One is an orphan, who has voluntarily enlisted in the school to seek revenge on her cheating girlfriend. The other is a single mother, desperately trying to reunite with her little daughter. Violence and anxiety are ever present, and in the end conditions could not be more unfortunate for anyone involved.

Tonårsflickor på Driven mercilessly examines the everyday life of a couple of disillusioned girls living on the outskirts of society. The terrifying and shocking story depicts a grim world filled with violence, sexual abuse (mostly lesbian), suicide, and unending doom. The anxiety-ridden atmosphere is reinforced by the color-reducing lens filter that casts the entire movie in shades of gray. In all possible ways, that is a penetrating and intense movie. Too bad Mai Zetterling had to go to England to get her funding for this movie—I guess Sweden was too busy paying for Lasse Åberg's Disney collection and other frivolities to care!

Alternative title: *Scrubbers*

Clockwise from top left: A
tailcoat you only wear once—
theatrical poster for Träfracken
(The Wooden Tailcoat)
Courtesy of Klubb Super 8;

Very dry poster for a the
late Lars Görling's greatly
misunderstood movie;

Essy Persson in 1966 as a
teasing nurse in Träfracken
Courtesy of Klubb Super 8

TRÄFRACKEN
[The Wooden Tailcoat]

(1966)

Director:
Lars-Magnus Lindgren

Cast:
Gunnar Björnstrand
Elsa Prawitz
Catrin Westerlund
Ulla Sjöblom
Heinz Hopf
Margaretha Krook
Essy Persson
Allan Edwall
Björn Berglund
Christina Lindgren
Åke Fridell
Gösta Prüzelius
Peter Lindgren
Elsa Textorius
Christina Carlwind
Hjördis Petterson
Picko Troberg
Bert-Åke Varg
Bo Hederström
Stefan Larsson
Mona Kampf

Several mysterious deaths occur in the area surrounding a hospital: a car crash that seems prearranged; a suspicious case of euthanasia; and an obvious murder. The investigation is complicated by the vast number of suspects, but eventually the senior physician (Gunnar Björnstrand) is identified as the culprit behind the heinous crimes. After he is exposed, he tries to kill his wife but falls to his death in the fracas. In the final sequence, the couple's daughter stands lonely and abandoned in the funeral parlor.

This crime thriller is structured like a Greek tragedy, with the undertaker as narrator. The cast consists of big names such as Gunnar Björnstrand, Margaretha Krook, Allan Edwall, Bert-Åke Varg, and of course Heinz Hopf, in an early appearance as a young doctor. First and foremost among the exploitation segments we see a few dirty segments of Björnstrand whipping and smacking around a young girl. He already seems so obviously like the killer, it actually comes as some surprise when it turns out he really is guilty.

Expressen's Lasse Bergström tried to halt future development of Swedish thrillers with his review: "Quite a festive atmosphere, between the caskets and the murders here. One step further, and the Swedish film detective will stay in his place, buried for good." Bergström must have been turning in his living grave with the later arrival of Swedish thrill rides such as *Smutsiga Fingrar* (see page 229) and *Thriller – En Grym Film* (see page 258). By the way, a "wooden tailcoat" is a colorful Swedish slang phrase meaning "casket."

Alternative title: *Sadist*

(1993)

Director:

Thomas Samuelsson

Cast:

Fredrik Dolk

Jacqueline Ramel

Mats Huddén

Gösta Bredefeldt

Katarina Weidhagen van Hal

Thomas Roos

Axel Düberg

Carina Jingrot

Robert Sjöblom

Jonas Uddenmyr

Hans Jonsson

Johan Paulsen

Olle Blom

Elisabet Höglund

TRYGGARE KAN INGEN VARA ....
[Nobody Can Be Safer ......]

One night while out jogging, Peter (Fredrik Dolk) stumbles onto the scene of a rape in progress, and he manages to bring the rapist down and alarm the police. Three years later, he has become a known author after publishing a book based upon his experiences. To finish his new novel, Peter takes off with his wife and newborn son to an idyllic isolated cabin in the very north of Sweden. Right away, strange things start to happen. A mysterious man sneaks around the house, the car breaks down without explanation, and Peter receives threatening letters warning that he should never have written his book. The country idyll soon turns into a living hell.

After the less-than-perfect *P. S. Sista Sommaren* (see page 193), Thomas Samuelsson had to wait five years until he managed to convince someone to let him direct a film again. The result was this odd rape-revenge thriller set in the blistering cold of Arvidsjaur in Norrland. Even though the theme sounds pretty rough, the film shies away from anything that would seriously shock and disgust. But in an interesting twist for *sensationsfilms* connoisseurs, Samuelsson cast Mats Helge Olsson regular Mats Huddén as the rapist, and he plays the part in his usual weird, uninterested style.

The critics uniformly murdered this picture. "Over a sickeningly weak plot, this miserable abomination is made even worse by its total confusion regarding spatial orientation, irrelevant camera movements, laughable reaction picture inserts, grotesque character motivation, and lousy acting. The film is a blatant amateurish job from the start to fisnish in every department; I have never seen anything as worthless," lamented Jan Aghed in *Sydsvenska Dagbladet Snällposten*.

Needless to say, Thomas Samuelsson was never allowed to direct a film again. With men like him out of the picture, the era of *sensationsfilms* came to an end.

TUPPEN
[The Rooster]

(1981)

Director:
Lasse Hallström
Cast:
Magnus Härenstam
Pernilla Wallgren
Maria Johansson
Allan Edwall
Annika Dopping
Åsa Bjerkerot
Suzanne Ernrup
Ing-Marie Carlsson
Weiron Holmberg
Roland Janson
Ellionor Bille
Ebba Malmström
Annika Christensen

While World War II rages in the rest of Europe, clumsy efficiency expert Cederqvist (Magnus Härenstam) arrives at rural textile factory to whip the female employees into shape. While eager to get laid, Cederqvist is far from a ladies' man, and his insecure manner fails to impress the girls. However, when the women realize they can use the consultant to boost their company status, things get going for Cederqvist. Suddenly, he is conquering women around the clock. In the end, the film is unclear about who actually used whom, but Cederqvist definitely gets far more than he asked for.

Cederqvist starts off as a shy voyeur but becomes sexually active in a way only a middle-aged man deprived of sex for most of his life can be. As his swagger grows, the viewer's attention span is tested, and Cedeqvist's sexual encounters reach a manic pace. The real strength of the movie is voyeurism, as many girls are exposed in full frontal nudity. Among those exposed is Pernilla Wallgren, now known as Pernilla August, familiar to modern audiences from *Star Wars* episode *I* and *II* (George Lucas, 1999 & 2002), where she plays Shmi Skywalker, the fully dressed mother of Darth Vader. *Tuppen* is her only nude appearance on the silver screen.

Lead actor Härenstam was famed in Sweden as one of three stars of the children's TV show *Five Ants Are More Than Four Elephants*. Meanwhile, with sidekick Brasse Brännström, he also did adult humor, touring bars around Sweden. When these two sleazebags released an album titled *Warning: Children*, tens of thousands of parents around Sweden got it all wrong. Moms and dads bought the album for their sons and daughters for Christmas, expecting a light children's album. Instead, kids were confronted with very explicit material drenched in alcohol and dripping with sex—one song consists only of swear words. Rather than being safely entertained, an entire generation was confused and destroyed forever, doomed to a life of sin. I know—because I was one of those kids.

This film premiered to mixed reviews in Sweden. Critics found the story too thin, and gags too few and far between. The acting is quite good overall, though, and Härenstam is especially entertaining as the corny and lovesick gentleman. Director Lasse Hallström already had *ABBA: The Movie* (1977) under his belt, and he later reaped a stack of Oscar nominations for movies with guys like Johnny Depp and Tobey McGuire, such as *What's Eating Gilbert Grape* (1993), *The Cider House Rules* (1999), and *Chocolat* (2000).

TVINGAD ATT LEVA
[Forced to Live]

Director:

Mats Helge Olsson

Cast:

Per Oscarsson
Mariana Lindahl
Mats Olsson
Roger Lundgren
Carl-Erik Proft
Taggen Axelsson
Jan Eliasson
Elsa Westerberg
Yvonne Swedberg

Author Jan Bergman (Jan Eliasson) is found unconscious by a young woman, Ann Malmström (Mariana Lindahl), and fellow author Bengt (Mats Olsson). The three suspect that a mysterious hermit (Roger Lundgren) whose life Jan has been researching could be involved in the assault. When they realize the hermit has already received a life sentence for the murder of his wife, it's time for the police to enter the picture. Everything ends in a big battle, in which the hermit kills a police officer before killing himself.

After his initial lingonberry western efforts, tireless genre enthusiast Mats Helge Olsson haunted cinemagoers with this outlandish thriller. The movie is a wonderfully ruthless shoestring production, intensified by Per Oscarsson's customary brilliant acting. After this movie, Mats Helge was inactive for four years. When he returned—with a vengeance, naturally—he completely gave up on the storytelling aspects of filmmaking in order to focus exclusively on daring action, as evidenced in *The Ninja Mission* (see page 182) and *Eagle Island* (see page 53).

TYSTNADEN
[The Silence]

This story concerns two very different sisters—one seriously ill (Ingrid Thulin) and the other sexually frustrated (Gunnel Lindblom)—isolated together in a bleak and nameless foreign city. A neglected boy and a small group of dwarfs are also involved. While conflict rages outside the window, the sisters confront each other in a gray hotel room.

Tystnaden is the production, and marks the exact moment, when sex and nudity became normal in Swedish film. If an internationally acknowledged director like Ingmar Bergman could portray sex in such an explicit way, then the last border had been crossed. Hordes of less serious filmmakers immediately abandoned all remaining inhibition about depicting whatever crazed and depraved ideas they thought would attract and scandalize a paying audience. The movie caused uproar wherever it was shown, but eluded the scissors of censorship. Today, the sexual content comes across as pretty innocent, but the power of *Tystnaden* lies in what it unleashed rather than in what it is.

(1963)

Director:
Ingmar Bergman
Cast:
Ingrid Thulin
Gunnel Lindblom
Jörgen Lindström
Håkan Jahnberg
Birger Malmsten
Eduardo Gutiérrez
Lissi Alandh
Leif Forstenberg
Eduardinis

Clockwise from top left:
Vaxdockan (The Wax Doll)*'s*
Per Oscarsson and his wax
doll Gio Petré
Courtesy of Klubb Super 8*;*

"An infernal examination of
erotic confusion"
Courtesy of Klubb Super 8*;*

Magnus Härenstam hovers
over all his ladies on the
Swedish Tuppen (The
Rooster) *poster*

VAXDOCKAN
[The Wax Doll]

(1962)

Director:
Arne Mattsson

Cast:
Per Oscarsson
Gio Petré
Tor Isedal
Elsa Prawitz
Bengt Eklund
Marie-Louise Nordgren
Dagmar Olsson
Mimi Nelson
Rick Axberg
Elisabeth Odén
Olle Grönstedt
Agneta Prytz
Lennart Norbäck
Mia Nyström
Mona Andersson

Lundgren (Per Oscarsson) is a lonely and disconsolate night watchman who fantasizes about female intimacy. One day, he steals a mannequin and brings her home to nurture and befriend. Lo and behold, the dummy—portrayed with stunning realism by Gio Petré—comes to life and wins Lundgren's heart. When his neighbors hear him talking to himself in solitude, and after he forgets to pay his rent, everyone suspects something is amiss. When a neighbor discovers his doll, Lundgren shoots and wounds the snooper in a fit of rage. Crazy with anger and frustration, he smashes his beloved doll to pieces and crawls along the floor, truly alone and certifiably insane.

The brilliant Per Oscarsson is supported here in this display of erotic confusion by two future stars of Swedish exploitation, Tor Isedal and Gio Petré. Isedal—along with David Carradine and Heinz Hopf—is one of the few actors to have worked with both Swedish film titan Ingmar Bergman and *sensationsfilm* auteur Mats Helge Olsson. This early dystopian portrait of a man slowly rotting from loneliness remains one of Arne Mattsson's most powerful efforts. However, with twisted films like this, Mattsson started alienating the critics, who had loved him up to this point.

Alternative title: *The Doll*

VECKÄNDA I STOCKHOLM
[Weekend in Stockholm]

(1976)

Director:

Anne-Mari Berglund

Cast:

Anne-Mari Berglund

Knud Jörgensen

Lene Bergström

This brightly colored and ultimately boring sex movie follows a young woman to Stockholm to visit her friend, and of course details her subsequent string of erotic experiences.

Since the plot is virtually nonexistent, and there is no dialogue to speak of, the only thing holding this mess together is a jazzy soundtrack and the hilarious narrator. The single interesting sequence involves the characters going to see a cartoon porn flick in a movie theater. Even this scene ends up with intercourse. Director Ann-Mari Berglund and her husband, Knud Jörgensen, just seem like a couple that filmed themselves having sex in order to get some cash. So Jörgensen probably deserves equal credit for the creation of this nudity-filled relic—although attaching a director credit to this film at all just devalues the meaning of "director."

Veckända i Stockholm crosses the divide from X-rated *sensationsfilm* to pure pornography—which was still a new phenomenon in Sweden in 1976. The Swedish feminist movement in the late '60s and early '70s fought to get porn out in the open. Nowadays, it is kind of the opposite. Some people are never satisfied. But the rash of brothels, porn, and child porn that the feminist movement helped bring about in the 1970s was probably not too healthy anyway.

VEM VAR DRACULA?
[Who Was Dracula?]

(1975)

Director:
Calvin Floyd
Cast:
Christopher Lee

Inspired by Raymond T. McNally and Radu Florescu's 1972 book *In Search of Dracula*, this odd documentary deals with the Dracula myth and phenomenon. The film is centered around Bram Stoker's classic novel but ventures out to examine many other aspects of the bloodthirsty character. The director visits Transylvania and learns traditional myths about vampires, and ways of protecting against them. Among other tidbits, viewers learn that Dracula is the only ghost who can perform sexual intercourse! The imagery is a mix of new material, sequences from other movies, and stock footage of spooky things. Everything is narrated by Christopher Lee, who portrayed Dracula in a number of British movies produced by Hammer Horror—and here Lee's voice is dubbed by Tor Isedal, veteran of many a *sensationsfilm*!

Falling short of being some kind of vampire-themed mondo movie, this is honestly a pointless documentary that sucks all the fun out of bloodsucking. Director Calvin Floyd apparently got hooked on horror classics, however, since he returned two years later with *Victor Frankenstein* (see page 273), his own version of Mary Shelley's well-known monster tale.

Alternative titles: *Dracula's Transylvania*; *In Search of Dracula*; *The Legend of Dracula*

Theatrical poster for misunderstood masterpiece
Vindingevals (Vindinge Waltz)
Courtesy of Klubb Super 8

"Dracula existed!" boasts the creepy poster for
Vem Var Dracula? (Who Was Dracula?)
Courtesy of Klubb Super 8

A rare Swedish attempt at gothic horor: Victor Frankenstein **Courtesy of Klubb Super 8**

VICTOR FRANKENSTEIN

(1977)

When Victor Frankenstein (Leon Vitali) is rescued by a ship in the Arctic Ocean, he exhaustedly tells the enraptured crew his tragic story of creating a monster that eventually destroyed his life. As the mad doctor finishes his wild tale, the monster suddenly attacks the ship. Victor confronts the beast but is killed. The monster heads out alone, crossing vast landscapes.

This Swedish-Irish coproduction of Mary Shelley's old monster story stars Per Oscarsson as the ghastly creation. In fact, Oscarsson is the only redeeming quality of the movie—he is always a great presence on film, even in monster gear. Director Calvin Floyd seemed to have not learned much about scaring people in the two years since making his Dracula documentary *Vem Var Dracula?* (see page 271). Four years later, his final film, *Ondskans Värdshus* (see page 188), was so trashed by critics that he stopping making movies altogether.

"In short, this is the most boring movie I have ever seen dealing with Frankenstein and his monster," Hans Schiller complained to the national audience in *Svenska Dagbladet*. Someone should have warned pesty child actor Jan Ohlsson, who appears here as Frankenstein's younger brother. He had been riding a wave of success, appearing a series of adaptations of *Pippi Longstocking* author Astrid Lindgren stories. After this, only made one more detested movie before being forced to get a desk job.

Director:
Calvin Floyd
Cast:
Leon Vitali
Per Oscarsson
Nicholas Clay
Stacy Dorning
Jan Ohlsson
Olof Bergström
Mathias Henrikson
Archie O'Sullivan
Harry Brogan
Tor Isedal

Alternative title: *Terror of Frankenstein*

(1974)

Director:

Joseph W. Sarno

Cast:

Marie Forså

Nadia Henkowa

Anke Syring

Ines André

Birgit Zamulo

Françoise Suehrer

Peter Hamm

Brit Corvin

Henrik Winston

Karin Lorson

Stefan Stein

Eleonore Leipert

Christa Jaeger

Marianne Dupont

Alo D'Armand

Marc Edwards

VILD PÅ SEX
[Wild for Sex]

Innocent teen girl Bibi (Marie Forså) arrives at her aunt's boarding house for young girls. Sounds innocent enough, but the place turns out to be overflowing with lust and desire. Soon Bibi finds herself the focal point of everyone's erotic urges. As time passes, she is seduced by most men and women of the house—the rest she seduces herself. Bibi enjoys being the center of attention at the wild ongoing sex party raging in her aunt's house, and everyone else seems pleased to be getting a piece of her young, beautiful body. What could go wrong? Well, jealousy sadly rears its ugly head, and in the end Bibi just feels used and left out.

Vild på Sex is a robust *sensationsfilm* with young and sensual Marie Forså as the leading actress. Well, it's hard to really call this acting, as the participants deliver their lines with such a lack of commitment that the movie starts to feel like a stark modernist play. When it comes to the sex, on the other hand, there is all the feeling in the world involved, and the actors moan and whine until the viewer fears they will burst. Countless sex scenes involve violent whipping, dildos, group sex, and tons of hot lesbianism. The intensity of the soft-core sex scenes almost makes them seem X-rated. But there's a difference, as director Joe W. Sarno proved during a great big part of his later career making adult films.

This is one of the few films to have ever premiered in the deserted town of Åmål—a place so boring that Lukas Moodysson made its blankness a major theme of his great teen angst drama, *Fucking Åmål* (US title: *Show Me Love*, 1998).

Alternative titles: *Baby Love*; *Confessions of a Sex Kitten*; *Girl Meets Girl*

VINDINGEVALS
[Vindinge Waltz]

Jürgen Schildt really laid everything on the line in his damning review for the national daily newspaper *Aftonbladet*: "The movie is rotten, totally incoherent, doomed from the start—to put it mildly. You cannot even call this a catastrophe. A catastrophe always has something magnificent about it, and the only thing magnificent about *Vindingevals* is its ability to bore. So let us briefly state that this is nothing but a series of perfect examples of bad artistic economy, forced gestures, and stiff actions, plus a few almost smothered groans from the basement where the Swedish Theatrical Association keeps their everyday spare parts."

Yes, *Vindingevals* is a confusing story of summer sex, sun, and madness set in turn-of-the-century southern Sweden. However, the film is by no means uninteresting. The movie consists of several bizarre elements, such as a dead horse, a gypsy (Diana Kjaer) who exposes her womanhood to little boys (for a few *öre* coins), a woman who pukes in her bed, a man dressed only in a hat covering his erect penis, an Australian with a whip, and—last but not least—the christening of an intoxicated man. The gypsy exhibitionist is surely the worst, though, as an *öre* equals 1 percent of the Swedish krona, an amount so worthless that it can't even be measured in fractions of a penny.

The cast brings together such trash movie veterans as Hans Ernback, Gio Petré and Diana Kjaer, and she looks naughtier than ever. As the icing on the cake, Mac Ahlberg is in charge of cinematography—this is a sleeper classic!

(1968)

Director:
Åke Falck

Cast:
Georg Rydeberg
Keve Hjelm
Diana Kjaer
Erik Hell
Hans Ernback
Gio Petré
Kent Andersson
Cay Bond
Tina Hedström
Mona Andersson
Peter Lindgren
Hans Wahlgren
Mats Olin
Oscar Ljung

(1962)

VITA FRUN
[The Lady in White]

Director:

Arne Mattsson

Cast:

Karl-Arne Holmsten

Anita Björk

Jan Malmsjö

Hjördis Pettersson

Lena Granhagen

Nils Hallberg

Nils Asther

Sif Ruud

Tor Isedal

Gio Petré

Elisabeth Odén

Distraught after being left out of her father's will following a family dispute, young girl Eva von Schöffer (Gio Petré) goes into a trance and soon drowns herself in a swamp. Afterward, the remaining heirs in her family witness a lady dressed in white sneaking around the mansion grounds, and they hear Eva's signature melodies being played on an eerie harpsichord. Instead of trying to deduce the cause of what's going on, everyone simply blames the "White Lady" for Eva's death, and they continue bad-mouthing one another and arguing over the inheritance. About fifty minutes into the film, architect/investigator John Hillman (Karl-Arne Holmsten) stumbles onto the scene by sheer chance. He is compelled to make some sense out of all this, but death and confusion still reign—until the prolonged finale, that is, which makes absolutely no sense at all.

Leaving behind the color Cinemascope photography of *Ryttare i Blått* (see page 213), the preceding film from his Hillman quintet, Arne Mattsson delivers a black-and-white suspense thriller in the vein of his original *Damen i Svart* (see page 49)—a very wise choice. Once again, he delves into horror motifs with staring eyes, coffins, shadows, face masks, and harrowing screams in the pitch-black night. In addition, the wonderfully unsympathetic trio of Nils Asther, Tor Isedal, and Jan Malmsjö all portray sleazy lunatics with great energy. Too bad Petré is killed off within the film's first minutes—that's a prime example of bad casting. All the cornball sequences with Nils Hallberg as Freddy fit very badly with the rest of the film's atmosphere of Bergmanesque doom. *Vita Frun* has its fair share of bizarre images—a doll with its eyes poked out, a mummified face mask—and creepy suspense. However, the killer's identity is far too obvious from the very first frames of the film. Not even a complete moron could avoid solving this case light-years ahead of Hillman.

Once again, Mattsson had a great success on his hands with *Vita Frun*. Several actors later admitted that the director started to develop a sadistic side during the shooting of this film. Filming in the cold swamp, he forced an almost hysterical Gio Petré to do take after take, nearly freezing the poor actress to death. His intensity later came to full light in such extraordinary films as *Smutsiga Fingrar* (see page 229). He concluded this calmer phase of his career, his "Swedish *giallo*" quintet, in 1967, with *Den Gula Bilen* (see page 82).

VITA NEJLIKAN
[The White Carnation]

(1974)

Director:
Jarl Kulle
Cast:
Jarl Kulle
Ingvar Kjellson
Margaretha Krook
Caroline Christensen
Siv Ericks
Gunwer Bergkvist
Gerd Hagman
Ann-Mari Adamsson-Eklund
Gunvor Pontén

An associate professor (Jarl Kulle) at Stockholm University leads a double life. Apart from his subpar academic career, he dedicates much of his time to women and parties. Problems arise, unfortunately, since his income by no means lives up to his expenses. He is forced to think strategically, and he starts seducing the right kind of ladies in order to help make ends meet. He performs his amorous deeds in a number of inventive ways, for example disguising himself as a pastor and as an art dealer. Not exactly a mastermind to begin with, the professor eventually develops problems keeping his different convoluted relationships separate, and reality quickly catches up with him.

Jarl Kulle treats himself here to a big confidence boost, directing himself as a successful womanizer in this easily digestible comedy. Not too much sensationalism to talk about—only a couple of breasts and a bottom flashing. As the movie drags on, Kulle's voice-over monologues become especially trying on the nerves. The director seemed all to eager to tame down the *sensationsfilm* genre just as it was taking off. That harmless impulse has served him well, as he remains one of Sweden's most loved actors. Along with half the other *sensationsfilms* fixtures in this book—including Heinz Hopf and Jörn Donner—Kulle redeemed himself in *Fanny and Alexander* (Ingmar Bergman, 1983). That Oscar was hardly enough for everyone, though.

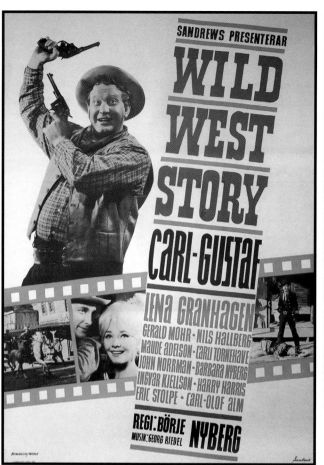

Clockwise from top left: *Swedish cowboy Carl-Gustaf Lindstedt ready to brawl on the poster for early lingonberry western* Wild West Story*;*

The murderous film War Dog*, where not even children are spared;*

Jarl Kulle as the very annoying lead character of Vita Nejlikan (The White Carnation)*;*

Video box for Arne Mattsson's fourth John Hillman movie, Vita Frun (The Lady in White)

WAR DOG

(1986)

Vietnam vet Charles (Timothy Earle) is mourning his brother Rick (David Lundberg), who fought together with him in the war. Unwilling to totally accept the government's claim that his brother is dead, Charles asks his friend Frank (Chris Masters) to examine the death certificate. As suspected, the paperwork turns out to be forged. Joined by journalist Dean Daniels (Gunnar Ernblad), the crew starts to investigate. Charles believes he is on to something big, and his hunch is confirmed when both Dean and Frank are brutally executed. Charles's former commander, Spacek (Bengt Fridh), has disappeared into the Vietnam jungle, where he is building his own private army. Using drugs and torture, Spacek has efficiently built a squadron of killing machines—and a brainwashed Rick is one of them. Charles is captured and tortured by Spacek's men, but he manages to break out and make a violent escape with his brother by his side.

This incredibly flipped-out action movie is an astonishingly violent, ruthless orgy of gunfights, explosions, blood, disembodied limbs, and nasty violence. The diligent use of slow motion is spectacular and never becomes tedious, as it does in most low-budget productions. The attitude toward violence against kids is completely apathetic, as children are shot and maimed for the camera just like everyone else. One fistfight between hard-boiled men is so brutal it makes *Fight Club* (David Fincher, 1999) look like Sunday school. The over-the-top approach is so complete that the lack of any other qualities is quickly forgotten. No need to worry about plot or believable dialogue. The portrayal of Spacek's "killing machines" is totally brilliant: Stoic men in black clothes and dark shades who never twitch or speak a word. They look considerably more like robots than Arnold Schwarzenegger ever did in *The Terminator* (James Cameron, 1984).

Up there with *The Ninja Mission* (see page 182), *War Dog* is undoubtedly among the very best Swedish action movies.

Alternative title: *Wardogs (The Assassination Game)*

Directors:
Björn Carlström
Daniel Hübenbecker
Cast:
Timothy Earle
Gunnar Ernblad
Bengt Fridh
David Gillies
Iréne Grönwall
Catherine Jeppsson
Wolf Linder
Sydney Livingstone
David Lundberg
Jan Lundberg
Chris Masters
Bill Redvers

(1964) WILD WEST STORY

Director:
Börje Nyberg

Cast:
Carl-Gustaf Lindstedt

Lena Granhagen

Gerald Mohr

John Norrman

Ingvar Kjellson

Barbara Nyberg

Carli Tornehave

Nils Hallberg

Nils Eklund

Ulf Johanson

Maude Adelson

Harry Harris

Old Joe (John Norrman) and his granddaughter share a small cabin in the wild western town of Small Land Hills. Over the years, Joe has fought many Indians, Mexicans, and outlaws with the help of his now-deceased partner, Revolver Kid Andersson. Old Joe's latest nemesis is a gang of bandits. Their leader, the seedy Gonzales (Gerald Mohr), is a bad man who lusts for women, cheats while gambling, fights dirty, and even dabbles in crooked politics. Soon Revolver Kid's son Lucky Andersson (Carl-Gustaf Lindstedt) arrives riding a donkey. He proclaims himself sheriff and sets out to defeat Gonzales and rescue Old Joe. Everything comes to a head during a violent bar fight, in which all uneven scores are settled.

This extremely slow and harmless comedy is noteworthy as the first Swedish attempt to make a kind of western movie. Since the filmmakers didn't dare try an actual western, they settled for a halfhearted parody. Apart from a burlesque *verité* number and some fighting sequences, not much sensational happens here. Carl-Gustaf Lindstedt was praised for his acting, and when Mats Helge Olsson brought back the Swedish western genre eleven years later, he followed tradition and cast Lindstedt in the lead role. That film—Olsson's *I Död Mans Spår* (see page 95)—spawned the term "lingonberry western." The exteriors of *Wild West Story* were shot in Yugoslavia, in locations that were later destroyed during the Balkan war in the mid-1990s.

YNGSJÖMORDET
[The Yngsjö Murder]

(1966)

Director:
Arne Mattsson

Cast:
Gunnel Lindblom
Gösta Ekman
Christina Schollin
Rune Lindström
Isa Quensel
Heinz Hopf
Elsa Prawitz
Frej Lindqvist
Tore Lindwall
Maritta Marke
Curt Ericson
Gösta Bernhard
Christian Bratt

Anna Månsdotter (Gunnel Lindblom) and her son Pär Nillson (Gösta Ekman) are respectively sentenced to death and life in prison after teaming up and killing Pär's wife, Hanna Johansdotter (Christina Schollin). Behind this nineteenth-century tragedy is a bitter feud based on incest, abuse, and anxiety. In the form of flashbacks, the film follows the final hours of Anna's life, which, after a painful court proceeding, lead to her lethal execution.

Arne Mattsson delivers a distressing and detailed reconstruction of the infamous Skåne murder of 1889. The movie is ruthless in its portrayal of prison, and the execution scene is brutally bloody and chill-inducing—especially by the standards of kind, understanding Sweden, where capital punishment was put out to pasture with a final guillotine chop around 1910. The film itself is not as tolerant of human vice.

Most terrifying—as many times before—is actor Heinz Hopf in the ice-cold role of the county chief. The acting overall is impressive; even the otherwise forlorn Gösta Ekman works really well in this depressing context. The production itself was characterized by gloom and doom, as producer Lorens Marmstedt and actor Christian Bratt both died while working on the movie.

Yngsjömordet is probably the last Mattsson film to earn positive recognition from critics. They abused all his productions after this—but from a *sensationsfilm* perspective, Mattsson's most earth-shattering and questionable creations still lay ahead of him. *Yngsjömordet* lay in wait to be rediscovered and remade for Swedish TV in 1986 by schlock master Richard Hobert.

Alternative title: *Woman of Darkness*

YOUNG PLAYTHINGS

(1972)

Director:
Joseph W. Sarno
Cast:
Christina Lindberg
Eva Portnoff
Margareta Hellström
Thomas Nervell
Göran Harrysson
Gunilla Mattisson
Britten Larsson
Teddy Lundberg
Sinikka Karlsson
Björn Brännemark
Karin Genberg
Jill Wernström

Gunilla (Christina Lindberg) is an innocent girl fascinated by her free-spirited friend Nora (Eva Portnoff). Unbeknownst to Gunilla, daring Nora is having an affair with Gunilla's husband, Janne (Thomas Nervell), and the two illicit lovers are scheming to get Gunilla to agree to a three-way relationship. For starters, Nora persuades her friend to move in with her, and coaxes her into taking part in sexual games. Meanwhile, Gunilla is spending more and more time with mysterious neighbor Brit (Margareta Hellström), a woman who sets up peculiar little erotic plays in her apartment. Both Gunilla and Nora are soon swept into the theatrical excesses, participating in purely pornographic productions with several others. Gunilla begins to feel liberated, and she generously agrees to share her man Janne with Nora. The three go for a wonderful honeymoon, but Gunilla and Nora soon long to be back with Brit and her bewitching exhibitionism. The members of the theater group, however, are driven to dementia from all the debauchery, and ultimately they all go completely insane.

This curious Joseph Sarno movie is actually an American production shot in Sweden almost exclusively using Swedish actors. It's one of Sarno's most interesting and wild creations, especially the crazy scenes from the pornographic theater. Among the inventive props is a rocking horse armed with two moving dildos. The film offers much nudity, especially on the part of lead actress Christina Lindberg. The dialogue is lousy and the lines are delivered with zero feeling, in thickly accented English. This could be a problem, but instead contributes to the delirious atmosphere of a very odd movie.

Alternative title: *The Red Queen*

A WORLD WITHOUT *SENSATIONSFILMS*

Some forty years after Arne Mattsson's *Hon Dansade en Sommar* brought moral panic to the world, the National Board of Film Classification (Statens Biografbyrå) finally surrendered its right to interfere with moviemaking in 1992, approving Peter Jackson's ultra-bloody splatter fest *Dead Alive* without cuts. Previous violent films as a rule had either been heavily edited or banned outright. From that point on, with head Gunnel Arbäck leading the retreat, the office slimmed down its formerly zealous mandate to a minimum—banning its final mainstream film, *Man Bites Dog* (Rémy Belvaux, etc.) in 1992, and demanding cuts for the last time from *Casino* (Martin Scorsese) in 1995.

The final moment of controversy for any Swedish movie came on March 26, 1993, with the theatrical release of brightly colored teen gangster film *Sökarna*. Like many of its predecessors, *Sökarna* began a huge national debate on the proper moral limits for filmmaking. The National Board of Film Classification did cut a scene of forced oral sex before allowing *Sökarna* to be shown, and that was the last time the board delivered a verdict on a Swedish film. Yet the new lax climate did not usher in a wild new wave of Swedish *sensationsfilms*. On the contrary, Sweden no longer seemed interested in producing films that rile the moral majority. When *Sökarna* finished its successful run, and came down from cinema marquees around the country, *sensationsfilms* took a last coughing breath and died.

Swedish cinema had already been running on fumes for quite some time, and finally the tank was empty—nothing exciting remained. A stream of intellectually and sensationally dead movies flooded theaters, enthusiastically backed by the moronic Swedish Film Institute. Gone was the daring sexuality of *Jag – En Kvinna 2. Äktenskapet*. Gone were the gung ho Cold War action spectacles of Mats Helge Olsson. Horny bearded Danes and their nude models fled the coop for greener pastures. The few kicker hooligans and *raggare* who survived into the mid-'90s were shadows of their former savage force. We were left with wave after gray wave of tired cops and contrived social "realism."

Where cheap celluloid and the sexual revolution spurred *sensationsfilm* production in the '70s, the combined landslides of digital technology and deregulation buried sound and image production in the '90s. Like everyone else, Swedes of all ages enthusiastically turned to the Internet, rather than film or video, for a constant stream of titillation. Sex films in particular, which had already long since moved out of theaters and into VCRs, were obliterated by porn-on-command. Digital previews of every sexual desire possible were cut up into tiny pieces to be enjoyed at the mere click of a finger. So it was good night forever for proper Swedish pornography after 1993. Rest in sleaze.

In 1992, Sweden's government abandoned its monopoly on land-based television transmission, and former satellite channel TV4 took its broadcast to the terrestrial airwaves. Suddenly, the two commercial-free public-funded TV channels were competing for viewers with all the vice and mindless entertainment commercial television could summon. The race for eyeballs began, and new channels such as TV3 and TV5 entered the market. Viewers were treated to countless cheap imported TV series, reality shows, and straight-to-television films. Pandora's box was open, and exploitation became normal, comfortably enjoyed in the living room with a drink in hand and a moronic smile on the lips. When beautiful young women got drunk and had sex for the *Big Brother* cameras, the trained actors and moviemakers with ties to Ingmar Bergman dabbling in kinky cinema became quaint relics. The public swallowed the bait, hook, line and sinker, and forgot that the days of shocking Swedish sin ever existed.

Meanwhile, the government put on its director's beret and got busy with funding filmmaking in force. As a result, the void left by nutty *sensationsfilms* was soon filled with tired, repetitive, and formulaic assembly-line movies. In 1972, only sixteen Swedish movies premiered theatrically, and by 1992, that number remained exactly the same. In 2002, however, the number of premieres jumped to 22, and by 2008 a staggering 38 Swedish movies were released—not counting the plentiful made-for-TV productions. As the quantity skyrocketed, the quality suffered. Under the operating principle "more movies means more money," production houses spit out as much inoffensive dreck as possible to draw a larger audiences. Mats Helge Olsson may have been a hack, but when he spilled his guts and worked his ass off in the '80s, relentlessly spitting out hilarious action flicks, his personality was unmistakable. Also, he worked on his own terms—without help from the government-sponsored Swedish movie machine.

Crime and detective films soon flooded the new markets. In 1993, director Hajo Gies picked up the story of Inspector Martin Beck where Bo Widerberg's *Mannen på Taket* ended. Hopeless comic actor Gösta Ekman took on the lead role in *Brandbilen som Försvann* (1993) and within a year starred in five more Inspector Beck movies. The producers ran out of original Beck novels to adapt, but returned in 1997 with Peter Haber as the new Inspector Beck, generating twenty-six more movies in the next twelve years about the increasingly washed up inspector's new adventures. The scripts quickly went from decent to horrible.

Greedy Swedish TV producers also spawned no fewer than thirty-six crime films dedicated to the adventures of Inspector Wallander—an even more washed-up version of Inspector Beck. Viewers barely noticed as three actors rotated through the Wallander role, and eventually Kenneth Branagh took up the character for a UK TV series. Reputable Swedish writers Henning Mankell and Håkan Nesser saw their work degraded by hack TV writers. When Sweden ran out of good crime authors, even the terrible ones got their potboilers turned into movies. At the bottom of the barrel, the nine films about Johan Falk had no literary origins and consequently no substance, just some rainy skies and the notoriously wooden actor Jakob Eklund. Directed by Mats Helge Olsson's old sidekick and pupil Anders Nilsson, the Falk series completely failed to revive any energy from the *sensationsfilm* period, when cops staggered without pants from one beating to the next.

At the same time that sex films were dealt a deathblow, and cop thrillers were homogenized to the consistency of pablum, the horror and action genre films suffered in the hands of talentless, self-aware nobodies. Once the only outlet for the most daring and ruthless directors, these genres became the gathering point for the most narcissistic mirror-gazing. Anders Jacobsson's *Evil Ed* (1997), appeared to be an expensive vanity project for the benefit of film-collecting insiders. The same is true of Martin Munthe's awful *Camp Slaughter* (2004), the most tame and toothless example of a slasher film imaginable—only dangerous for a lethal dosage of winks and nods. Munthe's thriller *Hjärta av Sten* (2000)—about a Russian hitman loose in Stockholm—contained decent actors like Brasse Brännström and Michael Nyqvist, but was too badly scripted to execute correctly. At least Munthe fared better than his peers. Atrocities such as *Blå Måndag* (Anders Lennberg, 2001), *Inte Bara Mördare* (Oscar Petersson, 2000), and *Farligt Förflutet* (Oscar Petersson, 2001) were good arguments for reopening the National Board of Film Classification to ban films on the basis of sheer boredom.

The two—count them, two—separate follow-ups to *Sökarna*, should have been stopped, for sure. *Blodsbröder* (Daniel Fridell, 2005) and *Sökarna – Återkomsten* (Lena Koppel/Torsten Flinck/Liam Norberg, 2006) were equally painful. Fridell was originally hired to direct an official sequel. After squabbling with star Liam Norberg, however, he just left the production and made his own movie. Both suck big-time—each lacks the nihilistic, alienating vision of the original. The stupid moralistic nonsense on display instead shows a total disrespect for the true madness of *Sökarna*.

Meanwhile, instead of learning useful crafts like storytelling and cinematography, young filmmakers bought digital video cameras and dubbed themselves directors. Abysmal dreck such as *Hundtricket* (Christian Eklöw/Christopher Panov, 2002) and *Kopps* (Josef Fares, 2003) spread to Sweden's theaters like a plague, returning to the status quo of forgettable lightweight comedies that ruled Sweden in the 1950s, prior to the advent of *sensationsfilms*.

Curiously, in an era when Hollywood has remade every American 1970s exploitation classic from *The Last House on the Left* (Wes Craven, 1972) to *I Spit on Your Grave* (Meir Zarchi, 1978) the first such remake in Sweden was *Kärlekens Språk*. Unexpectedly resurrected in 2004 by the talentless Anders Lennberg, this catastrophe stole its title and theme from the original movie, but paraded its brainless sensations without the dark heart and compelling soul of the perverted and disingenuous original. The main selling point was Swedish actress Regina Lund, known from generic TV series and films, parading around naked and introducing segments containing graphic masturbation and sex scenes. Lund has since become known as the most media-horny person in Sweden—she married herself in a plane over Iceland, then sold the story to the tabloids. This poorly tuned homage to the past proves that sensations alone cannot resurrect the spirit of *sensationsfilms*.

Fortunately, all is not completely lost. Though the various *sensationsfilms* genres were killed off one by one, a smattering of films after 1993 managed to survive on pure sensations. Though the general atmosphere was drab, director Bo Widerberg's swan song *Lust och Fägring Stor* (US title: *All Things Fair*, 1995) wandered deeply into his sleazy old mind. In a burst of slippery sensationalism, he placed his own son Johan in a series of dirty sex sequences—some with MILF-extraordinaire Marika Lagercrantz, some with a twelve-year-old girl—all directed in close detail. At the point when he requested that an underage girl strip naked for the camera, Bo Widerberg had clearly surrendered completely. Sadly, the *sensations*-maker died shortly after this film, so he couldn't continue to direct films as an even dirtier and older man.

The most interesting recent movie exploring sexuality is Lucas Moodysson's *Ett Hål i Mitt Hjärta* (US title: *A Hole in my Heart*, 2004). The curious story about the making of an amateur porn movie clearly contains some kind of message, but mostly comes across as just a bunch of really dirty scenes of perversion and filth. Not far from the legitimized smut of *Kärlekens Språk* and its sequels, *Ett Hål i Mitt Hjärta* remains one of a handful of quasi interesting modern Swedish movies. Too bad the brilliant leading man, Thorsten Flinck, wasn't born twenty years earlier—he could have accomplished miracles in the hands of directors such as Arne Mattsson or Jan Halldoff. Naturally, he cut his teeth on the silver screen with a brilliant performance in *Sökarna*—at the end of the *sensationsfilms* era.

The best Swedish film since 1993, Tomas Alfredsson's *Låt den Rätte Komma In* (US title: *Let the Right One In*, 2008) is something special—a genuinely scary horror film. This portrayal of a lonely underage kid who befriends an equally lonely vampire only contains a fraction of the perverse excesses of John Ajvide Lindqvist's magnificent novel, yet the film chills even the hardest of spines. The scene when stern pedophile Håkan (a great Per Ragnar) douses his own face with acid brings back the ancient *sensationsfilm* shock of *Smutsiga Fingrar*. The only setback is kind of a compliment; the film remains too slick and masterful to sidle up with the old *sensationsfilms* masters—never stumbling in the dark with unintentional comedy.

At the moment, the scent of change hangs in the air, thanks to massive renewed attention to Swedish sex and violence in a trilogy of films springing from three notorious novels by the late Stieg Larsson. The first part, *Män Som Hatar Kvinnor* (literally "Men Who Hate Women," 2009; known abroad by the less sensational title *The Girl With the Dragon Tattoo*), directed by Danish filmmaker Niels Arden Oplev, has taken the world by storm. The movie was born in a cauldron of *sensationsfilms*, and summons images from countless movies in this book with its lesbian sex, incest, senseless rapes, revenge scenarios, and *Stockholmsnatt*-style subway beatings. National Swedish television (SVT) commissioned a series by director Tomas Alfredsson based on Larsson's following two books, but after the success of Oplev's film the TV version was quickly cut and reedited into two feature films: *Flickan som Lekte med Elden* (US title: *The Girl Who Played With Fire*, 2009) and *Luftslottet som Sprängdes* (literally "The Air Castle That Got Blown Up"; US title: *The Girl Who Kicked the Hornet's Nest*, 2009).

Based on another popular book, Daniel Espinosa's nihilistic *Snabba Cash* (US title: Easy Money, 2010) is crime drama without any tired old inspectors—reason enough for praise! *Snabba Cash* tries to be different, with sharp pacing, a fresh storyline, and above all a sinister portrayal of Stockholm as a cold and dark place. The movie follows the style of *Sökarna* more closely than the official follow-ups, but lacks that film's freaky and nonsensical elements—essential to true *sensationsfilms*. Like *Låt den Rätte Komma In* and *Män Som Hatar Kvinnor*, this movie is slated for a Hollywood remake, with teen idol Zac Efron both starring and producing. Next, will Justin Bieber bankroll his own version of *Barnens Ö*, complete with copious frontal nudity? The teenyboppers of the US can only hope.

Unexpectedly, just as the night seems longest and darkest, *sensationsfilms* appear to have reached a new starting point in Sweden with Hannes Holm's *Himlen är Oskyldigt Blå* (US title: Behind Blue Skies, 2010). This film really embraces the ethics of the original exploitation era. In this strange drama, which premiered in Sweden in October 2010, many of favorite vices return to the slithering screen: gangsters, naked blonde girls, midsummer celebration, remote island locations, drugs, and porno clubs. Set in 1975 under an ever-shining sun, the film opens with a spectacular sequence in which a young guy with a massive hard-on in full focus tries to get oral sex from a girl. The premise is pure exploitation, and the exposed actor this time around is Stellan Skarsgård's son (and *True Blood* star Alexander Skarsgård's brother) Bill, yet another Skarsgård offspring following in his father's footsteps by using his penis to decorate the world of dubious cinema. With a film like this, I can sure see some light at the end of the tunnel.

Just as this tome of cinematic obscurities comes to a close, now comes the biggest shock of all: The earthshattering announcement that The National Board of Film Classification has finally admitted total defeat and disbanded as of January 1, 2011. In effect, this means there will be no film censorship whatsoever for anyone above the age of fifteen, or, oddly enough, under the age of one. Former censor Gunnel Arbäck, the woman who led the board for twenty-six years, welcomed the news: "I realized early on that the censorship was a limitation of free speech, and that we had useless tools to work with. Virtually every videocassette released in the early '80s should have been banned, according to our laws."

While Arbäck, who quit in protest in 2007, laughs at her former employees, Sweden contemplates a new dawn after exactly one hundred years of censorship terror. The Swedish Film Institute will celebrate the occasion by screening some forbidden gems of the past, among them the vilified *The Texas Chain Saw Massacre* (Tobe Hooper, 1974). Meanwhile, the National Board of Film Classification will gather their former employees for a quiet glass of beer at a dreary bar, probably surrounded by plenty of the old *sensationsfilms* stars they put out of business. Around here, though, it's nothing but champagne, as we honor the liberation of Sweden's cinema and complete the final book on Swedish film to be written during the era of censorship. From this day on, all cuts are to be restored and our work is truly done.

GLOSSARY OF CURIOUS SWEDISH CULTURE

DALARNA

The central region of Dalarna is definitely the most Swedish part of my country—home of weird folk music, traditional clothes, midsummer celebrations, moonshine, skiing, and the lustful blonde girls known as *dalkullor*.
Fäbodjäntan (see page 58)
Midsommardansen (see page 167)
Sound of Näverlur (see page 239)

DANMARK

A country located slightly southwest of Sweden. Denmark tried to unify Scandinavia in the fifteenth century, but Sweden didn't approve, and simply stole all the good parts (Skåne, Halland, and Blekinge). Still, Denmark had a sexual revolution on par with Sweden's, and produced a similar number of sleazy films, so we must still be related. You can tell us apart because the Danes tend to be bearded, and smoke more than Swedes. Danish is basically Swedish, spoken by an extremely drunk person with a hot potato in his mouth.
Dagmars Heta Trosor (see page 48)
Jag – En Älskare (see page 105)
Jag – En Kvinna 2. Äktenskapet (see page 108)
Jag En Markis – Med Uppdrag att Älska (see page 111)
Nyckelhålet (see page 184)
Sound of Näverlur (see page 239)
Swedish Wildcats (see page 253)

FALUKORV

Made in the Dalarna region, this thick sausage contains so little meat that it is generally regarded as a vegetarian dish. Every child in Sweden eats this at least once a week.
Fäbodjäntan (see page 58)

FINLAND

This country to the east of Sweden used to be part of the Swedish empire until the Russians took it in 1809 (leading Sweden to immediately invade Norway). We don't miss Finland much, though, since it has no natural resources and is inhabited by gloomy, violent, knife-wielding alcoholics. They also speak a language that nobody understands.
Il Capitano (see page 44)
Kronvittnet (see page 136)

FOLKÖL

A watery beer of 2.8–3.5% strength, this is the only alcohol sold in regular Swedish groceries. Naturally, this is the drink of choice for teenagers, since it is basically the only thing they can get. *Folköl* has caused a lot of alcohol-related damage to young bodies, since it is far more dangerous to get drunk on vast amounts of low-alcohol beer than on a few shots.
Punkmordet (see page 201)
Stockholmsnatt (see page 246)

FRITIDSLEDARE

A job that only exists in Sweden, where you hang out with teenagers all day, doing nothing at all. You get ten weeks of vacation. As you can guess, this is my choice of work, since it allows me to watch a lot of crazy films and write books.

GULDBAGGE

The top movie award in Sweden is not a gallant knight with a sword like an Academy Award, but rather a beetle made of copper. The annual awards show usually attempts to copy the Oscars, but any attempt at glamour in Sweden during freezing February just falls flat. During the '70s, the Guldbagge jury seemed pretty hooked on *sensationsfilms*, but those guys have all sinced been replaced.
Ett Anständigt Liv (see page 26)
Barnens Ö (see page 33)
Il Capitano (see page 44)
En Handfull Kärlek (see page 84)
Kaninmannen (see page 121)
Mannen På Taket (see page 163)
Ormen (see page 189)
Det Sista Äventyret (see page 220)
Tystnaden (see page 267)

KICKERS

A youth culture that emerged in the mid-'80s, somewhat connected to the arrival of hip-hop music and break dancing. The real kick for these guys was beating people up using karate moves picked up from Bruce Lee films. Like the bad guys in *The Karate Kid*, the kickers roamed the streets of Stockholm beating the hell out of anyone—metalheads, punk rockers, old people, homosexuals, and even each other.
Stockholmsnatt (see page 246)
Sökarna (see page 232)

KOLLEKTIV

Hand in hand with the blossoming Swedish prog scene, the '70s saw thousands of Swedes taking socialism to heart, cohabitating in enormous households. The idea was nice, but by the 1980s it had all fallen apart. All that was left where communes once stood were the stains of myriad STDs, unlistenable protest music, and many families torn apart.

Kärlekens XYZ (see page 127)

Sams (see page 214)

Smoke (see page 228)

KRÄFTSKIVA

Crayfish party. Whereas midsummer is a happy celebration of the arrival of summer, *kräfskiva* is the sad party mourning its end. At a *kräftskiva*, Swedes eat crayfish while wearing stupid hats, singing stupid songs, and drinking tons of booze. At night, all of Sweden is swept in complete mayhem with violence, delirium, and countless brief sexual relationships.

Lejonet och Jungfrun (see page 142)

LUCIAFIRANDE

St. Lucy's party. Every year on the morning of December 13, people dress in white and walk around with candles in their hair, singing religious hymns about an Italian saint. And at night? All of Sweden is swept in complete mayhem with violence, delirium, and countless brief sexual relationships.

Mannen Från Mallorca (see page 161)

Sommarens Tolv Månader (see page 238)

Svart Lucia (see page 250)

LUMPEN

The Swedish military service used to be mandatory for boys. Since Sweden is a big country with a small population, it would be impossible to protect the borders if anyone wanted to attack. So the government kind of gave up on training everyone for war. Nowadays, only the most macho enlist, and everybody else drinks beer and watches *sensationsfilms*.

Det Sista Äventyret (see page 220)

Jag Är Nyfiken – Gul (see page 104)

MIDSOMMAR

Sweden is the only country in the world that really celebrates midsummer, and we do it in style. During the day the kids are the focus, and there is a lot of dancing around trees and singing of stupid songs. As the evening comes, however, the adults take over in a drinking frenzy you wouldn't believe. The nights are a good chance to catch up on complete mayhem with violence, delirium, and brief sexual relationships.

Hon Dansade en Sommar (see page 92)

Midsommardansen (see page 167)

Mördaren – En Helt Vanlig Person (see page 173)

Sound of Näverlur (see page 239)

NEUTRALITET

Swedes are nonconfrontational by nature, and neutral as a matter of policy. That is why we find more lovemaking than roughhousing in this book. Sweden hasn't been at war since 1814. Together with Switzerland, it is the only country in Europe not involved in either world war. Especially World War II is a bit of an embarrassment for Sweden, as German troops were allowed to travel through the country to Norway by train. In other countries, movies depicting the '40s usually focus on the perils of war, but in Sweden the main focus—as per usual—was carefree sexuality.

Ormen (see page 189)
Tuppen (see page 265)

NOBELPRISET

The annual Nobel Prize ceremony is as glamorous as Sweden gets, the rare occasion when anyone actually cares about the country. We outsourced the peace prize to Norway, which turned out to be a big mistake. Instead of hosting a dignified ball, they hire performers like Will Smith, and throw the awards at guys like Henry Kissinger instead of someone deserving. I guess they just don't know any better.

Inkräktarna (see page 100)
Res Aldrig på Enkel Biljett (see page 206)

NORRLAND

The northern region of Sweden is basically a deserted expanse of small, boring villages and strangely silent people—mostly males who enjoy loads of drinking. The Alaska of Sweden.

Ådalen 31 (see page 18)
Blödaren (see page 37)
Blood Tracks (see page 40)
Ingen Kan Älska som Vi (see page 98)
Nordexpressen (see page 183)
Rymdinvasion i Lappland (see page 211)
Skräcken Har 1000 Ögon (see page 225)
Tryggare Kan Ingen Vara (see page 264)

NORGE

Located slightly to the west of Sweden, Norway used to be a part of the Swedish empire, until 1905, when we kind of let them go. Though the place is full of Christian nutcases, we really miss Norway, due to its wonderful nature, the oil reserves, and all the great black metal bands. They also speak Swedish, even if the people tend to call it Norwegian.

Het Snö (see page 88)
Mannen i Skuggan (see page 162)

RAGGARE

A group of juvenile delinquents that emerged in the late '50s, inspired by James Dean films and rockabilly. They originally did nothing but drive cars around trying to pick up girls, but in the late '70s they took up the hobby of beating up punk rockers. *Raggare* are a kind of a motorcycle gang without motorcycles, organization, personal hygiene, or anything really. Today *Raggare* still exist basically as a pathetic shallow approximation of an extinct youth movement.

Chans (see page 46)
Raggare! (see page 202)
Raggargänget (see page 203)
Sound of Näverlur (see page 239)

SÄPO

The less effective Swedish version of the FBI, SÄPO is frequently accused of being both radically right-wing and incompetent. In 1985, Swedish prime minister Olof Palme was murdered openly on the street. Mirroring the foggy investigation following the Kennedy assassination, a murderer is yet to be found.

Mannen från Mallorca (see page 161)
Slagskämpen (see page 227)

SFI

Founded in 1963, the Swedish Film Institute is supposed to support the production and distribution of Swedish movies. They also grant funds for movie production, and in a small country like Sweden, that aid is invaluable. Unfortunately, the Film Institute parts ways with the rest of us when it comes to good taste, so for the last few decades tax money has been thrown at movies that suck instead of *sensationsfilms*.

Besökarna (see page 36)
Förvandlingen (see page 70)
The Frozen Star (see page 72)
Övergreppet (see page 192)
Slagskämpen (see page 227)
Sökarna (see page 232)
Sommarens Tolv Månader (see page 238)

SKÅNE

The southern region of Sweden, Skåne is known for racism and its collection of very old historical airports. Filled with moonshine-smelling rednecks and hillbillies waving guns in everyone's faces, this really is the Texas of Sweden.

Blödaren (see page 37)
Eagle Island (see page 53)

Grossisten (see page 80)
Yngsjömordet (see page 281)

STATENS BIOGRAFBYRÅ The National Board of Film Classification set age limits for movies prior to theatrical release, and in theory they also cut films that were too over the top. The Board shut down completely on Jan. 1, 2011, after not censoring any nonpornographic movie since 1995. In the glory days of *sensationsfilm*, they played a key role in movie production. One of the main reasons *sensationsfilms* became so sexual is that the Board was way more lenient toward sex than it was to violence. Sweden compensated for the lack of blood with a lot of boobs, instead of the other way around like the US.
491 (see page 17)
Dom Kallar Oss Mods (see page 51)
Kärlekens Språk (see page 126)
Lämna Mej Inte Ensam (see page 140)
Det Sista Äventyret (see page 220)
Smutsiga Fingrar (see page 229)
Sökarna (see page 232)
Sommaren med Monika (see page 236)
Thriller – En Grym Film (see page 258)
Tills. Med Gunilla Månd. Kväll o. Tisd. (see page 260)

SYSTEMBOLAGET The Swedish Alcohol Retail Monopoly. At eighteen, any Swede can drink in bars or ruin their kidneys at home with weak *folköl*. Not until age twenty can Swedes legally enter a *systembolaget* store and gain access to the world's largest selection of alcoholic beverages. Even the crummiest shacks by the side of the road offer more fine French wines than any wine store in Paris. Since the *systembolaget* stores are few, and closed most of the time (including weekends), Swedes tend to stockpile loads of booze just to be safe. Hedging our bets, we also make a lot of moonshine.
Slagskämpen (see page 227)

TORPARSTUGA A traditional Swedish cabin, consisting of one small dark room with no windows. The only true *torparstuga* in the US is located in Swedesboro, New Jersey, so you should check it out if you ever pass by. While you're there, visit Old Swede's Inn and sample the Swedish nachos—a dish that tastes great but doesn't exist in any form in Sweden whatsoever.
Wild West Story (see page 280)

ROGUES GALLERY

MAC AHLBERG (director)

Born in Stockholm on June 12, 1931, Mac Ahlberg became one of Sweden's most prominent directors of *sensationsfilms*. In the late '60s and early '70s he directed a slew of fantastic sexploitation flicks, including *Jag – En Kvinna 2. Äktenskapet* and *Jorden Runt med Fanny Hill*. He was always hated or ignored by the critics, and during the end of the '70s the quality of his films sank overall. He often used the alias Bert Torn during this period, probably to distance himself from the products. After directing the disastrous *Gangsters* in Italy, Ahlberg kind of said "fuck you" to the European film community. He went to Hollywood and sought his fortune as a cinematographer on films such as *Ghoulies* (Luca Bercovici, 1985), *Re-Animator* (Stuart Gordon, 1985), and *Beverly Hills Cop 3* (John Landis, 1994). For his twisted ideas and great supply of energy, Ahlberg is a giant worthy of all the praise in the world. Together with Bo A. Vibenius and Arne Mattsson, he truly is one of the master directors of Swedish *sensationsfilms*.

Jag – En Kvinna (1965)

Jag en Markis – Med Uppdrag att Älska (1967)

Jag – En Kvinna 2. Äktenskapet (1968)

Fanny Hill (1968)

"Jag" – En Kvinnas Dotter (1969)

Nana (1970)

Porr i Skandalskolan (1974)

Flossie (1974)

Justine och Juliette (1975)

Jorden Runt med Fanny Hill (1975)

Bel Ami (1976)

Molly – Familjeflickan (1977)

Gangsters (1979)

TORBJÖRN AXELMAN (director)

Born in Eskilstuna on April 28, 1932, Axelman entered the film business with the strange comedy *Oj Oj Oj Eller 'Sången om den Eldröda Hummern'* (Literally "Wow Wow Wow, or Song of the Fiery Red Lobster", 1966). He wrote, directed, and starred in that film alongside many prominent Swedish film actors of the time, including Lasse Åberg, Jan Halldoff, and Ardy Strüwer. Axelman soon turned to sex and violence, with the sensation-trio of *Lejonsommar, Het Snö,* and his masterpiece *Kameleonterna.* Then Axelman struck up a friendship with American singer Lee Hazlewood, directing him in the quartet of *Cowboy in Sweden* (1970), *Smoke, Nancy & Lee in Las Vegas* (1975), and *Må Vårt Hus Förskonas från Tigrar* (1975). After a five-year break, Axelman's awful comeback *Flygnivå 450* bombed, and he was never allowed to work in cinema again— apart from a 1981 TV production. In 2008, Torbjörn Axelman returned to the headlines, when at the age of seventy-six he shot and wounded some repo men who entered his house. After a hostage situation, it took an entire police squad to bring the old-timer down.

ULF BRUNNBERG (actor)

Born April 7, 1947, in Stockholm, Ulf Brunnberg threw himself into the world of acting in 1968, and immediately became entangled in the *sensationsfilm* scene. Before 1976, he pulled off a row of great performances in such films as *Lejonsommar*, *Het Snö*, *Smutsiga Fingrar*, and *I Lust och Nöd*. The performance of his life is *Kameleonterna*, where he is just brilliant as the wild director Malcom Fyhring. During the late '70s he concentrated on lightweight TV productions, and in 1981 he became a huge star after the titanic success of the comedies *Varning för Jönssonligan* (Jonas Cornell) and *Göta Kanal eller Vem Drog ut Proppen?* (Hans Iveberg). Brunnberg nicely portrayed a sleazy manager in Staffan Hildebrandt's teenager drama *G*, and since then has contented himself with theater and occasional sequels to his two 1981 comedy hits. Fun facts: Brunnberg starred in Neil Simon's nude play *Oh, Calcutta!* in the early '70s, and one diligent newspaper drama critic took care to note: "Brunnberg has the biggest one."

Lejonsommar (1968)

Kvinnolek (1968)

Komedi i Hägerskog (1968)

Het Snö (1968)

Kameleonterna (1969)

Smoke (1971)

Smutsiga Fingrar (1973)

I Lust och Nöd (1976)

G (1983)

MARIE EKORRE (actress)

Born December 11, 1952, in Ludvika, Dalarna. Marie Ekorre stumbled into the world of Swedish *sensationsfilms* at the age of eighteen. Her first roles were as "naked girl" in *Lockfågeln* and "hooker #4" in *Smutsiga Fingrar*. She followed up with another anonymous role, that of "a girl" in *Stenansiktet*, then expanded her résumé by appearing in many German sexploitation films. Finally, in Mac Ahlberg's great *Jorden Runt med Fanny Hill*, Ekorre got to play a character with a name—Anita. Then Ekorre finished her short but intense career in exploitation cinema with starring roles in the Danish-Swedish co-productions *Nyckelhålet* and I *Lust och Nöd*. She is great in these films, so it is a shame that she quit acting prematurely. As one of the princesses of Swedish *sensationsfilms*, she is dearly missed.

ANDREI FEHER (director)

Born May 26, 1916, Fehrer started his career as a promising cinematographer in his native Romania, but in the late '70s he went to Sweden and directed a slew of porno movies. All of these were created under the pseudonym Andrew Whyte, probably since he was ashamed. He shouldn't be too embarrassed about his first film *Kärleksvirveln*—since this is a genuinely sleazy and high-quality *sensationsfilm*. In 1995, Fehrer tried to make a comeback in the US, releasing the thriller *Kiss of Death*. Nothing came of that.

Kärleksvirveln (1977)

Gräsänkor på Skandalsemester (1980)

Ta' Mej Doktorn (1981)

Pilska Julia på Bröllopsresa (1982)

Hetaste Liggen (1983)

The Porno Race (1985)

Dreams of Love (1985)

MARIE FORSÅ (actress)

Maric Forså was born December 13 (St. Lucy's holiday), 1956, in Farsta—one of the rougher suburbs of Stockholm. Her stint in film began with a brief nude sauna scene in the silly comedy *47:an Löken Blåser På* (Literally "The 47 Onion Blows On", 1972). Right away, a line of Swedish, American, and German exploitation filmmakers lined up to cast her in many sexually explicit films over the next five years. Though she had no acting talent whatsoever, she starred in Joe Sarno's *Vild på Sex* and Mac Ahlberg's sleazy quartet of *Flossie, Justine och Juliette, Bel Ami,* and *Molly – Familjeflickan*. She often used the name Maria Lynn. After *Molly*, Forså appeared uncredited and only half-naked in bit parts in Jan Haldoff's *Chez Nous*, and Lasse Hallström's *Jag är Med Barn* (1979). Though Forså repeatedly has stated that she never participated in any hard-core scenes, there are a few inserts in *Lifterskan* that appear to make the case otherwise. Marie Forså was one of the princesses of Swedish *sensationsfilms*, and it's a shame her career didn't last longer.

JAN HALLDOFF (director)

Born September 4, 1939, in Stockholm, director Jan Halldoff started his career with a couple of mild dramas in the 1960s—and then the discovery of Christina Lindberg made them both naked movie sensations thanks to *Rötmånad*. Having found his niche, Halldoff continued with pretty dirty stuff such as *Firmafesten*, *Stenansiktet*, *Chez Nous,* and *Lämna Mej Inte Ensam*. After 1982, he suddenly disappeared from the film scene altogether, like many other personalities within the *sensationsfilm* world during the early '80s. He died in 2010 and is missed.

Rötmånad (1970)

Firmafesten (1972)

Stenansiktet (1973)

Det Sista Äventyret (1974)

Jack (1976)

Chez Nous (1978)

Lämna Mej Inte Ensam (1980)

HEINZ HOPF (actor)

Born November 11, 1934, in Stockholm, Heinz Hopf studied medicine before entering drama school in 1955. His film career started with *Rasmus, Pontus och Toker* (1956), an adaption of Pippi Longstocking author Astrid Lindgren's beloved children's book *Rasmus på Luffen*. In 1958 Hopf became employed at the national theater stage Dramaten, playing roles in Shakespeare and Brecht productions. Things soon turned dirty for the slick-looking Hopf, however, and he played countless sleazy parts in such films as *Morianerna*, *Ann och Eve – De Erotiska*, *Exponerad*, and *Smutsiga Fingrar*. His crowning performance came in *Thriller – En Grym Film*. His ruthless portrayal of a sadistic rapist/pimp shocked the world. After *Tabu*, Hopf took a five-year break from filmmaking. He also left the theater in 1979, due to stage fright and, allegedly, escalating alcoholism. However, Hopf returned in grand style in Ingmar Bergman's Oscar-winning drama *Fanny och Alexander* (1982). Afterward, Hopf starred in two substandard Swedish slasher films, *Mask of Murder* and *Månguden*, before ending his glorious *sensationsfilm* career with *The Hired Gun*—a curious Arne Mattsson/Mats Helge Olsson collaboration. He stuck to TV roles, probably ending his career by playing an East German Stasi agent in the 1990s series *Rederiet*. Heinz Hopf sadly passed away on January 23, 2001, after suffering from throat cancer for some time. Hopf is dearly missed by any fan of Swedish *sensationsfilms*, and he represents well the duality of the genre: A king of Swedish sleaze who was also a respected name within the legitimate theater.

TOR ISEDAL (actor)

Born July 20, 1924, in Norrköping, Tor Isedal was one of Sweden's most productive actors ever. He appeared in everything from Oscar-winning dramas to pure exploitation. He launched his career in high class, appearing in two of Ingmar Bergman's best films: *Det Sjunde Inseglet* (1957) and *Jungfrukällan*. He soon descended into a world of baser entertainment, appearing in *Vita Frun*, *Kameleonterna*, *Exponerad,* and the lingonberry Western *I Död Mans Spår*. Though seldom a leading man, Isedal always marked his films with his unique stern presence. Tor Isedal died at the age of seventy-five in 1990, remaining very active before the camera until the very end. Next to his tireless friend Arne Mattsson, Tor Isedal earns the award for most entries in this book.

Jungfrukällan (1960)

Vita Frun (1962)

Vaxdockan (1962)

Morianerna (1965)

Ormen (1966)

Komedi i Hägerskog (1968)

Kameleonterna (1969)

Kyrkoherden (1970)

Midsommardansen (1971)

Exponerad (1971)

Dagmars Heta Trosor (1971)

Sängkamrater (1975)

Justine och Juliette (1975)

Lejonet och Jungfrun (1975)

I Död Mans Spår (1975)

Vem Var Dracula? (1975)

Victor Frankenstein (1977)

Bödeln och Skökan (1986)

DIANA KJAER (actress)

Vindingevals (1968)

Fanny Hill (1968)

Skottet (1969)

Kyrkoherden (1970)

Som Hon Bäddar Får Han Ligga (1970)

Dagmars Heta Trosor (1971)

Lockfågeln (1971)

Firmafesten (1972)

Baksmälla (1973)

Born February 5, 1945, in Stockholm, Diana Kjaer made her cinema debut in *Vindingevals*, as a gypsy who exposes herself to young boys. After that, she was unstoppable. Kjaer reigned over the Swedish *sensationsfilm* world with intensely sexual performances. Among her great roles are parts in *Fanny Hill*, *Skottet* and *Firmafesten*. One of the very sexiest women in Swedish film history, she could also really act—which is more than you can say about many other actresses at the time. Though she was truly great, Diana Kjaer basically stopped acting in the late '70s. Her last performance was as a prostitute in a neglected Finnish drama from 1981, after which she rarely acted again—a loss for us all. Diana Kjaer tragically passed away on January 31, 2005, at the young age of 59. She remains one of the brightest shining starlets glimmering in the Swedish *sensationsfilm* sky, and she is missed by all of us.

MARIE LILJEDAHL (actress)

Born February 15, 1950, in Stockholm, Marie Liljedahl had a short but intense acting career. After appearing as a girl on a beach in a Greek comedy, she made her Swedish *sensationsfilm* debut in Joe Sarno's *Jag, En Oskuld*. She then appeared in two Italian exploitation films, two German sex comedies, and Spaniard Jesús Franco's *Eugenie... the Story of Her Journey Into Perversion* (1970), before returning to Sweden to star in Arne Mattsson's *Ann och Eve – De Erotiska*. After that, she concluded her acting career with Joe Sarno in the wild *Någon att Älska*. It's tragic that Liljedahl's principal acting career only lasted three years, producing a mere four Swedish *sensationsfilms*. She possessed a presence that few other actresses could touch, and she remains a strong runner-up for Christina Lindberg's position as queen of Swedish exploitation cinema.

Jag, en Oskuld (1968)

Eva – Den Utstötta (1969)

Ann och Eve – De Erotiska (1970)

Någon att Älska (1971)

CHRISTINA LINDBERG (actress)

Rötmånad (1970)

Exponerad (1971)

Maid in Sweden (1971)

Smoke (1971)

Young Playthings (1972)

Swedish Wildcats (1972)

Anita – Ur en Tonårsflickas Dagbok (1973)

Thriller – En Grym Film (1974)

Sängkamrater (1975)

Jorden Runt med Fanny Hill (1975)

Attentatet (1980)

Sverige åt Svenskarna (1980)

Gräsänklingar (1982)

Born on December 6, 1950, in Gothenburg, this gorgeous and voluptuous brunette posed in bathing suits for several magazines while still in high school. She went on to nude photo sessions for magazines such as *Playboy* and *Penthouse*, and became *Penthouse* Pet of the Month in June 1970. Her public debut as an actress came that same year, when director Jan Halldoff utilized her good looks to launch his sexploitation classic *Rötmånad*. After proving that her photographic presence transferred very well to the silver screen, Lindberg became the star of a slew of sexploitation classics, including *Exponerad*, *Maid in Sweden*, and *Anita – Ur en Tonårsflickas Dagbok*. Her crowning performance was Bo A. Vibenius's ultra-raw rape-revenge film *Thriller – En Grym Film*. Afterwards, Lindberg studied journalism and only dabbled occasionally in bit parts, mainly in comedies. She became a devoted animal rights activist and developed her talents as a mushroom picker—releasing the instructional short video *Christinas Svampskola* (literally "Christina's Mushroom School," 1993). Today, Lindberg is the editor-in-chief for Sweden's official aviation magazine *Flygrevyn*, and she appears frequently at film festivals speaking about her glory days. In 2009, Lindberg unexpectedly surfaced in the short film *Ingen Kom Ner*, a welcome sighting after a long absence from the cinema. Christina Lindberg is the undisputed queen of Swedish *sensationsfilms*, the only Swedish actress since the days of Greta Garbo and Ingrid Bergman to achieve a divine cult status among fans.

CAMILLA LUNDÉN (actress)

Born May 5, 1967, in Stockholm, Camilla Lundén made a bombastic entrance on the Swedish *sensationfilms* scene in 1987 as Paolo Roberto's girlfriend, Nilla, in the notorious *Stockholmsnatt*. After that, for some reason, no filmmaker but Mats Helge Olsson would touch her. He made her a star through no-budget action films such as *Animal Protector*, *Fatal Secret*, *The Mad Bunch* and *Grottmorden*. No other filmmaker picked her up after Olsson's untimely exit from cinema, until poorly regarded Rickard Hobert put her in *Glädjekällan* (1993). Since then, she has starred in virtually nothing but Hobert films and TV productions. Today she stars in an awful series of crime films about Inspector Johan Falk. Camilla Lundén's talents were surely always minimal, but she nonetheless made a solid impact within the world of Swedish *sensationsfilms*.

Stockholmsnatt (1987)
Animal Protector (1988)
Fatal Secret (1988)
The Mad Bunch (1989)
Grottmorden (1990)

ARNE MATTSSON (director)

Born on December 2, 1919, in Uppsala, Arne Matsson dedicated his entire life to the cinema. With his directorial debut in 1944, he was immediately recognized by critics and audiences, and his early popularity grew and grew, culminating with *Hon Dansade en Sommar*—winner of the Golden Berlin Bear at the Berlin International Film Festival in 1952. This film-kickstarted the Swedish *sensationsfilm* era, as its depiction of a naked girl was considered extremely daring. Mattsson continued his successful career with a series of thrillers in the late '50s and early '60s, but his films turned darker and the critics turned against him. In the late '60s and early '70s, Mattsson produced his most extreme and interesting films, such as *Morianerna*, *Mördaren – En Helt Vanlig Person*, *Ann och Eve – De Erotiska,* and above all the incredible *Smutsiga Fingrar*. The last is a masterpiece of dirty crime cinema, but by this time Mattsson was hated by critics and all but abandoned by audiences. Before long, he was only allowed to work in cinema occasionally, leading to a life in the shadows as director of neglected low-budget films such as *Mannen i Skuggan* and *Mask of Murder*. He ended his career in the farthest reaches of the backyard of the Swedish film industry, assisting the talentless Mats Helge Olsson on the no-budget action films *The Mad Bunch* and *The Hired Gun*. On June 28, 1995, Arne Mattsson died with little fanfare from the industry. In the world of Swedish *sensationsfilms* he is a true hero—he will always be a monarch within our kingdom!

MATS HELGE OLSSON (director)

Born on May 10, 1953, in Lidköping, Mats Helge Olsson was the black sheep of Swedish filmmaking. Olsson started his wild career with the two lingonberry westerns *I Död Mans Spår* and *The Frozen Star*. These films made little impact, so Olsson tried the action film instead with *The Ninja Mission* (1984). This formula worked far better, and Olsson quickly followed up with a slew of similar, but worse, films such as *Eagle Island, Fatal Secret,* and *Animal Protector*. In 1989, he codirected two no-budget action films, *The Mad Bunch* and *The Hired Gun*, with the far more talented Arne Matsson. Olsson also made the slasher films *Blood Tracks* and *Grottmorden*, the children's ghost movie *Spökligan,* and the awful action-comedy *Nordexpressen*. That last effort effectively stopped Olsson from ever directing again. Since he never relied on public funds but always secured the budgets for his films himself, Mats Helge Olsson has repeatedly proclaimed himself "Sweden's only professional filmmaker"—a claim that rings completely false when you see the quality of his films. The professional director is reputedly also hearing-impaired and has trouble breathing after all the dangerous smoky explosions engineered in the course of his films. Cough on, you crazy diamond!

I Död Mans Spår (1975)

The Frozen Star (1977)

Tvingad att Leva (1980)

The Ninja Mission (1984)

Blood Tracks (1985)

Eagle Island (1986)

Spökligan (1987)

Silent Chase (1987)

Fatal Secret (1988)

Animal Protector (1988)

The Mad Bunch (1989)

The Hired Gun (1989)

Russian Terminator (1990)

Grottmorden (1990)

Nordexpressen (1992)

GIO PETRÉ (actress)

Mannekäng i Rött (1958)

Ryttare i Blått (1959)

Vita Frun (1962)

Vaxdockan (1962)

Älskande Par (1964)

Kattorna (1965)

Den Onda Cirkeln (1967)

Jag – En Kvinna 2. Äktenskapet (1968)

Vindingevals (1968)

...Som Havets Nakna Vind (1968)

Fanny Hill (1968)

Ann och Eve – De Erotiska (1970)

Born November 1, 1937, in Stockholm, as Ann-Mari Birgitta Bengtsdotter Petré, Gio Petré started her career in respected comedies and dramas, such as Ingmar Bergman's *Smultronstället* (1957). She went on to more commercial fare, starring in three Arne Mattsson thrillers from the late '50s and early '60s. Before long, she found herself in pure sleaze, and she remains immortalized for her wonderfully intense performance as Siv Holm in Mac Ahlberg's masterpiece *Jag – En Kvinna 2. Äktenskapet*. She continued to appear in great films during the end of the '60s, including some directed by Arne Mattsson, before calling it quits in the early '70s. Nobody who has seen Gio Petré in a Swedish *sensationsfilm* will ever forget her presence—and she is actually a very fine actor as well.

JAN-OLOF RYDQVIST (actor)

Born in Stockholm on January 26, 1930, Jan-Olof Rydqvist is one of the sleaziest character actors in the Swedish film industry. For some reason, he managed to get uncredited bit parts in several Swedish comedies and dramas throughout the '40s and '50s. His sole attempt to become a writer, *Stöten*, flopped in 1961, probably due to the fact that he was a sworn Nazi and genuinely disturbing to be around. Then he disappeared for almost a decade, before Torgny Wickman found use for his creepy appearance—a mixture of drooling retard and a child molester. Rydqvist returned in the dirty *Eva – Den Utstötta*. Today, Jan-Olof Rydqvist is nearly a household name for his roles in *sensationsfilms* such as *Smutsiga Fingrar, Anita – Ur en Tonårsflickas Dagbok, Sängkamrater,* and *Kärleksvirveln*. Shortly after the last one was finished in 1977, Rydqvist died on his birthday. According to popular legend, nobody came to to his party, and he reputedly ate and drank himself to death with all the extra food and drink on hand. The actresses of Swedish *sensationsfilms* could finally relax, but he remains sorely missed by fans.

Farlig Frihet (1954)

Eva – Den Utstötta (1969)

Smutsiga Fingrar (1973)

Anita – Ur en Tonårsflickas Dagbok (1973)

Sängkamrater (1975)

Kärleksvirveln (1977)

JOSEPH W. SARNO (director)

Jag, En Oskuld (1968)

Kvinnolek (1968)

Någon att Älska (1971)

Siv, Anne & Sven (1971)

Young Playthings (1972)

Swedish Wildcats (1972)

Den Pornografisk Jungfrun (1973)

Vild på Sex (1974)

Lifterskan (1975)

Kärleksön (1977)

Fäbodjäntan (1978)

Born March 15, 1921, in Brooklyn, Joe Sarno was a pioneer of '60s sexploitation films and then of '70s hardcore pornography. He jet-setted the world in search of financial backing for his film projects, directing several classic Swedish productions, including *Jag, en Oskuld*, *Någon att Älska*, *Swedish Wildcats*, *Vild på Sex*, and *Lifterskan*. He became a legend in Sweden by directing the most notorious Swedish sex movie of all time: *Fäbodjäntan*. During the '80s, this was the film everybody saw; parents, grandparents, and children alike—often uncomfortably in the same room. Over his vast career, Joe Sarno directed the best actors of Swedish *sensationsfilms*—Christina Lindberg, Marie Liljedahl, Heinz Hopf, Ulf Brunnberg, Marie Forså—and for that he is as integral a part of Sweden as meatballs and IKEA. After a lifetime of sinful bliss, Joseph W. Sarno passed away in 2010 at the age of seventy-nine in his beloved Manhattan. Rest in sleaze!

BO A. VIBENIUS (director)

Born in Stockholm on March 29, 1943, Bo A. Vibenius walked a strange path through the Swedish film industry. He started as an assistant director to Ingmar Bergman on the critically acclaimed *Persona* (1966) and *Vargtimmen* (1968). He then decided to write, produce, and direct films himself, beginning with the bizarre children's movie *Hur Marie Träffade Fredrik, Åsnan Rebus, Kängurun Ploj och...*. Then he spent five years planning and executing *Thriller – En Grym Film*—the apex of Swedish *sensationsfilms*. *Thriller* shocked the world, and inspired filmmakers for decades. Quentin Tarantino based much of his *Kill Bill* films on *Thriller*. Vibenius followed his extreme film with the much weirder and more pornographic *Breaking Point*, a film of great sleazy intensity. For some reason, he never directed a feature film again. He did work in production management for the major films *Mannen på Taket* (1976) and *Tabu* (1977). After serving as assistant director of *Raskenstam* (1983), he disappeared from the film world forever. Somwhere along the line, he reputedly won a medallion for excellent shooting as a tank commander in the Swedish Army. Though he only directed two exploitation films, both are unforgettable and unsurpassed, and thus Bo Arne Vibenius is the reigning king of Swedish *sensationsfilms*.

Hur Marie Träffade Fredrik, Åsnan Rebus, Kängurun Ploj och... (1969)

Thriller – En Grym Film (1974)

Breaking Point (1975)

TORGNY WICKMAN (director)

Born April 22, 1911, in Lund, Torgny Wickman initially tried to make a career directing unsuccessful dramas and comedies in the mid-'50s. Just when it seemed Wickman would get a break, he suddenly struck gold with his highly sensational sex education film *Kärlekens Språk*. Hot on the massive international success of that film, he made the sleazy *Eva – Den Utstötta*, *Kyrkoherden,* and then a sequel to his initial success, *Mera ur Kärlekens Språk*. Pushing the limits of productivity in 1970, he also made his weirdest and most sensational film, *Skräcken Har 1000 Ögon*—combining sex and horror in a way for which the world was not yet prepared. After this intense period, his pace slowed, and apart from two more sequels to *Kärlekens Språk* he only managed four more films before calling it quits. In 1972, Wickman made a pornographic short film in 3-D, *Drömsex i 3-D* ("Dreamsex in 3-D)—maybe now the world is finally ready for that. Short films remained his passion in life, and he reportedly made over 1,600 of them. Wickman died on September 23, 1997, leaving behind many great achievements within the magical world of Swedish *sensationsfilms*.

ACKNOWLEDGMENTS

Thank you to Tobias Pettersson; Tommy Olsson; Ronny Bengtsson; Rickard Gramfors; Anders "Hambone" Mauritzon, for images and expertise; Ralph Lundsten; Victoria Klesty; Agnes Cavallin; Pelle Gråbergs and Jonas Åhlander, for access to their massive sleazy collections; Wes Benscoter; Boarne Vibenius; and the inimitable Christina Lindberg.

Additional thanks to the caretakers of the precious *sensationsfilms* legacy. Support these institutions with your last *öre*: Thomas E and Seriesamlarna/Nordic Posters [Nordicposters.com]; Studio S [Studiosentertainment.se]; Donald May, Jr., and Synapse Films [Synapse-films.com]; and especially for their kind support, Klubb Super 8.

TWENTY *SENSATIONSFILMS* TO SEE BEFORE YOU DIE

1951: **HON DANSADE EN SOMMAR** (Arne Mattsson)

This sunny but tragic romantic drama started the Swedish *sensationsfilms* era. The film's depiction of free sex and nudity—especially the naked breasts of Ulla Jacobsson—stirred up lots of excitement. The film became a huge international hit, and a headache for censors everywhere.

1960: **JUNGFRUKÄLLAN** (Ingmar Bergman)

The grim theme of vengeance in this violent medieval drama became the blueprint for the forthcoming rape-revenge subgenre. In Sweden, the press rightfully called it sensationalistic, but Ingmar Bergman still earned Oscar, Golden Globe, and Cannes awards.

1967: **JAG ÄR NYFIKEN – GUL** (Vilgot Sjöman)

The message of this challenging political drama was probably lost on audiences whose heads were spinning from all the nudity and the frank portrayal of sexual liberation. Under the English title *I Am Curious (Yellow)*, the film unexpectedly became a massive international hit and to this day remains one of the most successful of all Swedish films.

1968: **DOM KALLAR OSS MODS** (Stefan Jarl)

This magnificent documentary finds two teenage boys at the absolute bottom of the social ladder, living for nothing but friendship, music, and beer. A scene of authentic intercourse is arguably the first of its kind in a nonpornographic feature. This unpolished sex act caused a massive debate in Sweden, and initally the film was banned. The stars were arrested at the premiere for causing a ruckus.

1968: **JAG – EN KVINNA 2. ÄKTENSKAPET** (Mac Ahlberg)

This nihilistic sexual drama delves into the destructive relationship between a young girl and her older husband. The film brought the Swedish *sensationsfilm* to full flower, as it is draped in dubious sex, perversions, and Nazi memorabilia.

1969: **KÄRLEKENS SPRÅK** (Torgny Wickman)

Posing as a dry sex instruction film, *Kärlekens Språk* is just an excuse to revel in sex and sexual abnormalities. This became a huge hit in theaters worldwide, and spawned countless sequels of even more questionable merit. It is the first feature film to intimately display sexual intercourse in long, loving detail.

1969: **KAMELEONTERNA** (Torbjörn Axelman)

Set in the world of the Swedish culture establishment, this is a psychotic thriller where morbid visions, depraved sexuality, and violence come together in perfect proportions.

1973: **STENANSIKTET** (Jan Halldoff)

A washed-up politician who seeks revenge on society hires a bunch of indifferent preteens to serve as his hitmen. This incredibly bleak vision shows a civilization about to collapse; the hostile suburbs of Stockholm drain the humanity out of inhabitants. At this point, *sensationsfilms* had started to incorporate social commentary amidst all the sex and vice.

1973: **SMUTSIGA FINGRAR** (Arne Mattsson)

This brutal crime thriller lives in a nightmarish world of drugs, prostitution, violence, and murder. Originally banned outright, but now available, *Smutsiga Fingrar* has heaps of both the nuttiness and the shocking scenes that make *sensationsfilms* great.

1974: **THRILLER – EN GRYM FILM** (Bo A. Vibenius)

The quintessential and by far most extreme rape-revenge film, a movie that tacks inorganic hard-core sex scenes onto extreme violence. The defining film of Swedish *sensationsfilm* queen Christina Lindberg, *Thriller* also inspired Quentin Tarantino greatly in his *Kill Bill* films. Outside the works of Ingmar Bergman, this is probably the best known of all *sensationsfilms*.

1974: **INKRÄKTARNA** (Torgny Wickman)

When a young hippie couple enters an upper-class mansion, the narrative elements of this incredible film are soon lost. Instead, we are treated to a carousel of sex, misunderstandings, and future Abba movie *Mamma Mia!* star Stellan Skarsgård's dangling willy.

1975: **JORDEN RUNT MED FANNY HILL** (Mac Ahlberg)

A delirious sleaze fest about a young girl traveling the world of erotic cinema, this film delivers nudity and sex to the max, thanks to starlets Christina Lindberg and Marie Ekorre.

1975: **BREAKING POINT** (Bo A. Vibenius)

This monumentally delirious creation is the wildest and strangest Swedish *sensationsfilm* ever—and definitely must be seen to be believed. Even then, it remains nearly impossible to fathom. Imagine a jarring fabric of hard-core pornography, futuristic bleakness, compulsive model train play, and perverted pranks melting into a wonderland of dirty madness.

1977: **KÄRLEKSVIRVELN** (Andrei Fehrer)

This supercharged hard-core sex film takes place in a demented world of dirty old criminals and fifteen-year-old nymphomaniacs. The best and vilest of the Swedish porn films, from an era when these things were done as dirty as possible for a reason.

1978: **FÄBODJÄNTAN** (Joseph W. Sarno)

Set in the picturesque region of Dalarna, where an everlasting sun shines on all the little red cabins, this sex film became a massive hit, even though it is genuinely unarousing. Probably the scene in which a thick sausage is used for sexual purposes did it.

1979: **ETT ANSTÄNDIGT LIV** (Stefan Jarl)

In the shocking sequel to Jarl's documentary *Dom Kallar Oss Mods*, virtually everyone from the first film has been degraded to the point that they are drug addicts in the gutter. Filled with death and desperation, this is probably one of the most intense and tragic movie experiences possible. Sweden had a lot to answer for at the time.

1984: **THE NINJA MISSION** (Mats Helge Olsson)

Made on a shoestring budget, according to the filmmakers this hyper-charged action film topped the charts in the US for years. It doesn't say a whole lot that this is hack director Mats Helge Olsson's most accomplished film. The scene where a man chokes on his own vomit while putting on a gas mask is unforgettable.

1985: **BLOOD TRACKS** (Mats Helge Olsson)

Olsson's hilarious attempt at the slasher genre displays the decimation of a ridiculous hair metal band (played by Sweden's answer to Hanoi Rocks, Easy Action) during a mountain-side music video shoot. Lots of blood is spent, and a naked girl is rescued from a avalanche as slowly as possible. *Blood Tracks* is atrociously bad and very entertaining.

1987: **STOCKHOLMSNATT** (Staffan Hildebrand)

This dramatized semi-documentary about '80s street gangs of "kickers" in Stockholm was funded by the government to convince kids to stop kicking apart phone booths across Sweden. Instead, director Staffan Hildebrand got it all wrong, and naturally all the violence in our country escalated instead.

1993: **SÖKARNA** (Daniel Fridell)

The end of the *sensationsfilm* era came with this bleak, futuristic, and delirious thriller about young criminals stalking the good citizens of Stockholm. The dramatic mix of sex, violence, and drugs made this the last film to stir up moral panic in Sweden. After this, it was all over for cheap thrills at the local cinema.